Praise for *The Real Deal on Retirement*

"*The Real Deal on Retirement* offers anyone seeking to navigate the complex terrain of retirement planning a real solution. John breaks down the essentials of retirement planning into manageable steps. He empowers readers to take charge of their financial futures by simplifying concepts such as asset allocation and risk management. If you are looking to refine and augment your strategy, this book provides invaluable advice and tools to build a solid financial foundation for your retirement."

—Walker H., senior vice president,
Financial Independence Group

"John VanWeelden looks beyond the traditional asset-based retirement planning and reveals powerful methods of creating a stable, tax efficient retirement plan, unique to each individual's needs. This book demonstrates the benefits of focusing on cash flow to better generate a worry-free retirement. Whether you are a novice or experienced investor looking for alternatives to help mitigate the risks associated with conventional retirement investing, this book is for you . . . highly recommended reading."

—Frank F., retired engineer, Cintas

"I want to make sure that my wife and I age gracefully and enjoy our later years, knowing that our retirement plans are solid. Worry is not on my list of retirement goals! VanWeelden provides valuable insights on taxes, health care, and investments, providing a playbook for people to take action today. It's an encouraging and eye-opening read for anyone planning for retirement."

—Todd M., director, Valvoline

"My wife and I have been clients of John VanWeelden for fifteen years. He has positioned us exceptionally well for our retirement. We are now focusing on the legacy we'll leave our three children, with confidence we'll avoid the pitfalls John identifies. While reading his new book, *The Real Deal on Retirement*, I recognized features of the retirement plan he has laid out for us and got an even better understanding for why and how it has worked so well. The book is ideal for those approaching retirement, but it would also be a good read for those starting their career to prepare for retirement well ahead of time, and for retirees who want to address the flaws in their traditional approach to retirement planning."

—**Ivan W., retired senior engineer, GE**

"John VanWeelden nails it in *The Real Deal on Retirement*. Using everyday language and examples, he blows up myths and all-too-common misconceptions about how to plan for the financial side of retirement. No gimmicks, no tricks, no new-fangled tools or apps—just common sense applied to the 'long game' of building and preserving wealth through good markets and bad. His ideas are well-proven and an important wake-up call to those of us who grew up learning about and employing traditional approaches. Spoiler alert: there's a better way to improve your odds of having sufficient income through your retirement and this book lays it out for you!"

—**Cameron M., president, Performance Advisors, LLC**

"This book clearly illustrates what my wife and I have always felt: John is genuinely invested in our retirement success. *The Real Deal on Retirement* is your road map to designing a retirement income plan that coordinates everything from Social Security claiming strategies to advanced tax planning in order to optimize both your retirement cash flow and financial legacy. John is skilled at mapping retirement resources, using Income Stability Ratio as his north star."

—**Jim L., retired director, Ethicon Endo-Surgery**

"John's book is a comprehensive yet easy read that should benefit any retiree. His grasp and explanation of active risk management is superb. He presents insightful concepts (the speedometer of risk) and strategies with a focus on long-term income flow, which are totally consistent with how he advises my wife and me, and puts them into practice. Undoubtedly you will learn much and get answers to questions you may never think or know to ask . . . but should."

—Dave S., retired senior manager, Procter & Gamble

"*The Real Deal on Retirement* by John VanWeelden is a transformative guide and a must-read for anyone serious about securing their financial future. It delivers straightforward, sincere insights into retirement planning and investing, stripping away the complexities to offer actionable, practical advice that you can start implementing today. By cutting through the jargon, this book empowers readers to achieve a financially worry-free retirement, making it an indispensable resource for anyone looking to ensure a comfortable and secure future, and leave a financial legacy for their children."

—Billy D., retired senior leader,
Procter & Gamble; Management Consultant

"John has developed an efficient and thorough methodology for addressing the needs for both planning and action when it comes to the management of family resources in pre-retirement, early retirement, the long haul, and end-of-life phases of our lives. He is continuously in the teaching mode, with information, counsel, and flexibility to wrestle with your personal and family situations, as they affect your resources."

—Michael H., retired director, GE Marine Engines,
GE Aircraft Engines; executive vice president, DG Fuels, LLC

"*The Real Deal on Retirement* is a commonsense approach where John brings together the perfect combination of art and science to deliver optimal returns while mitigating downside risk. This proven recipe is a must-read to help you meet your financial retirement ambitions."

—Aaron K., senior manager, Amazon

"*The Real Deal on Retirement* spells out the dangers of chasing returns in retirement. John does an excellent job of explaining the importance of prioritizing asset preservation and income stability, which often results in more money and more retirement income stability, especially when markets are volatile. This book is an enlightening comparison of the traditional approach to investment planning, Modern Portfolio Theory, and a more comprehensive and personalized approach that prioritizes risk management. The Income Stability Pyramid is an especially helpful tool for envisioning these concepts."

—John W., vice president, Standard Textile Co.

"*The Real Deal on Retirement* exposes (with substantiating explanation) the deficiencies of conventional retirement planning methods and related investment precepts. VanWeelden's refreshing approach addresses volatility head-on, while also emphasizing the importance of carefully crafting and consistently adjusting retirement plans to unique personal circumstances and retirement objectives. *The Real Deal on Retirement* is well-organized and easy to read with a conversational approach that inspires one to read on. It's complete with valuable supplemental planning that's often neglected or misunderstood, spot-on quotes, and timely-infused humor."

—Monte C., retired real estate manager, The Kroger Co.

"John VanWeelden has written a must-read book for anyone who has begun their retirement strategizing and planning. John's primary point of emphasis is ensuring that you have sufficient, stable, increasing, tax efficient, and lifetime income. John's strategy is to maximize cash flow and minimize risk versus the typical cookie-cutter asset growth–based financial plan. John incorporates risk management techniques that not only build lifetime retirement income but also protect your assets from the inevitable crash. Read this book and learn from one of the best!"

—Greg S., director, Great American Insurance Group

"Wow! I have been consulting with financial advisors on their businesses for over thirty-five years and John's book nails it. One of the best I've read, it approaches retirement planning from a holistic perspective, not just focusing on one strategy or product to solve the problem. What is especially unique is John's inclusion of tools and resources. He includes a 'Taking Action' checklist at the end of each chapter and has incorporated QR codes throughout, which guide you to additional resources. *The Real Deal on Retirement* will be immensely helpful to many people looking for answers."

—David H., vice president, Financial Independence Group

THE **TRUTH** ABOUT RETIREMENT
INCOME PLANNING AND INVESTING

★ THE ★

REAL DEAL

ON
RETIREMENT

JOHN D. VANWEELDEN

MBA, CAP, AIF, NSSA

RIVER GROVE
BOOKS

Published by River Grove Books
Austin, TX
www.rivergrovebooks.com

Distributed by River Grove Books

Design and composition by Greenleaf Book Group and Mimi Bark
Cover design by Greenleaf Book Group and Mimi Bark

Publisher's Cataloging-in-Publication data is available.

Print ISBN: 978-1-63299-797-5

eBook ISBN: 978-1-63299-798-2

First Edition

This book is dedicated to my wife, partner, best friend, and life coach, Diane, without whom I would likely never have pursued a career in retirement services, much less written this book. Over the years, her encouragement and selflessness in every aspect of life, toward me and so many others whom she has touched, has enhanced our lives immeasurably.

And also to Alex and Mary Aitken, a.k.a. "Nana and Papa," who demonstrated and taught me the not-so-common-sense basics of money management, financial stewardship, and personal fiscal responsibility—much of which became the foundation of all we teach today at VanWeelden Financial Group.

The measure of intelligence is the ability to change.

—ALBERT EINSTEIN

CONTENTS

A TALE OF TWO COWORKERS

The individual's decumulation phase is the nastiest,
hardest problem I've ever looked at.

—WILLIAM F. SHARPE,
   NOBEL PRIZE-WINNING ECONOMIST

So why another book on retirement? On the one hand, many could argue it's the last thing we need. There are literally thousands—and new ones being published practically every day. On the other hand, I would argue it's exactly what's needed. Why? Because most all the other books seem to be preaching from essentially the same gospel. And it's the wrong one. My goal for this book is to present a different way of looking at the unique financial challenges of retirement and to propose simple but highly effective solutions to achieve your retirement dreams.

This book is the result of more than 25 years of research and practical, hands-on experience working directly with retirees throughout two and a half of the most financially turbulent decades in history. It's all about

teaching you how to retire with confidence, maximizing all you've accumulated throughout your working years, regardless of whether you have
far more money than you'll ever need or you're just hoping to make what
you have last the rest of your lifetime. It's all about achieving your retirement dreams and minimizing the chances that some unforeseeable future
derails those dreams.

LUCK IS NOT A PLAN

Since they say a picture is worth a thousand words, I think the best way to
illustrate my point is for you to consider/imagine the following scenario
based on a John Hancock piece from 2015:

- You are age 65.
- You think you're ready to retire.
- Your life expectancy is 30 years.
- You have exactly $1 million of retirement savings.
- You've determined that, in addition to your Social Security and/or
  pension, you need another $50,000 a year (in today's dollars and
  adjusted annually for inflation) from your million-dollar portfolio
  of investments in order to live comfortably throughout retirement.

Although everything you've read and everyone you've spoken with says
your $1 million should be enough to retire comfortably, you decide to hire a
financial advisor, just to be sure. After some preliminary data collection and
testing, based on your age and personal risk tolerance, the advisor recom-
mends a retirement portfolio composed of 60% equities (stocks) and 40%
fixed income (bonds). They also explain that the historical average rate of
return for a 60% stock/40% bond portfolio is just over 8%, so generating
your target 5% per year should be no problem. They even show you a color-
ful statistical summary of their analysis, depicting your expected outcome.

Based on this information, you leave the advisor's office feeling extremely confident. You rush home and excitedly tell your spouse, "We have enough! We can retire!" You briefly summarize that although you need about 5% of your retirement savings value per year, your new advisor has designed a portfolio that's historically returned just over 8%. So you've got it made. A celebration is in order!

The next day at work, you share your wonderful experience with a coworker who is 10 years younger than you, and proudly announce your retirement.

Fast-forward 10 years later. Your coworker is now also ready to retire. Remembering the conversation you had with them 10 years prior, they go see the same advisor you did, hoping for a similar outcome. Coincidentally, they also have exactly $1 million saved, just as you did. Let's also assume they have the exact same monthly income need and that there's been zero inflation over the past 10 years. (I realize this last assumption may be a tough one to swallow, but try to suspend your disbelief so we can keep the math as simple as possible. In the end it all works out the same, so long as the assumptions are the same for all parties involved.) The advisor creates the exact same plan for your coworker, and they are equally excited to see that they have more than enough to retire.

Now let's fast-forward once again, this time 30 more years into the future, so we can evaluate what's happened over each of your respective lifetimes. Table 0.1 breaks this down on an annual basis. (I am using historical data dating back to 1969 as a starting point so that we have a full 30-year history of market returns prior to 2000, since some people claim more recent events of the past two decades (like the dot-com bubble of 2000 and the Great Recession of 2008) were "one-offs" that will never happen again. Although I believe this to be naïve thinking, by going back to 1969, I've eliminated that time period from impacting this illustration. Both you (coworker number one) and your coworker (coworker number two) started with $1,000,000, with 60% invested in stocks and 40% in bonds and 5% in annual withdrawals.

| | | Original Investment $1,000,000 | | | | |
| | | Coworker One (YOU) | | | Coworker Two | |
Age	Year	ROR	Year-End Value	Year	ROR	Year-End Value
65	1969	-2.6%	$921,680	1979	14.7%	$1,091,720
66	1970	5.3%	$914,490	1980	23.9%	$1,288,990
67	1971	10.5%	$952,190	1981	3.4%	$1,262,820
68	1972	12.9%	$1,014,470	1982	16.6%	$1,398,480
69	1973	-6.6%	$884,100	1983	16.6%	$1,554,260
70	1974	-12.6%	$702,190	1984	7.3%	$1,588,800
71	1975	25.1%	$800,850	1985	22.0%	$1,856,300
72	1976	16.5%	$851,070	1986	13.9%	$2,032,230
73	1977	-2.4%	$743,240	1987	5.7%	$2,062,320
74	1978	6.3%	$696,600	1988	12.2%	$2,225,370
75	1979	14.7%	$694,870	1989	22.1%	$2,624,020
76	1980	23.9%	$742,220	1990	1.2%	$2,557,530
77	1981	3.4%	$636,700	1991	20.8%	$2,988,080
78	1982	16.6%	$603,910	1992	6.1%	$3,065,740
79	1983	16.6%	$561,450	1993	7.3%	$3,180,260
80	1984	7.3%	$454,800	1994	2.0%	$3,133,510
81	1985	22.0%	$401,980	1995	24.6%	$3,788,840
82	1986	13.9%	$302,860	1996	16.3%	$4,290,720
83	1987	5.7%	$159,410	1997	21.2%	$5,075,020
84	1988	12.2%	$11,760	1998	19.1%	$5,920,940
85	1989	22.1%	Exhausted	1999	14.3%	$6,642,490
86	1990	1.2%	Exhausted	2000	-0.8%	$6,459,690
87	1991	20.8%	Exhausted	2001	-3.8%	$6,081,200
88	1992	6.1%	Exhausted	2002	-9.3%	$5,384,130
89	1993	7.3%	Exhausted	2003	18.9%	$6,263,190
90	1994	2.0%	Exhausted	2004	8.2%	$6,637,900
91	1995	24.6%	Exhausted	2005	3.8%	$6,747,610
92	1996	16.3%	Exhausted	2006	11.2%	$7,351,490
93	1997	21.1%	Exhausted	2007	6.1%	$7,642,780
94	1998	19.1%	Exhausted	2008	-20.5%	$5,914,020
		Average ROR: 10.5%			Average ROR: 9.6%	

Table 0.1: Data based on two 31-year periods ending on December 31, 1998 and 2008, respectively. Each portfolio assumes a first-year 5% withdrawal that was subsequently adjusted for actual inflation. Each portfolio also assumes a 60% stock/40% bond allocation, rebalanced annually. Stocks are represented by the S&P 500. The Standard & Poor's 500 Index (S&P 500) is an unmanaged group of large company stocks. It is not possible to invest directly in an index. Bonds are represented by the annualized yields of long-term treasuries (10+ years maturity). Inflation is represented by changes to the historical CPI. Past performance does not guarantee future results. This illustration does not account for any taxes or fees.

The chart illustrates what happened to each of your investment portfolios during each year of your respective 30 years of retirement, assuming you both invested in the exact same portfolio of 60% stocks, represented by the S&P 500 index, and 40% bonds, represented by long-term treasuries. You each also withdrew exactly $50,000—or 5% of your portfolio value—the first year and adjusted that withdrawal each year, based on the change in the Consumer Price Index for that year, to account for inflation.

As you analyze the chart, notice the following:

- Both of you experienced exactly 26 years of positive annual returns.
- Both of you experienced exactly 4 years of negative returns.
- Both of you far exceeded the expected 8% average rate of return over your 30-year retirement.

Moreover, you outperformed your coworker in every single statistical category:

- Your average rate of return was higher, 10.5 versus 9.6.
- The average of your "up" years was 13.6%. And the average of your coworker's up years was 13.1%.
- The average of your down years was -6.1%. And the average of your coworker's down years was -8.6%.

To summarize, your overall average was better, your positive-year average was better, and your negative-year average was better.

But as you can see from the chart, your results were not better. In fact, they were far worse. You ran out of money in 19 years! You're completely broke. Your portfolio has $0 in it, and therefore, you have no more income. Your coworker, on the other hand, didn't run out of money. In fact, they eventually died with almost six times the amount of money they started with; a $5,914,020 legacy they left for their children!

So what happened? Luck. Plain and simple. Good luck for your coworker. Bad luck for you. Despite all your planning and statistical analysis and your strong performance metrics over those 30 years, all of which far exceeded your highest expectations, it all came down to luck. You see, since you retired 10 years apart, the unique sequence (order) of investment returns over each of your 30 years of retirement dictated both their success and your failure.

Although this is a fictional example, the underlying numbers are very real, representing the actual historical performance of a typical retirement portfolio comprised of 60% stocks (represented by the S&P 500) and 40% bonds (represented by the Bloomberg U.S. Long-term Treasury Index) over each of the stated 30-year periods of time.

As you can see, this approach to retirement planning simply doesn't work. Because luck dictates the results. And luck is not a plan. In fact, the results would likely be much worse today, given the unprecedented market volatility we've seen over the past two and a half decades, and our current rising interest rate environment, which we'll touch on later in the book.

So in the words of Harry Callahan, aka Dirty Harry, the question is, "Do you feel lucky"?

Or would you rather take another path with your retirement? If you choose the latter, continue reading, because the whole point of this book is to help you understand why the current approach to retirement is flawed and how to avoid this type of result—running out of money simply because of dumb luck—happening to you.

WHAT YOU WILL GET FROM THIS BOOK

Unfortunately, the aforementioned scenario is far too common, largely due to the increased systemic market volatility we've all witnessed over the past 25 years; (part of the "new normal" I'll explain later in this book) It's precisely why I felt the need to develop a completely different approach—one that doesn't rely on luck. I've witnessed the devastation that can happen to people who blindly follow the traditional retirement model, so I've written this book to help you avoid becoming yet another victim. It's your key to successfully navigating retirement.

For too long we've all been trained to think in terms of pursuing growth—finding the next big thing in the stock market, the next high-flyer on the NASDAQ, or the blue chip that keeps on giving. Meanwhile, we have treated risk management—avoiding losses—as merely a passing afterthought. Retirement changes all of this, turning it on its head. When you retire, risk management *must* become the primary driver, with achieving reasonable gains following as a distant second.

Whether you have far more money than you'll ever need or you're just hoping what you have will last a lifetime, this book is about maximizing your outcome and minimizing what could go wrong along the way. In the pages ahead, I'll teach you how to make this change. I'll show you how to turn away from the woefully inadequate, flawed traditional paradigm. You'll discover a more reliable approach—one that isn't just "a better mousetrap," because a better mousetrap isn't what you need. You need an altogether unique paradigm for thinking about retirement. By the end of this book, you'll walk away with a healthy new perspective for achieving retirement success, regardless of where you are in your retirement planning journey.

This book is intended primarily for those who are already retired or are planning to retire within the next five years. However, for those of you a bit further from your intended retirement date, or even just starting out in your career, read on, because you will need to decide whether to follow the status quo or begin now to forge ahead on a road less traveled, one designed to position you for a worry-free retirement.

HOW TO USE THIS BOOK

I've divided this book into four parts:

Part 1 is called The New Normal. It's an overview of the core problem with today's retirement paradigm—a misdiagnosis of the problem itself—as well as an overview of an alternative approach that will help you plan for and enjoy a financially worry-free retirement.

Part 2 provides a clear, effective process for creating stable, increasing, tax-efficient lifetime income while maintaining flexibility and maximizing your residual estate—that is, your margin of error during your lifetime and your financial legacy upon your death.

In part 3, I'll bust some of the oldest retirement planning and investing myths while providing a better way of thinking about and overcoming each underlying issue.

Part 4 pulls it all together, revealing some additional key concepts for you to consider when designing your own retirement income plan.

You'll get easy-to-follow strategies that I've developed over the years to help you avoid the mistakes that await those who blindly follow the myths, hype, and propaganda of the mainstream financial media.

Don't Skip the End-of-Chapter Exercises

This book is intended to be a highly interactive and participatory process. At the end of each chapter, I'll highlight various key concepts and encourage you to take the necessary steps to implement what you've learned.

To get the most from this book, I encourage you to take the suggested action at the end of each chapter. I'll include QR codes for you to access worksheets and other helpful information, as well as a link to a short video summary of the main points of the chapter.

Hopefully I've gotten your attention. You may even be wondering: How can this traditional approach to retirement be so wrong if everyone does it this way? And if it puts people at risk, why would anyone do it this way?

Those are excellent questions, and they come with surprising answers, ones that I plan to address in the pages ahead. So relax, take a deep breath, and open your mind to the possibility that there is indeed a better way . . .

Use your mobile phone to hover over the QR code below and follow the link, which will take you to a login page to establish a user ID and password that will enable you to complete the various exercises at the end of each chapter and to track your progress as we go (www.therealdealonretirement.com).

Taking Action

Before moving on to chapter 1, use the QR code below to access your personal progress portal.

1. You'll be prompted to establish a unique user ID and password to access all the video shorts, worksheets, and resources for each chapter.

2. Complete the **Retirement Readiness Questionnaire**, found under "Introduction." This will help you evaluate your current state of readiness to make the transition into retirement, even if you're already retired. (It's never too late to do the right things.)

   a. What is your personal Retirement Readiness score?

   b. How do you feel about that? Are you surprised?

   c. What do you feel are the most glaring areas of need/shortfall?

   d. What appears to be the area(s) in which you are best prepared?

PART 1

The New Normal

CHAPTER 1

A CRASH COURSE IN RETIREMENT PLANNING

The reason investors do so poorly over time
is the inability to manage risk. Risk is never a function
of how much money you make when markets are rising.
It is a measure of your ability to survive the crash.

—LANCE ROBERTS

My first indication that something was awry came when I was working for a large national financial advisory firm back in 2000. I had recently made a major career change to pursue my dream of being a financial advisor. I was just 34 years old, and the raging tech stock boom of the nineties had many acting as if everything had changed and that there would never again be another major market correction, because as always, "this time was different." There was a new economy, ushered in by the internet. Growth and prosperity were rampant, while annual investment returns of 20% or more were the new normal.

But we all know what happened next. Reality set in, as it always does. Over the next two and a half years, from 2000 to 2002, the S&P 500 fell a full 50%, from its high of around 1,552 to a low of approximately 776. Witnessing the devastating effects the bursting of the dot-com bubble had on people who had recently retired or were planning to retire soon thereafter, I got my first glimpse of just how ineffective the traditional approach to retirement planning and investing is. It simply doesn't provide the peace of mind most retirees are looking for. And for those who thought it did, that peace of mind has proven to be a false sense of security.

I'll never forget the looks on the faces of even the most senior advisors at the firm as they processed the reality of what was happening to their clients' retirement portfolios. Their hard-earned savings were evaporating before their eyes, and their retirement dreams were being destroyed. Those advisors had no answers for their clients. How would they ever recover? Should they cash out now or stay the course? How much worse could it get? Now what?

Coming out of the aforementioned crash of 2000–2002, the market's strong performance between 2003 and 2007 made short work of most people's memories. Despite the fact that it would take over 13 years for the S&P 500 to meaningfully breach its 2000 high after the dot-com debacle, by late 2007 many investors had once again grown infatuated with the stock market's record over the five years since.

CHARTING MY NEW PATH

So in late 2007, when I began to recommend taking a more cautious approach in response to the burgeoning subprime debt crisis overseas, many people were unwilling to listen, concerned they might miss out on any part of the ongoing bull market.

But once again, you know what happened next. The so-called subprime crises spread like wildfire, contaminating far beyond the limits of subprime debt and infecting markets worldwide. The global economy tanked, taking with it the US stock market. From its high of 1,565 on October 9, 2007, to its low of 677 on March 9, 2009, the S&P 500 lost over 56%. This time the wreckage took place in about half the time of the 2000–2002 crash: 17 months versus 31.

S&P 500

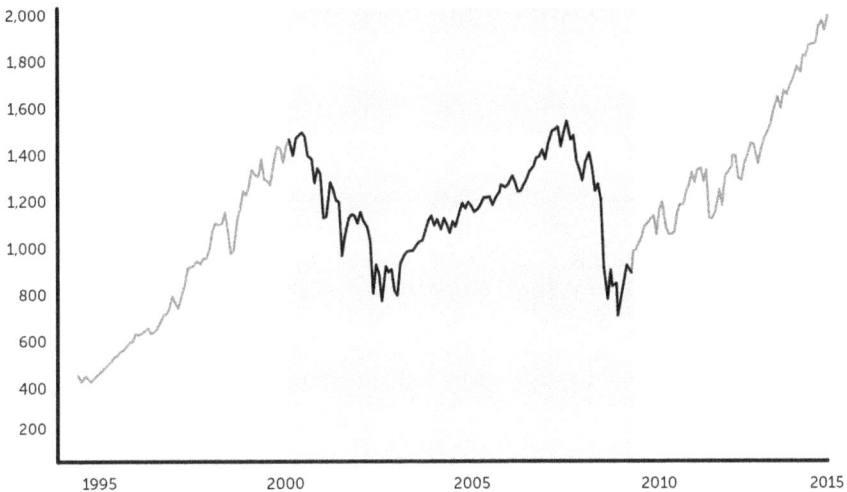

Figure 1.1: For investors, the period from 2000 to 2009 was a retiree's worst nightmare.

By this time, I had moved from the large national firm to a smaller regional firm and had begun following many of the principles in this book that I'd been developing since 2000. I had quickly learned that choosing not to follow the status quo was difficult, if not impossible, while remaining associated with a large firm.

Although I operated my personal advisory business like that of an independent advisor, in reality my affiliation limited my ability to be truly independent. Everything from their subsidized educational opportunities, to their compensation plan, to their compliance program made deviating from their "endorsed" practices difficult, if not impossible. In retrospect, I now understand that this was not unique to my particular situation, but rather it was, and is, true of most any large firm. In the end, you're either totally independent or you're not.

Once again, retirees were looking for answers because their traditional plans were failing—largely because they weren't plans at all, something I'll expound upon later in this chapter. They were just analyses, which merely quantify the problem or situation. A plan, on the other hand, is meant to not only identify the problem, but also solve it. And that's what these retirees didn't have.

"WE'VE ALWAYS DONE IT THAT WAY"

Unfortunately, the financial industry has long established most of its accepted systems, processes, and rules around what I refer to as the "traditional" approach to financial planning and investing—by which I mean things like asset allocation, diversification, dollar-cost averaging, tax deferral, and the like. These and many other basic concepts form the foundation of what I call the financial industry "mousetrap"—the chassis upon which most all mainstream financial planning and investing emanates. This foundation includes everything from advisor education, training, and oversight, to regulation and enforcement. This means most advisors "grow up" in this environment, are taught this singular approach, and are expected to adhere to it and replicate it.

In fact, there's such a "plug and play" mentality surrounding this conventional methodology that robo-advisors and online calculators are becoming popular alternatives for implementing these inadequate strategies. Rather than consulting with a live advisor in person, someone planning their retirement can simply plug their numbers into an online calculator and, like magic, their (hypothetical) financial future is laid out before them. After all, anything that can be boiled down to a rote set of rules or formulas can be implemented just as well (if not better) by a computer algorithm rather than by an intelligent, thinking human being, right?

This traditional approach that is so ingrained among investment firms and so easily replicated lends itself rather easily to a cookie-cutter approach. As a result, these robo-advisors and online calculators have become increasingly popular. Individuals and, disturbingly, advisors themselves think, "Well, I can just plug the information in and it'll spit out the prescribed strategy."

The unfortunate result is that, more and more, the vast majority of retirement plans and investment portfolios look similar, if not entirely identical, once you peel back the layers of the onion. Even though that sameness is not a good thing.

TIMES HAVE CHANGED

The shortcomings of this entire conventional reality that I've just described are compounded by the current global economic environment, which has grown especially challenging for retirees.

This is largely due to the following seven issues, of particular concern to most retirees, in which we have recently entered uncharted waters:

- Market volatility
- Inflation
- Interest rates
- Taxes
- Health care costs
- Longevity
- Vanishing pensions

I will tackle each of these here and give special emphasis to how they specifically impact retirees.

Market Volatility

Stock market volatility has been extraordinary over the past two and a half decades, going back to the late nineties with the dot-com bubble. Since then, the level of instability has been unprecedented, including significant equity declines in 2008, 2011, 2015, 2018, 2020, and 2022. This extreme volatility of the stock market has been exacerbated by the recent rise in interest rates, which is devastating for fixed-income investments and thus equally so for bond prices. Most recently, 2022 saw one of the worst years ever for both stocks and bonds combined.

And as I'll explain in chapter 10, this creates an even bigger problem for retirees, since bonds are traditionally relied upon as the "shock absorber" for stocks within the most commonly utilized investment approach today, based largely on something called Modern Portfolio Theory (MPT), which I'll describe later in this book. The result is a seemingly insurmountable obstacle to generating stable, increasing, tax-efficient retirement income, so long as you are committed to that conventional approach to retirement planning and portfolio design.

Inflation

The purchasing power of the dollar has declined approximately 84% since 1970 and 96% since 1910. This obviously presents significant problems for successful retirement planning.

First, and most obviously, if your dollars buy fewer and fewer material goods and services year after year, that means your retirement income must proportionately increase year after year to keep pace. As I'll demonstrate in chapter 4, it's hard enough to generate stable, tax-efficient income year after year, let alone need that same income stream to increase each and every year for the entire length of your 20- to 30-year retirement. Imagine living today on the same monthly income you required back in the 1990s!

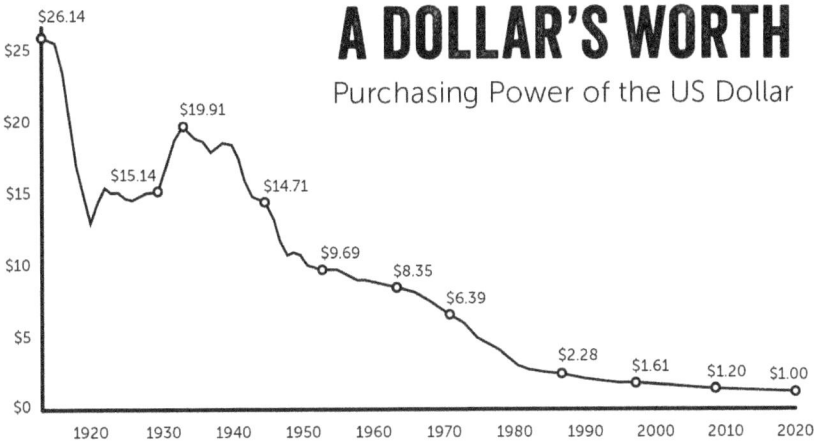

A DOLLAR'S WORTH
Purchasing Power of the US Dollar

Figure 1.2: The Value of Today's Dollar at Various Times throughout the Past 100 Years
Source: Department of Labor: Bureau of Labor Statistics

Second, this decrease in purchasing power brings into focus an uncomfortable truth about historic equity market returns over time. Perhaps much of the increase in US equity market valuations over the past 30-plus years is less the result of an overall increase in the value of all the underlying companies and more a result of a decrease in the value of the underlying currency in which those stocks are being priced. Inflation increases the price of everything, right? That includes stocks.

In other words, generally speaking, no one gets excited when the prices of goods and services go up, exclaiming "the economy is doing great!" But everyone does get excited when the value (price) of their 401(k) increases. But what if the value is rising for the exact same reason—as a function of inflation? And what if the purchasing power of your investments hasn't increased anywhere near equal to the rate of inflation over time? That would mean you're falling further and further behind every year, but you don't know it because of the illusion of the increasing value of your retirement savings portfolio.

Interest Rates

For the vast majority, if not all, of your and my adult working lifetime, interest rates have generally been decreasing. But that changed in rather dramatic fashion when 2022 saw a massive spike in rates as the Federal Reserve tried to calm inflation. The good news is that if you're able to retire debt-free, you won't be paying the higher interest rate to creditors. Instead, you'll be benefitting from higher interest rates on your guaranteed savings vehicles, such as checking, savings, money markets, certificates of deposit (CDs), and fixed annuities.

Historical 30–Year Mortgage Rates
1971–2023

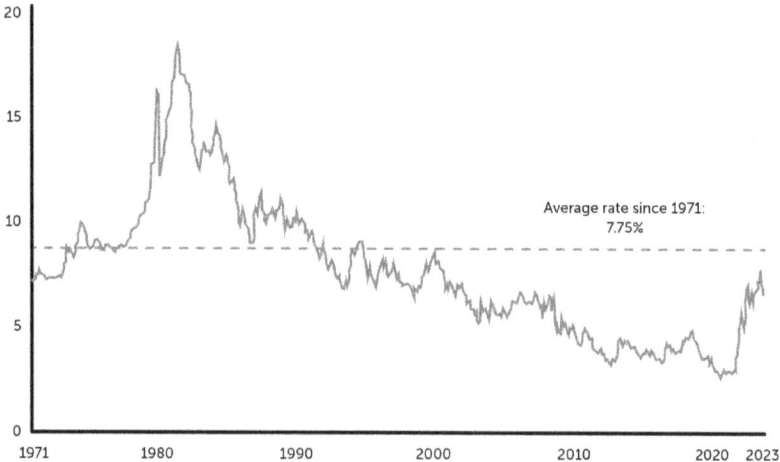

Figure 1.3: Source: Yahoo Finance and Bloomberg

But as I have alluded to, 2022 also revealed the significant downside to this recent trend as it relates to traditional retirement planning. Generally declining interest rates means that bonds have historically behaved a certain way and could be relied upon to play a specific role in your retirement portfolio. But for the first time in decades, rising rates resulted in major downward volatility for fixed income securities like bonds at the same time equities were in freefall.

The result? The year 2022 was the worst year for stocks and bonds combined since the late 1960s. And since the traditional approach to retirement planning assumes bonds to be conservative investments, acting primarily as a shock absorber for stocks, many conservative investors were in for quite a surprise when both the equity and fixed income portions of their retirement savings experienced major losses.

US Stocks vs. Bonds Returns 1926–2022

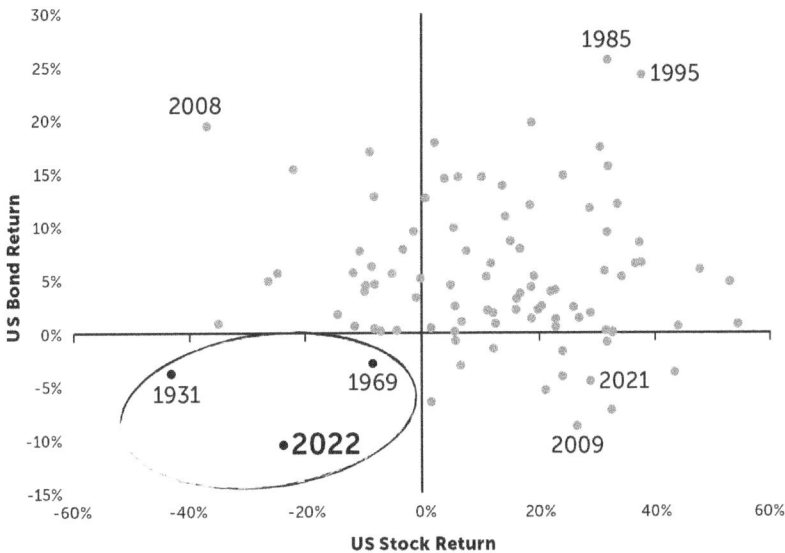

Figure 1.4: US Stocks versus Bonds Returns 1926–2022
Source: Bloomberg, Lombard Odier

And this trend doesn't appear to be momentary, as has occasionally happened in the past. But it is likely to be ongoing for the foreseeable future since the Fed would risk losing control of already soaring inflation by reducing rates again on any significant basis, apart from a few likely cuts heading into the next election to temporarily boost the economy in favor of the incumbent administration. (It wouldn't surprise me if the recent, dramatic increase in rates was precisely to ensure sufficient ability to reduce rates again, should the need arise.)

Taxes

Contrary to what you've undoubtedly been told for the entirety of your working life to encourage you to plow savings into your tax-deferred retirement accounts, taxes will likely be your single largest expense during retirement. And that assumes Congress leaves tax rates where they currently are. However, I've met very few people who think tax rates will not be higher in the future than they are today.

I'll elaborate on the dire need for long-term tax planning in chapter 13. For now, suffice it to say, the debt situation in the US is such that there seems to be no end in sight for Congress's need to tax and borrow. After all, those are the only two ways they have to pay the bills related to their ever-increasing expenditures and liabilities. The government's lavish tax-and-spend habits create obvious complications for retirement income planning, since, as they say, "It's not what you earn, but what you keep" that matters.

Overall Spending in Retirement

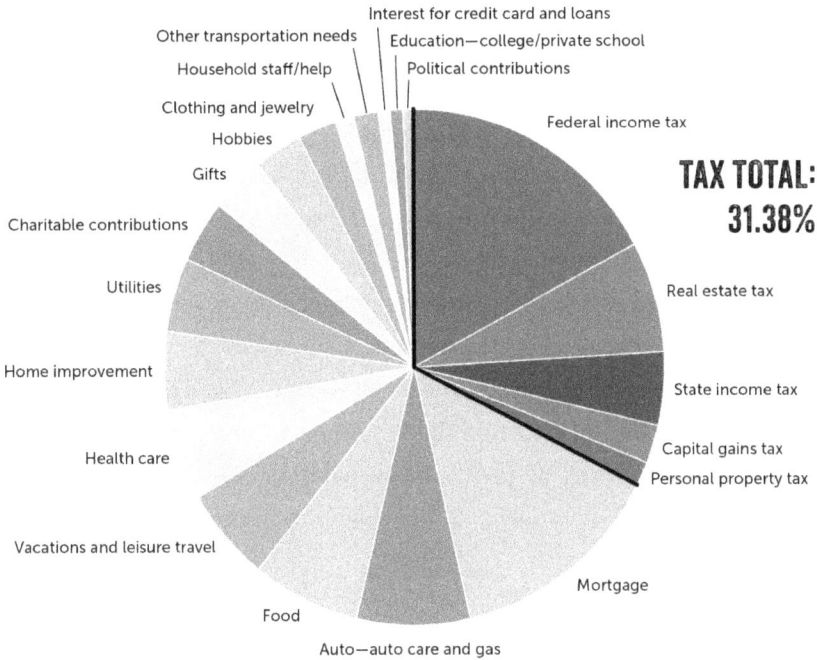

Interest for credit card and loans
Other transportation needs
Education—college/private school
Household staff/help
Political contributions
Clothing and jewelry
Hobbies
Federal income tax
Gifts

TAX TOTAL: 31.38%

Charitable contributions
Utilities
Real estate tax
Home improvement
State income tax
Health care
Capital gains tax
Personal property tax
Vacations and leisure travel
Mortgage
Food
Auto—auto care and gas

Source: research study by Lincoln Financial Group and Spectrem Group, Oct. 5–8, 2009

Figure 1.5: Overall Spending in Retirement

Health Care Costs

Health care will likely be your second-largest expense during your life-time, just behind taxes. And like taxes, it's reasonable to assume health care costs will continue to consume an ever-increasing portion of your wealth and income in retirement, unless you happen to know exactly when you're going to die and can plan accordingly.

This reminds me of a particular client who I first started working with some 15 years ago. At that time, he informed me he had a certain chronic and incurable illness that would likely prevent him from living more than another five to 10 years or so. So I asked him this one simple question: "If you are alive in 11 years and you're out of money, is that okay?" Needless to say, we ran his plan out to well into his 90s.

Not so needless to say, however, is that just last month he was in for his annual review at age 86! And he was recently told that his condition is in remission—something he didn't think was possible 15 years ago. Of course, his treatments have cost him a pretty penny, but it's all in the plan, so he's in great shape—both physically and financially!

This example underscores the need for your retirement plan to include a high level of attention to both Medicare and long-term health care planning, as well as plenty of available liquidity for unplanned health care needs.

Longevity

Back in 1935, when the United States Social Security Administration was first formed and the Social Security insurance program enacted, the average life expectancy was just 63 years, and the earliest you could claim Social Security was age 65. So back then, most people didn't even live long enough to collect any Social Security. The program was meant to cover those who outlived their anticipated life span. Today, people are living longer than ever. The average life expectancy for a 60-year-old is now well into their 80s. Moreover, I routinely see people with access to quality housing, nutrition, and medical resources living well into their 90s and even 100s. So if you're on the doorstep of retirement now, you should probably plan for a good 25 to 30 years of retirement.

Living longer sounds great, so long as you have a decent quality of life. However, in reality, increasing longevity serves to multiply every other financial risk related to retirement, simply because you're living longer and increasing the likelihood of something happening. Consequently, we always plan for all of our clients to live into their 90s, if not longer. This aligns with our general philosophy of being ultraconservative with all our assumptions when it comes to retirement income planning.

Vanishing Pensions

Pensions were once extremely common, serving as the bread and butter of retirement income for most workers as recently as a couple of decades ago. But pensions are a dying breed. Only about one-third of our recently retired clients currently have pensions that represent a significant source of income for their retirement. And many that do have them are concerned about their pension's long-term viability, due to some of the issues many pension funds and pension guarantee entities are facing. My own father is a great example of this. At age 88, he's been relying on his pension much longer than he ever expected. And every year he worries that this will be the year it goes away. Thankfully, that has not been the case.

Ironically, but not surprisingly, the issues facing those entities are the same issues facing retirees without pensions, who are managing their own retirement savings portfolios. You likely know of someone who lost all or a portion of their pension during the last decade or two. This risk serves to increase the burden for retirees to find reliable ways to create their own stable, increasing, tax-efficient retirement income, which I'll elaborate on throughout this book.

As you can imagine, these seven issues substantially complicate the already significant problems facing the traditional approach to retirement planning, greatly adding to its shortcomings. Since many of these seven weren't as prevalent in the past, retirement income planning was historically much simpler.

Let's face it. If everyone had a large, stable pension, two Social Security checks, and a life expectancy of 65 to 70 years old, I probably wouldn't be writing this book.

THE DEFINITION OF INSANITY

Despite all these factors, the traditional approach to retirement has remained largely unchanged, resulting in many unfortunate outcomes, over the past couple decades in particular. Moreover, the financial industry and mainstream media continue to preach the same worn-out mantras that may have been effective back in the day but are completely inadequate given this "new normal." And many approaches to retirement planning and investing that purport to be truly unique or "outside the box" are really just putting lipstick on the same old pig, with perhaps some limited variation sprinkled in for the sake of perceived differentiation.

Albert Einstein is often quoted as having said, "The definition of insanity is doing the same thing over and over while expecting a different result." And that's effectively what's happening with retirement planning. I continue to see retirees constantly utilizing the same approach that used to work when retirement was a fairly simple, straightforward proposition, despite the fact that today's new normal has rendered that approach completely inadequate. The fact of the matter is, as I sit here writing this book, the vast majority of retirees, as well as most advisors, continue to embrace the old traditional mindset. Little thought is given to new, truly innovative retirement solutions.

Having witnessed so many disappointing outcomes while cutting my teeth in the industry for my first several years, I made a conscious decision long ago to identify and develop processes and strategies to address this state of affairs and help retirees maximize their likelihood of success, leaving as little as possible to luck. As one of my clients (a literal bridge builder) once stated of our approach, "You've spent the last couple decades developing and implementing strategies that anticipate that one moment in time that may never happen, but if it does, we know we'll survive."

And he's right. That, understandably, was his approach to building bridges. He built them for that one moment in time that probably won't ever happen, but if it does, the bridge will survive. I believe this is how you must approach retirement planning in light of today's new normal—given the seven issues identified earlier. You must build the plan as if whatever could go wrong will go wrong, and then make sure your plan will still work. Then, if nothing goes wrong, you're way ahead of the game. But if things don't go as planned, which is likely in some form or fashion, you're still okay. That's precisely what the rest of this book is about.

The current retirement planning model is broken and woefully inadequate. Times have changed, but retirement planning hasn't. Most retirement plans leave far too much of the outcome to luck. These changes have resulted in unprecedented hardship for many retirees over the past 25 years. You need a different approach that reflects today's reality.

Taking Action

Before moving on to the next chapter, use the QR code (page 9) to access the chapter 1 resources, then:

1. Complete the **Investment Priorities** and the **Personal Goals and Objectives** worksheets for chapter 1. These will help you identify your retirement planning priorities as you move forward.

2. If you are married, have each spouse complete one and then compare your results.

   a. You may be surprised by the differences in your answers.

   b. Discuss the areas in which you differed significantly to better understand each other's perspectives.

   c. Try to do them again from a "combined" perspective, trying to arrive at a consensus.

There will be cases where you cannot reach consensus. That's okay. This exercise will help initiate discussion about important planning topics that you may not have discussed in depth before. That's an important part of the process.

CHAPTER 2

A CASE OF MISTAKEN IDENTITY

If I have an hour to solve a problem,
I'll spend fifty-five minutes thinking about the problem,
and five minutes thinking about solutions.

—ALBERT EINSTEIN

N ow that you understand the increased retirement challenges presented by today's world a little better, let me put the retirement
planning problem itself into perspective. The core problem with today's
traditional retirement planning paradigm is that it misidentifies the
problem altogether, and a misidentified problem is difficult to solve.

You see, retirement is currently treated as an asset problem. This is evidenced and reinforced by a variety of slogans and marketing campaigns
throughout the financial industry, such as "What's your [retirement]
number?," inferring all you need to do is save a certain amount of money
to ensure you're able to retire confidently. It's also the topic of focus of
many industry books, articles, and financial calculators—all of them

focused on how much you need in terms of assets or retirement savings to retire confidently.

In social settings, when people find out I'm a retirement advisor, the most common question I get is, "How much should I have saved up in order to retire?" That's a perfect example of the fact that people have been conditioned to think this way about retirement and how to know if they're ready.

ALL THINGS ARE NOT EQUAL

Having spent a lot of time pondering the issue of what amount of money do people need to retire, I believe the main reason for this way of thinking is because it's simple. People like simple. *How much do I need? Do I need a million? Do I need two million? Do I need three million?* It's a simple question with presumably a simple answer. And all things being equal, simpler is better. But all things are never equal. And therein lies the problem. Reducing the equation to a single variable—savings—is not sufficient to be remotely predictive of success. And in some cases, it's not even relevant.

But that way of thinking is easy. And easy is important if you are marketing financial services or most anything else. The simpler you can make the problem seem, the easier it is to communicate your proposed solution, and the more likely you'll be to successfully compel someone to take action.

A great example is the fast food giant McDonald's. When you watch or listen to a McDonald's commercial, you constantly hear about the price of their food. Everybody used to know they could go to McDonald's and get a 99-cent hamburger or buy any number of items on their Dollar Menu for a buck, or a meal for $5 (before inflation took over, of course, and the Dollar Menu became the $1 $2 $3 Dollar Menu). But I've never heard a McDonald's commercial talk about the nutritional value of their food, right? Let's face it, talking about the nutritional value of their food would be a much more complicated discussion than simply saying, "Our burgers cost 99 cents." Which conversation makes it easier to induce someone to action?

By simplifying the discussion, it's easier to convince their target market to purchase their solution. Quite frankly, even if they were able to make the nutritional value argument in a simple, coherent, and understandable fashion, they would likely lose the argument to someone else, which is a whole other problem. It's all about directing their target market's focus toward the variable that enables them to most easily win the argument and thus compel their audience to take the desired action.

The same can be said for most any industry, including the financial industry. Think of a company like Vanguard, known for having inexpensive mutual funds. Why are they known for that? Because they tell you all the time, "We have low fees, and low fees are all that matters." They are making their argument from the position that all things *are* equal, so all that matters is cost. You never hear Vanguard talk about generating the best risk-adjusted returns from their funds, or their managers' ability to actively mitigate losses, or how competitive their products are from a performance standpoint compared to other companies.

Although Vanguard does have some actively managed funds, they are mostly known for their low-cost, passively managed index funds, which are all about low price since they don't actually aim to outperform their respective index. By commoditizing mutual funds (their product), price becomes the only factor in the eyes of their target market. Whether this characterization is actually true is irrelevant so long as they can convince you it is.

So instead of getting into the much more complicated conversation about net realized returns, or active versus passive management, or our managers versus theirs, it's much easier to simply say they're inexpensive, because they can win that argument quickly and easily, which appeals to the vast majority of their target market—the "do-it-yourselfers." The problem, of course, is that low cost is only the best choice when all other things are equal, which is never the case in real life. It's possible, even likely, that a different strategy could deliver a better net result over time, despite a higher fee. But that would be a much more complicated conversation, difficult to communicate in a 30-second commercial or in a static, single-page ad to their target market. I can attest firsthand to the effectiveness of this approach, having spent countless hours over the years "unteaching" people many of the erroneous principles they have unwittingly embraced as a result of years of "steeping" in the mainstream financial media.

RETIREMENT IS A JOURNEY

In similar fashion, many financial services firms benefit by reducing the retirement planning conversation to as few variables as possible. Those simplified arguments are easier to make, and to win. That's extremely important when attempting to appeal to a massive audience. In reality, however, evaluating any value proposition should involve far more than price alone. That's just one side of the equation. It must also involve value, which is much more difficult to define.

My point, of course, is that this oversimplified traditional approach to retirement planning is the wrong approach. "How much do you need?" or "What's your number?" are the wrong questions. They greatly underestimate the entire problem. They treat the issue as monolithic instead of multifaceted, which it truly is. More specifically, the asset-based approach treats retirement as an event rather than a journey. So long as you have $X saved at a given point in time, you'll be fine.

But retirement *is* a journey. In fact, it's a journey of ever-increasing length, given today's ever-increasing life expectancies. Any worthwhile plan must be built for the entire journey, not simply to satisfy a particular equation at a single moment in time. This, of course, makes retirement planning a much more involved process, but given the extraordinarily high stakes, it's a worthwhile one.

ONE SIZE DOESN'T FIT ALL

Although the core issue with the traditional approach is that it treats retirement as an asset-based problem, that's just the tip of the iceberg in terms of its actual shortcomings. For example, one major flaw of taking the asset-based approach is that it doesn't consider all of the various types of resources you might have.

Think about it this way. If you say, "How much do I need saved in order to retire?" and I say, "$2 million," most likely our conversation's over. You either have that amount saved or you don't. But what that conversation doesn't do is address all the various types of resources you might have and how each of them can be converted into your ultimate goal: retirement income.

Understanding the various types of assets, as well as any sources of non-asset-based income you might have, like Social Security or a pension, is critical. You can certainly imagine how differences in the amounts of those types of resources would have a dramatic impact on how much you might need to have saved. But the asset-based conversation doesn't address any of that—certainly not with sufficient detail to adequately guide your planning process. I have clients with tremendous guaranteed monthly income generated by things like Social Security, pension payments, rental income, guaranteed annuities, or royalty payments—but less in the way of liquid assets. And I have others with tremendous liquid assets but less in the way of guaranteed monthly income. And of course, some have both. But their plans all look quite different.

Another problem with the asset-based approach is that it doesn't consider your unique personal income needs, which undoubtedly vary from person to person. Probably the second most common question I get when identified as a retirement advisor in social settings is, "How much monthly income does the average person need during retirement?" or "I think we'll need $X per month in retirement. Is that normal?"

What you require to live comfortably is unique to you, just as it is to every other individual. And it may or may not vary throughout your lifetime. You can't compare yourself to your neighbor or any "average" person. Remember, the so-called average person doesn't exist. Do you have debt you need to service? Will it be retired at some point? If you're retiring early, how will you pay for medical insurance prior to qualifying for Medicare at age 65? What if your health care spending needs are different from your neighbor's? What if you live longer than they do? What if your spouse dies prematurely? How much of a financial legacy do you want to leave your heirs? These are just a few of the more obvious differences that must be contemplated.

Nor does the asset-based approach consider the fact that history likely will not repeat itself. Most traditional planning assumptions are based on historical averages. And even if your averages end up being similar to historical averages, which is highly unlikely, your specific retirement years will undoubtedly be unique from all of those historical scenarios, as in our coworkers example in the introduction. They will differ with respect to the sequence of investment returns, inflation, and interest rates, to name just a few variables. What if inflation is different than it was? What if the markets behave differently than they have in the past? What if we have another 2008–like event? What if interest rates are different? What if your life expectancy is different?

One somewhat extreme example of the uniqueness of every situation is one of my favorite clients, a couple who own a successful business. Early on in our relationship, they were quite concerned about their lack of "retirement savings." All their friends had large retirement 401(k)s and IRAs. Everything they read said they should too. All they had was their business, some real estate, and two very tiny IRAs. Conventional wisdom said they were way behind in saving for retirement. Even their accountant was encouraging them to pour money into retirement accounts to reduce their current tax bill and save for their future. It would have been easy to just set them up with a retirement plan and plow as much of their annual profits into it as possible. But based on their business model and personal retirement objectives, their wisest course of action was to forego the short-term gratification of saving a few tax dollars and satiating their need to keep up with the Joneses. Instead, we focused on reaching their retirement objectives through their business. Their annual business profits were far more stable, tax efficient, and largely within their own control.

Fast-forward to today. They are now "retired" wealthy absentee business owners with more cash flow than they'll ever need. And based on today's tax laws, they will leave a far larger financial legacy to their children than they ever could have achieved through a traditional retirement savings account. Meanwhile, many of their friends' retirement fates hinge on the future of stock and bond markets over the next 30 years.

Hopefully you can see how oversimplified the traditional asset-based approach is and why it so often fails. Oversimplifying the problem is extremely dangerous because not only can it create a false sense of security, but it can also be unnecessarily discouraging, generating a false sense of despair for someone who thinks they will never have enough, when a more thorough analysis may indicate otherwise. Many a person has initiated a conversation with me by saying, "I don't think I'll ever be able to retire," only to find out at the end of our process that they could comfortably retire tomorrow, if they were so inclined, with a high level of confidence. In fact, this very scenario played out just last week with a couple who were completely shocked to learn how secure their retirement prognosis actually was, provided they simply implemented the retirement income plan and risk mitigation strategies we proposed. Those are fun meetings!

THE LUCK OF THE DRAW

I can speak forever about the shortcomings of the traditional approach to retirement planning and why you should consider an alternate path.

In the introduction I painted a picture using the simple example of two similar retirees who followed identical paths but who experienced dramatically different outcomes, because sometimes the most compelling argument isn't actually an argument, but an observation. The reason a picture is worth a thousand words is because it enables you to complete the narrative in your mind and draw your own conclusions.

So before you continue on, if you haven't already read the book's introduction, please do so now. It's critical that you understand the illustration provided there, because it lays the foundation for this entire book. It provides a context in which to place everything I'm going to share, including these next paragraphs.

In the example, the two coworkers did the exact same preparation. They worked for the same company, they made the same amount of money, they retired with the same life expectancy, they had the same monthly expenses, and they had the exact same amount of retirement savings. In short, they had *the exact same everything*, resulting in the exact same retirement "number" and the exact same high probability of success.

But even after we eliminated all those variables that for any two real individuals would have differed greatly and reduced the entire scenario to one single, solitary variable (the year in which they retired), they still experienced dramatically different outcomes.

Why? Because they used the traditional asset-based approach, which focused on how much they had saved, what an "appropriate" portfolio should look like, and how it had performed *historically*. It was not based on identifying the actual cash flow required to fund their retirement, then analyzing all their various resources to create a detailed, annualized plan for how to proactively generate the income that was needed each year and how to mitigate the various threats along the way.

Instead, they were subject to the luck of the draw—that is, their particular 30 years of retirement and how the stock and bond markets performed over those specific years, which was impossible for them to know until it was literally too late.

So for you, the question then becomes, Do you know precisely what the next 30 years are going to look like? If not, the traditional approach won't work for you. It's far too simple. And it's not proactive. The traditional approach is nothing more than a probability analysis. You won't know until you know. And then it will be too late.

THE COOKIE-CUTTER APPROACH

As you read this, some of you might be thinking, "That's me. That cookie-cutter approach is exactly what I have." If so, your process likely looked something like this: Your advisor (or these days your robo-advisor or online calculator) might have asked you some variation of these three questions: How much money do you have saved? How much annual income do you need during retirement? How much risk are you willing to take? This last question is usually answered via a questionnaire that attempts to identify your tolerance quantitatively on a scale of, say, 1–10.

During the next step, an investment strategy was likely recommended, based almost exclusively on your age, risk tolerance, and Modern Portfolio Theory (MPT), which I'll discuss more in chapter 10. Then your very predictable MPT allocation was likely sprinkled with some added "proprietary twist" from your particular advisor in an attempt to differentiate themselves from others wanting to manage your money in essentially the same manner.

Lastly, you were told that so long as you adhere to the prescribed asset allocation, history suggests your money should last a certain amount of time. If it appears your money will outlast you, then in theory, your plan is complete and you're said to be in good shape. If, on the other hand, it looks like your money might not outlast you, then you need to do one of the following—

- Delay retirement,

- Spend less, or
- Take on more risk (in the form of more equity/stock exposure).

Any one or a combination of these adjustments should help to increase your odds of success.

So in other words, you're told that if it doesn't appear you're likely to generate enough returns in your portfolio to provide for the rest of your projected lifetime, and you're unwilling to postpone retirement or reduce your desired standard of living, you need to take more risk, because traditionally speaking, higher risk equals higher return, right?

To the contrary, in the pages ahead I'll show you that taking more risk at this point in your life is actually the worst thing you can do. I'll explain why and tell you what you should do instead.

DO YOU REALLY HAVE A PLAN?

Once again, many of you right now are thinking, "Oh my gosh, that's me. That's my plan." But of course, it's not a plan. It's nothing more than a probability analysis. And the idea that increasing risk will increase your likelihood of success is equally troubling. You're transitioning into retirement, moving from your *acquire and grow* phase into the *protect and distribute* phase of your lifetime (see Figure 2.2), and you either have enough or you need to take on more risk. Really?!

To say that approach is problematic is an egregious understatement. It's a costly accident waiting to happen. It's exactly what's happened to so many retirees over the past two and a half decades, specifically since 2000. Since that time, it's common for people to seek our help because they have an advisor who "had always done a great job"—until the market dropped precipitously, like it did in 2000, 2008, 2018, 2020, and 2022, after which their plan was thrown completely off and now they're seeking damage control.

Just think about it rationally. What are the odds that something

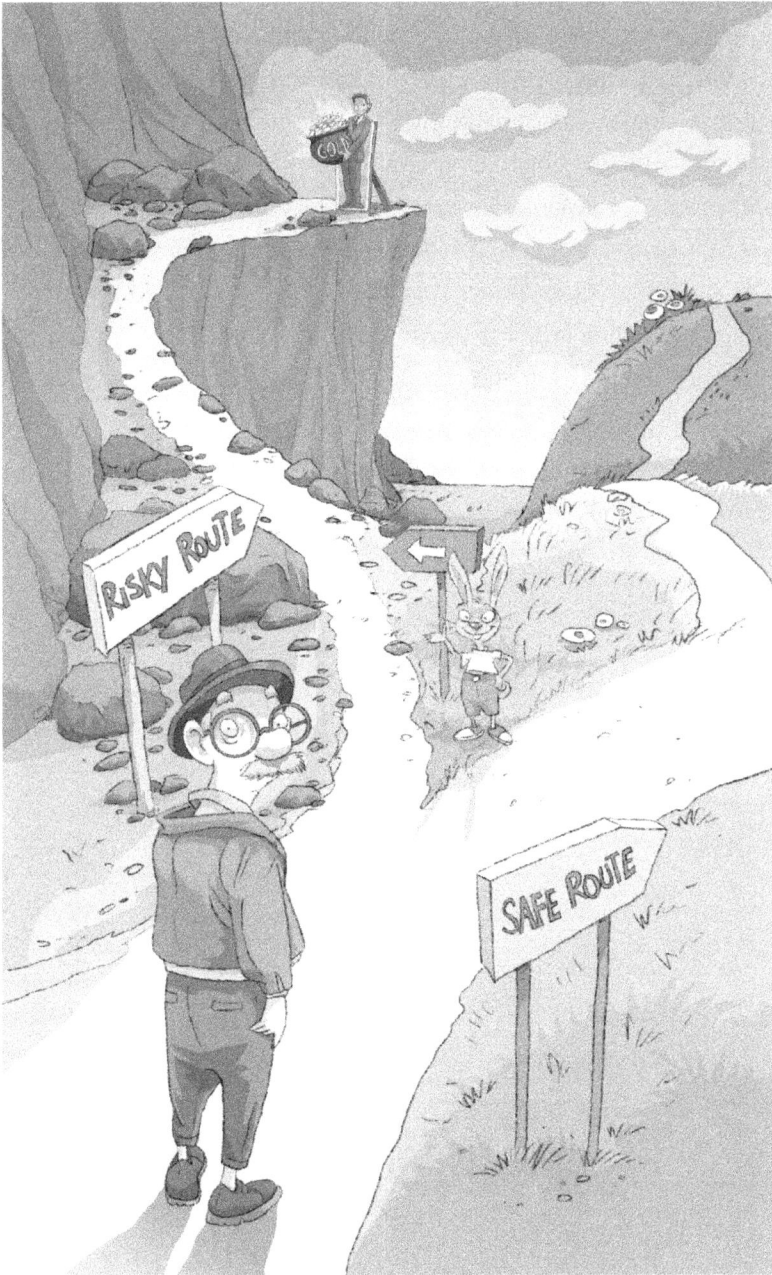

Figure 2.1: The Perils of Taking More Risk

unexpected is going to happen over the course of your 30-year retirement? Unexpected things happen every day—accidents, illnesses, economic downturns, inflation, deflation, wars and rumors of wars—right? Nevertheless, most of these traditional planning models assume the future will simply be an average of all the unexpected things that have happened in the past. As such, the typical retirement plan assumes nothing truly unique will ever happen. This rather naïve perspective is exacerbated by the fact that you are moving from the acquire and grow phases of your life to the protect and distribute phases of your life. The very things that determine "success" for your pocketbook have been turned upside down. So now, as you enter retirement and need everything to be more predictable than ever, all the rules have changed.

THE RETIREMENT WEALTH LIFE CYCLE
THE RULES ARE DIFFERENT

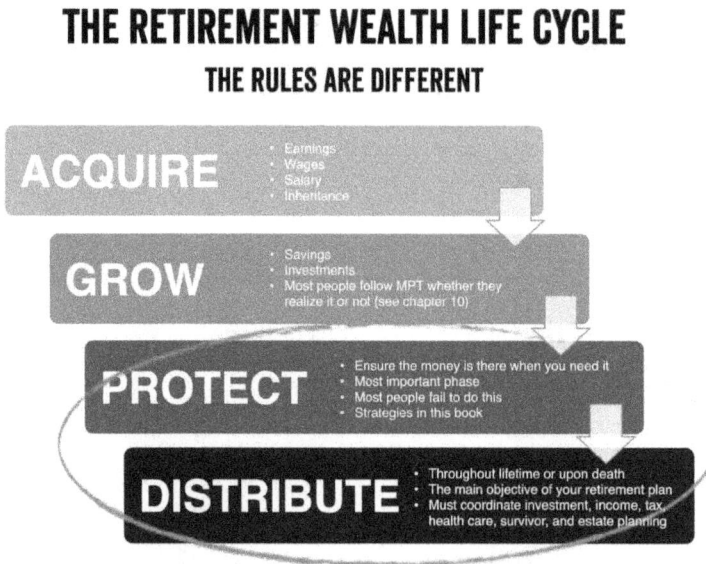

ACQUIRE
- Earnings
- Wages
- Salary
- Inheritance

GROW
- Savings
- Investments
- Most people follow MPT whether they realize it or not (see chapter 10)

PROTECT
- Ensure the money is there when you need it
- Most important phase
- Most people fail to do this
- Strategies in this book

DISTRIBUTE
- Throughout lifetime or upon death
- The main objective of your retirement plan
- Must coordinate investment, income, tax, health care, survivor, and estate planning

Figure 2.2: The Retirement Wealth Life Cycle

You no longer have "forever" for the averages to work themselves out. By definition, the rules and the math are different. The stakes are higher. And you only get one chance. What happens if a really bad economic downturn occurs just prior to your retirement? What if one occurs shortly after you retire? Or 10 years down the road? Or 20? What will be the long-term effect on you personally? How do you know you will survive it financially? Even if you have more money than you'll ever need and you're not concerned about "surviving," how do you know you're maximizing the likelihood of your personal definition of success?

Unlike when you were working and could just keep your head down, earning paychecks and shoveling savings into your retirement accounts at a reduced "buy low" price when the market was down, you are now consuming your assets and likely not adding new savings regularly. Unfortunately, none of those potentialities are adequately addressed with the current traditional planning approach. Hence the need for a different approach.

THE DISORDER OF OPERATIONS

So far, I've established how misdiagnosing the problem of when to retire based solely on the amount of assets one has is an oversimplification of the problem and, ultimately, lands people in retirement plans that aren't really plans. But perhaps the most damaging result is something I refer to as "the disorder of operations." In other words, within the context of this traditional approach, the investment strategy dictates everything. It dictates how much income you're likely to generate, how long your money should last, and how much volatility you're likely to experience along the way. This is completely backward.

The investment plan should be an outflow of your retirement income plan, not the dictator, as most are. Instead of the investment plan determining the income plan, the retirement income plan should be dictating the investment plan.

It Works Much Like Algebra

In algebra, (2 + 4) x 6 = 36, but 2 + (4 x 6) = 26. The order of operations matters and can lead to a distinctly different outcome. The retirement income plan should always come first and dictate the investment plan. To do it the other way around, which most people/advisors do, will potentially lead to a very different and undesirable result.

As you'll discover in chapter 10, this backward approach is largely due to the extraordinarily limited and antiquated approach most advisors take to portfolio design, especially for retirees. It typically looks something like this: time horizon x risk tolerance = investment strategy. The investment strategy itself is then based on MPT. It is typically composed almost entirely of stocks, bonds, and cash, along with scant amounts of other asset classes like commodities and real estate, albeit in the form of individual securities, mutual funds, or exchange traded funds (ETFs).

The only variable that ever changes in this equation is time horizon. As the investor ages, one year at a time, the overall allocation is slightly tweaked. That's it. This leaves you at the mercy of the markets. Again, this is a horribly backward approach that relies far too much on luck. Your projected outcome is based solely on history and historical averages. That's like buying one set of clothing based on the average historical temperature!

The Problem with Averages

But if you understand the simple math of averages, you'll understand that the problem with averages is just that: they're averages. The definition of an average, in and of itself, means it isn't necessarily even an actual scenario that's ever occurred. Rather, it's a hypothetical of all those scenarios lumped together. It's not real.

It's much like saying the average body weight of a room full of people is 145.6 pounds, when it's possible (even likely) that no one person in that room weighs exactly 145.6 pounds. For example, a room with two people could be composed of two people weighing 147.6 and 143.6 pounds, or a baby weighing 8 pounds and a pro athlete weighing 283.2 pounds. In both cases, the average is 145.6 pounds. Doesn't tell you much about the actual composition of the room, does it? It's just the average—every person's weight added up and then divided by the number of people in the room. It's a concept, not a real thing. It has no bearing whatsoever on your own weight even if you are in that same room, does it?

In similar fashion, as I'll expound upon further in chapter 8, a historical average rate of return of X% tells you nothing of what actually happened and whether your investment portfolio would have survived it.

In the same way, when you use these historical averages to build your expectations for the future, what you must realize is those historical averages didn't necessarily happen that way. It was an average of a wide variety of extremely different scenarios that occurred over time. The question then becomes, why would you base your entire retirement success on something so nebulous? My opinion, of course, is that you shouldn't. Doing so means your retirement plan isn't actually a plan, but rather you're playing roulette with your retirement.

Misidentifying the problem as an asset-based problem oversimplifies the issue and leads to a disorder of operations, where the tail ends up wagging the dog. What you should be doing instead is addressing your retirement as a cash flow problem, which we will cover in the next chapter.

Taking Action

Before moving on to the next chapter, use the QR code (page 9) to access the chapter 2 resources, then:

1. Create a list of all your major assets (exclude depreciating assets like cars, boats, and RVs, etc.) as well as any debts. Conservatively estimate the value of each.

2. Create a separate list of your non-asset-based income resources, such as pensions and Social Security benefits. Conservatively estimate the value of annual income to be generated by each upon your full retirement.

PART 2

The *REAL* Keys to Retirement Income Planning

CHAPTER 3

CASH FLOW IS KING

Money comes and goes, but cash flow
is the heartbeat of your financial success.

—JOE HUNT,
   THE BILLIONAIRE BOYS CLUB

S o at this point, maybe you're thinking, "Okay, I get it. I understand what the problem is, but what's the solution?" It should come as no surprise to you by now that I would suggest the solution, in a nutshell, is to begin to view retirement as a cash flow problem rather than an asset problem. The focus must be squarely on your income, not your assets. Had the two coworkers described in the introduction proactively focused on exactly how to generate the necessary income for each year of their anticipated retirement rather than on the value of their assets, they likely would have had a much different outcome. Instead, they ended up simply guessing whether or not they "had enough," based on the historical performance of their investment strategy.

DON'T BET YOUR FUTURE ON A CRAPSHOOT

The traditional asset-based approach to retirement is a passive approach; it relies on building a portfolio of traditional securities, taking a "buy and hold" posture, and relying on historical data to project the likelihood of your success. Generally speaking, with that approach you either have it or you don't. And even if you think you do, you won't know for sure until your investment returns actually play out over time. As mentioned previously, your options for altering your projected outcome are limited to postponing retirement, spending less, or taking on more risk. Everything else depends largely on how financial markets perform during the various years of your retirement. Suffice it to say, it's a bit of a crapshoot.

A cash flow focus, on the other hand, is much more active—even proactive. It requires that you evaluate all your various resources, both asset-based and non-asset-based, focusing almost exclusively on the most efficient manner in which to turn each into an income stream throughout the course of your retirement. This is the essence of a retirement income plan, which is the key to a financially successful retirement. You're being purposeful, you're being proactive, and you're *creating* your desired outcome versus allowing the markets to dictate it to you.

It all starts with understanding that the most important question has nothing to do with your balance sheet. Rather, it's all about your income statement, or cash flow. Put simply, *retirement is a cash flow problem.* Thinking about it that way will help you avoid a great many of the financial problems retirees have faced throughout the last few decades.

To put this concept into perspective, a retirement plan is something you might do many years before retirement, during the acquire and grow stages of your retirement wealth life cycle (see Figure 2.2, page 40). It is much more nebulous and usually asset-focused. With retirement so far away and with so many variables involved, it's understood that this type of planning cannot be precise, nor should it be. Rather, the goal is to ensure you'll be close enough to the target to be able to make the proper adjustments to accomplish your objective when the time comes.

Unfortunately, most people never advance beyond this approach. They just tweak their asset allocation when it's time to retire. A retirement income plan, on the other hand, is much more specific and income-focused because now it's time to hone in on the target and ensure you hit the bull's-eye. So what exactly does an effective retirement income plan look like? You're about to find out.

YOUR RETIREMENT TRIPTIK

I've heard the following quote numerous times throughout my tenure as a retirement specialist: "The average person spends more time planning their annual vacation than they do planning their retirement." I'm honestly not sure if it's true, but based on my experience, I don't doubt it. It does say a lot about human nature. Essentially, we have a hard time looking very far into the future. We much more readily grasp things in our immediate future. Planning for a vacation feels doable and exciting, and the gratification is almost immediate. But planning for a 30-year retirement feels less so.

Many of you reading this book are likely old enough to remember taking family summer vacation road trips back in the seventies. I was in grade school. My family owned a series of enormous, gas-guzzling station wagons back then. They were the vehicle of choice for suburban families, long before do-it-all minivans took that title away. Seat belts were still optional, and the back seats could be folded down to create the rough equivalent of a full-sized bed—sufficient sleeping quarters for young siblings during the lengthy drives. I grew up in Cincinnati, Ohio, where we could simply take Interstate 75 due south, all the way to Florida. It was, and still is, a popular vacation destination for Ohioans, given the virtually uninterrupted expressway route to any number of popular Florida destinations.

Back then, the traditional approach to taking a trip like that would include a visit to your local AAA office. AAA had offices in most every town throughout the country. You could tell them where you wanted to go and they'd supply a large fold-out map of the portion of country containing your route. Remember those? They were usually large enough to cover the better part of a kitchen table, or the dashboard of the family wagon. I remember my father from time to time strategically folding the map into small, manageable segments to match the corresponding portion of our trip while rolling down the highway, eyeballing his route to ensure we stayed on track. (Eventually the much more manageable spiral-bound flip charts replaced those enormous maps, but the concept was the same.)

The AAA agent would take a yellow highlighter and highlight the entire route for you, including places of interest that you might want to stop at along the way: attractions, gas stations, restaurants, lodging, rest areas, as well as any major construction or any other obstacles that might fall along the designated route. For example, since there was almost always construction in Atlanta, they'd circle that city and designate one or more alternate routes for us to bypass the delays. In the end, despite the lack of today's global positioning system (GPS) using satellites, to which we've all grown accustomed, you had an actual, detailed road map of your exact route. It had all the specifics laid out for you including estimated timing, all your planned stops, and even some contingency options in case certain things went wrong. These detailed route maps were called "TripTiks." (I'm told electronic versions are offered by AAA today, though I have neither seen nor used them.)

Anytime we'd get off at an exit, usually to eat or get gas and use the restroom, my dad would pull out that TripTik to see exactly where we were, how far we had gone, and how much farther we had to go. Most importantly, he'd confirm that, indeed, we were still on the correct path. If we got sidetracked for some reason or delayed by things like flat tires, extended traffic jams, detours, or breakdowns, my dad always made sure we got back to that yellow highlighted path, one way or another. It was our plumb line. With a TripTik in hand, not only did you know you were going to get there, but you had a really good understanding of exactly how and when you were going to get there, because of all the details AAA provided. For the most part, you were in control; you determined your own success. And our family never failed to make it to our intended destination. Some trips were smoother than others, but we always made it.

Contrast this approach to simply telling your travel agent that you own a late-model (1970s) station wagon, you have four family members, and you wish to travel to Florida for summer vacation. They reply, "Take 75 south. And stay on 75 south. No matter what happens, just stay on 75 south. History suggests there's a 90% chance you'll eventually get there." While much of the time you will indeed get there, the TripTik approach is likely to improve your odds of success and enhance the efficiency and predictability of the process.

Sure, it's theoretically possible you might get to your destination faster by winging it—just putting your head down, putting the pedal to the metal, and hoping everything goes perfectly. On the other hand, you might not get there at all. Following the TripTik provided travelers an air of certainty because all the details were clearly spelled out well in advance of embarking, and the most likely obstacles were accounted for.

In much the same way, the retirement income plan approach is superior to the traditional, asset-based approach. Just as the TripTik functions as your road map to success for your family vacation, your retirement income plan functions as your road map to success for your retirement. Both plot out your path in painstaking detail, mapping out each and every turn of your journey and preparing you for the various detours and pit stops along the way.

DESIGNING YOUR RETIREMENT INCOME PLAN

There are two main objectives in designing your retirement income plan:

1. *Ensuring you have sufficient, stable, increasing, tax-efficient, lifetime income*

    As you will soon discover, each of those adjectives is critically important, because not all income is created equal. It must be sufficient, stable, increasing, tax-efficient, and of course, it must last your entire lifetime. That's your number one objective.

2. *Maximizing your projected residual estate, preferably also in the most tax-efficient manner possible*

    Whether or not your goal is to leave a substantial financial legacy to your beneficiaries, it's important to maximize your projected residual estate—that is, the funds you'll have left over at the end of your lifetime—since you don't know how long you'll live or what unexpected events you might encounter along the way. Think of it this way—during your lifetime, your projected residual estate is your "margin of error" for dealing with unexpected events. Only at the end of your life does it actually become your financial legacy.

To draw from our TripTik analogy, reliable income is akin to an efficient, smooth-running car, which enables you to arrive at your destination safely with little to no unexpected issues. Maximizing your residual estate, on the other hand, is like the money you have in your wallet ensuring you always have sufficient excess resources to deal with any unexpected events you encounter along the way, or to enjoy at your destination. After all, remember the TripTik is just the road map to your destination. The beach vacation is your ultimate goal. Likewise, your retirement income plan is your road map to the ultimate goal of a fulfilling, peaceful retirement. Your retirement income plan is the means, not the end.

Always Plan to Have Money Left Over

In terms of how this translates to your actual retirement income plan itself, here are three rules:

1. Map out your entire financial future. You should map out exactly where your income's going to come from each and every year, for the rest of your life, while also understanding how much extra liquidity—or wiggle room—you'll have at any given time.

2. Know how much you expect to have left over at the end of your life. While you're alive and living off your money, this is your margin of error for any unexpected financial needs you may encounter along the way. When you die, this money becomes the financial legacy you'll leave to your heirs and/or beneficiaries. Since you don't know what the future holds or exactly how long you'll live, you should always plan for the largest margin of error possible—that is, the largest projected residual estate value.

3. Be as flexible as possible. You need to have the means and be willing to make adjustments to your retirement income plan along the way. That way, when life throws you a curve, you'll have the ability to respond without throwing off your entire plan.

As you read this, you may be thinking, "This sounds extremely complicated." Well, it is and it isn't. On one hand, it's quite naïve to assume you could plan out your entire life's most efficient annualized cash flow and simultaneously maximize your residual estate on a napkin, right? So some level of complexity should be expected. But I'm also a big believer in the idea that all things being equal, simple is better.

Yet, as previously noted, I'm an equally big believer in the idea that all things are never equal. So if you want a highly effective, accurate income plan for your retirement, one that enables you to focus your energy on living the retirement of your dreams versus worrying about your money and the vagaries of the stock and bond markets, it will take some effort and it won't be as simple as some might have you believe.

But once you understand the key elements of an effective retirement income plan, you'll see this process is not that complex. That doesn't mean I'm going to offer you a bunch of shortcuts. Your future is far too important for that.

An Effective Retirement Income Plan Should—

- Be specific
- Be lifelong
- Maximize income
- Minimize taxes
- Maintain flexibility
- Include survivorship and estate planning considerations

Figure 3.1 illustrates what a comprehensive retirement income plan might look like at a very high level, depicting all income sources for each year of your projected lifetime.

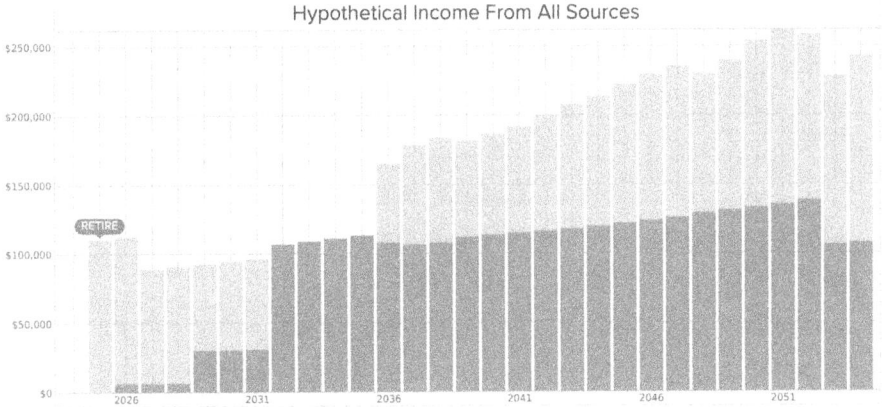

Figure 3.1: Retirement Income Plan ©2024 InvestCloud, Inc. InvestCloud and RetireUp are registered trademarks of InvestCloud, Inc. All rights reserved. Used with permission.

The following table shows the underlying breakdown of all cash flow, net of taxes, for a selection of the above years.

Year	Age	Social Security	Pensions	Income Salary & Other	Qualified	Non-Qualified	Taxes	Net of Taxes	Goal	Surplus/ Shortfall
2024	63/62	$0	$0	$0	$0	$0	$0	$0	$0	$0
2025	64/63	$0	$0	$0	$123,818	$0	$13,537	$110,280	$110,280	$0
2026	65/64	$0	$7,260	$0	$119,180	$0	$13,831	$112,609	$112,609	$0
2027	66/65	$0	$7,260	$0	$91,310	$0	$9,428	$89,141	$89,141	$0
2028	67/66	$0	$7,260	$0	$93,281	$0	$9,616	$90,924	$90,924	$0
2029	68/67	$25,478	$7,260	$0	$68,455	$0	$8,449	$92,743	$92,743	$0
2030	69/68	$25,987	$7,260	$0	$69,969	$0	$8,618	$94,598	$94,598	$0
2031	70/69	$26,507	$7,260	$0	$71,513	$0	$8,790	$96,490	$96,490	$0
2032	71/70	$99,614	$7,260	$0	$0	$0	$0	$106,874	$98,419	$8,455
2033	72/71	$101,607	$7,260	$0	$0	$0	$0	$108,867	$100,388	$8,479
2034	73/72	$103,639	$7,260	$0	$0	$0	$0	$110,899	$102,396	$8,503
2035	74/73	$105,712	$7,260	$0	$0	$0	$0	$112,972	$104,443	$8,528
2036	75/74	$107,826	$7,260	$0	$63,208	$0	$13,205	$165,089	$106,532	$58,557
2037	76/75	$109,982	$7,260	$0	$80,946	$0	$19,494	$178,694	$108,663	$70,031
2038	77/76	$112,182	$7,260	$0	$86,026	$0	$21,416	$184,052	$110,836	$73,216
2039	78/77	$114,426	$7,260	$0	$77,359	$0	$17,454	$181,591	$113,053	$68,538
2040	79/78	$116,714	$7,260	$0	$82,026	$å0	$19,234	$186,767	$115,314	$71,453
2041	80/79	$119,049	$7,260	$0	$86,034	$0	$20,722	$191,620	$117,620	$74,000
2042	81/80	$121,429	$7,260	$0	$94,654	$0	$23,413	$199,930	$119,973	$79,957
2043	82/81	$123,858	$7,260	$0	$102,074	$0	$25,214	$207,979	$122,372	$85,606
2044	83/82	$126,335	$7,260	$0	$106,155	$0	$26,187	$213,564	$124,820	$88,744
2045	84/83	$128,862	$7,260	$0	$114,744	$0	$28,275	$222,591	$127,316	$95,275

Table 3.1

All You Need Is 30 Days

That's not too much, is it? With the right advisor, if you make it your primary focus for about 30 days, you'll be able to design a terrific retirement income plan. Once complete, your goal will then be to place it on "cruise control" so you can sit back, relax, and enjoy your retirement journey, reviewing and updating your plan annually, making any necessary adjustments to ensure you stay on track.

There are a number of highly effective professional software options out there today that have the capability of making the entire retirement income planning process fairly straightforward and—wait for it—even pleasant. Many of my clients tell me they used to dread financial planning meetings but that our process actually made it quite enjoyable, such that they now look forward to our annual meetings.

On the other hand, there are also a lot of retirement planning software programs that are nothing more than investment planning software with an income modeling component, composed of lots of numbers and spreadsheets, emanating from the prerequisite MPT portfolio. That won't cut it, because once again, the order of operations is reversed. This is usually what you'll get from an advisor who's more of a "jack of all trades," working with anyone who walks through their door with money.

A true retirement specialist can create a thorough, detailed, and accurate retirement income plan for you. These are the professionals who will have the proper technology that will make planning your future effective and yes, enjoyable.

THE RIGHT TOOLS FOR THE JOB

When I was a kid, one of the lessons my dad taught me was, "Everything's easier when you have the right tool for the job." My mom used to say it was his way of passively suggesting he needed another tool. He also said it was important to have everything organized and in its proper place so you could always find it whenever you needed it. As I've learned throughout my own lifetime, he was right on both counts.

When it comes to the retirement income planning process, there are a number of tools we always use over and above our actual retirement income planning software. One of the most important is our Income Stability Pyramid (see Figure 3.2). It helps us organize your income-producing resources in accordance with the stability of their underlying cash flow over time so you can clearly see and understand the various types of resources you have at your disposal, and literally picture how stable your retirement income will be. Throughout my 25 years of retirement income planning, I've never met someone who didn't want their retirement income to be as stable as it was during their working years, if not more so, regardless of how much money they had. When it comes to retirement income planning, stability is key. Enter the Income Stability Pyramid.

THE INCOME STABILITY PYRAMID

VARIABLE
Stocks & bonds
Mutual funds & ETFs
Commodities
Derivatives

STABLE
Short-term bonds
Actively Risk Mitigated (ARM) brokerage
Certain variable annuities
Certain variable life insurance
Most home equity

GUARANTEED
Wages/earnings
Social Security & pension
Most deferred compensation
Certain rental income
Home equity via HECM

Royalties
Guaranteed life insurance
Guaranteed annuities
Cash equivalents

Figure 3.2: The Income Stability Pyramid

The Income Stability Pyramid is a strategic approach to visualizing and creating your stable, increasing, tax-efficient lifetime income. The pyramid has three components—

1. Guaranteed Income (base)
2. Stable Income (middle)
3. Variable Income (top)

At the Base: Guaranteed Income

As many ancient cultures have demonstrated when building pyramids, it is critical to start with a broad, stable foundation, which is one of the reasons those pyramids have endured for thousands and thousands of years. Chances are if you're reading this book, you want your retirement income to be stable, like an ancient pyramid. To do so, you will need to create an income plan that has a strong and steady base.

At the base of the pyramid is your guaranteed, or promise-based, income. The key fact about these resources at the bottom of your pyramid is that they are not directly affected by market volatility. Examples would be Social Security payments, most pension income, deferred compensation, earned income, royalties, guaranteed savings vehicles (checking, savings, and money market accounts), traditional CDs, guaranteed annuities, and certain cash value life insurance. I will explain each of these in further detail in the next chapter.

Of course, the guarantee of income is only as good as the entity behind that guarantee, so we limit the base of the pyramid to income-generating resources for which we have a high level of confidence that those promises can and will be kept. Most importantly, they are all at the base of the pyramid because the income generated from them is not directly impacted by traditional investment markets such as the stock market or the bond market. This base level represents your most reliable income, so it stands to reason that you want as much of it as possible, given the particular circumstances of your overall financial situation.

It's important to remember that not all guaranteed income is equal. For instance, some may be stagnant while some may have built-in adjustments for cost of living and inflation. Some may die with their owner while some may have spousal continuation options. These are just a couple of examples of how even guaranteed income sources can vary widely.

At first glance, it might seem simple enough to just find a way to convert every asset you have to a base-level guaranteed income–generating asset upon retirement. But as we've mentioned and will continue to discuss, as important as the lifetime income component is, it must be balanced with the need for liquidity to address future unplanned or unexpected events, as well as the possible desire to leave a financial legacy for your beneficiaries. For these reasons and others, the goal is to create a strong base of guaranteed income, but not exclusively so.

In the Middle: Stable Income

The second, or middle, level of the pyramid includes your "stable" income. This is income that's not guaranteed, but you have a high level of confidence that it's going to be there. So this income either has low market risk exposure or there is a highly effective risk-mitigation strategy in place to minimize the underlying market risk. Said another way, it has to be generated in such a way that you're confident it is highly stable over long periods of time—even if it's not guaranteed. Some examples of stable income include business income, rental income, royalties, short-term bonds, and other highly risk-mitigated investments. The key defining factor is that the income is truly stable and can be relied upon with a high level of confidence, even though it's not technically guaranteed.

One key that is a bit difficult to grasp at times, but is nonetheless fundamental to the process of categorizing resources in relation to their income stability, is determining their likelihood to have a negative impact on your quality of life, or purchasing power, due to market volatility. The more likely the income associated with a particular resource is to experience a negative event that directly impacts your standard of living, the higher up the Income Stability Pyramid it should be placed.

For example, if you plan to live in your current home indefinitely and are generating monthly, tax-free retirement income from your home equity via a home equity conversion mortgage (HECM), its price fluctuation will have little to no impact on your overall standard of living, so you would likely categorize it as stable or even guaranteed, depending on the structure of the HECM. However, if you plan to move in three to five years and use the proceeds from your current residence to buy your forever home, the price fluctuation over that three-to-five-year period could have a highly significant impact on your future standard of living, which would place it in the variable category, as explained in the following section.

At the Top: Variable Income

At the top of the pyramid you should place income that's generated from any asset or resource that is directly impacted by financial markets or other, typically uncontrollable external variables. The idea is that a significant decline in the value of these assets is both possible and would also have a significant impact on your standard of living. For most people, this equates to traditional investments like stocks, bonds, mutual funds, exchange-traded funds, commodities like gold, silver, or oil, as well as other securities. These are the most common types of investments people accumulate during their working years. Not coincidentally, they are also the most common types of investments available within the vast majority of retirement plans, such as 401(k)s, 403(b)s and the like, where most people have put the bulk of their savings for retirement.

The key determining factor for whether to list these types of assets at the top versus the middle level of the pyramid is your ability to mitigate risk. Assets like these, held at the top of the pyramid, typically rely solely on asset allocation and diversification for risk management, which history has proven to be insufficient for purposes of creating truly stable income over long periods of time. This reality is exacerbated by the fact that most qualified retirement plans offer limited investment options, further reducing your ability to adequately manage risk.

Unfortunately, this is the only risk mitigation most people are familiar with and have access to. Asset allocation and diversification are not active risk-mitigation techniques. Nor are they sufficiently effective for retirees. Rather, they are passive approaches that rely solely on a lack of correlation between the various underlying risks for each individual security. In other words, you simply hope they won't all drop in value at the same time. The unreliability of this approach as one's sole risk management technique was evidenced numerous times throughout the past 25 years, most recently in 2022, when stocks and bonds had their worst combined year in over half a century. As a result, these types of assets almost always occupy the top tier of the Income Stability Pyramid. In order to be listed in the middle of the pyramid, there would need to be some additional, highly effective risk-mitigation strategy in place.

To summarize, the general overriding idea is that the income generated at the top of the pyramid is unpredictable and can be extremely variable in nature. The income generated from the middle of the pyramid is much more stable, but not guaranteed. And the income at the bottom of the pyramid is guaranteed, or promise-based. So as you can imagine, when transitioning into retirement and designing your own retirement income plan, you generally want to "push" your income sources down the pyramid, creating a wide base in order to make your pyramid as stable as possible.

ENJOYING A WORRY-FREE RETIREMENT

Because not all income is created equally, it's important to categorize your retirement cash flow based on the Income Stability Pyramid. One helpful outcome of the retirement income planning process is the ability to compare the before and after of your Income Stability Pyramid. While the pre-retirement income planning pyramid is typically quite top heavy with stocks, bonds, and other more risky investments, forming an inverted pyramid, the post-retirement income planning pyramid should be more appropriately bottom heavy, resembling a more traditional pyramid shape.

Unfortunately, I've seen far too many "plans" collapse, essentially due to an upside-down Income Stability Pyramid.

Retirement is a cash flow problem. The income stability pyramid is a critical piece of the solution to that problem. With respect to creating a worry-free retirement relative to monthly income/cash flow, the relationship between the base and the remainder of the pyramid is critical. After all, the goal is to never have to think, or certainly never to need to worry, about your retirement income. Ever.

The Real Deal: How Much Will You Need in Retirement?

In the next chapter, I will teach you how to calculate the magic number known as **ISR—your Income Stability Ratio**. To do this, you must first ascertain your annual retirement income need. If you already have a strong handle on your monthly or annual need, great. If not, you can use the following simple process to estimate your monthly need:

1. On average, how much money is currently landing in your bank account each month?
2. On average, how much of that do you have left at the end of each month?
3. The difference is your current monthly need.
4. Multiply this number by 12. This is your current annual need.

5. Add any non-monthly expenses you haven't taken into consideration in the above calculation, if any. (One example might be real estate taxes.)

6. Last, add or subtract any expenses that will be added or subtracted as a result of your retirement. (Examples include debt that you may retire or additional travel expenses you may want to include.)

Congratulations! You've now got a good initial estimate of your annual retirement income need. This is, of course, a guesstimate, but it's a good starting point for your planning process and likely a pretty accurate one. Over time, you'll be able to tweak this number to better reflect your actual experience.

Taking Action

Before moving on to the next chapter, use the QR code (page 9) to access the chapter 3 resources, then:

1. Try placing each of the resources you identified in the previous chapter into your own **Income Stability Pyramid**. Only include those resources that have the ability to provide retirement income at some point in your lifetime.

2. Estimate how much annual income you'll need (in today's dollars) during retirement. (Refer to the "How Much Will You Need in Retirement?" text box, earlier in the chapter.)

   a. Use today's dollars, without regard for future inflation.

   b. This exercise is simply a **needs** assessment. It should be completed without regard to any specific income resources.

   c. What method did you use for calculating your need?

d. Did you find this process difficult?

e. What level of confidence do you have in your estimate (from 1–10)?

CHAPTER 4

BUILD A STRONG FOUNDATION

You can't build a great building on a weak foundation.

—GORDON B. HINCKLEY

When it comes to designing your retirement income plan, it's all about working your way up from the base of the Income Stability Pyramid or guaranteed income level. Step one is to assess what guaranteed income resources you already have. Step two is to optimize them. These are two quite different processes. Identifying your guaranteed income sources is fairly straightforward. However, optimizing those resources can be much more tricky, depending on the underlying resources in question.

My use of the word *optimize* is purposeful. I prefer *optimize* to *maximize*, since maximization of any particular income stream within a vacuum may be quite simple but it may not lead to the best overall outcome. Determining the optimal strategy for your unique situation is quite another matter, as it requires you to evaluate the interrelationships between all your income sources to understand how they affect one another—relative to everything from taxation to risk correlation to survivorship and estate planning.

Let's start by taking a slightly deeper dive into some of the most common types of income that qualify as guaranteed income for the base level of your Income Stability Pyramid.

TYPES OF GUARANTEED RETIREMENT INCOME RESOURCES

The following are some of the most common types of guaranteed retirement income resources you may find at the base of your Income Stability Pyramid. Although this list is by no means exhaustive, you'll get the idea—

- Social Security
- Pensions
- Deferred compensation
- Disability payments
- Earnings
- Certain rental income
- Certain trust payments
- Guaranteed life insurance income
- Guaranteed annuity payments
- Legal settlement payments
- Certain royalty payments
- Income from guaranteed savings vehicles (CDs, money markets, savings)
- Guaranteed Home Equity Conversion Mortgage (HECM) income payments

Social Security

Social Security (SS) was originally designed to provide income to a select minority of individuals who had outlived their life expectancies, but it has evolved well beyond that today. Given the changing US demographics since its introduction, SS is now considered a staple retirement income source for the vast majority of Americans and their spouses. Perhaps this is as it should be, given that SS benefit payments are largely the recipient's own money coming back to them, albeit at a fairly paltry return since they have been required to pay into it over their working lifetime. Social Security income payments are guaranteed by the Social Security Administration, an agency of the US government.

Generally speaking, SS provides income for the life of the retired worker. It includes cost-of-living adjustments and is tax-favored in that it is never 100% taxable. There are spousal and family benefits as well.

These are just the basics, but I'll discuss SS in much greater detail in chapter 7.

Pensions

This is a source of retirement income typically provided by a particular company, trade organization, or government agency. It can be paid out in place of, or in addition to, Social Security. It's typically guaranteed by the underlying company, pension fund, and/or entity, such as the Pension Benefit Guarantee Corporation. The fact that pension income may or may not have a significant impact on your Social Security income is a prime example of why coordination of all your retirement income resources is so critical.

Pensions and pension options are extremely varied, but for simplicity's sake, we'll touch on these characteristics that are most common:

- Most pensions begin around age 65 and last for the life of the recipient, though this can vary widely.

- Many have options for reduced monthly benefits in exchange for spousal continuation of benefits upon the death of the primary pensioner. This is an important option to consider for married couples, given the additional security it provides the surviving spouse in the event the pensioner were to die prematurely.

- Most pensions do not have cost-of-living adjustments, but there are exceptions.

- Usually 100% of the pension payment is taxable on the federal level, with some exceptions, but taxation varies greatly at the state level.

Deferred Compensation

This is guaranteed by an employer via a deferred compensation agreement, just as it sounds. It's an arrangement to defer compensation from the time it's earned until a later date—typically retirement—at which time it's usually paid over a specific period of time, normally several years. Deferred compensation is 100% taxable, since it is simply a deferral of normal wages. It is guaranteed by the employing entity and may be held in a special trust until payments begin.

Disability Payments

Disability payments are financial benefits that individuals who cannot work or have limited ability to work receive due to some sort of impairment, be it mental or physical. These payments can help with meeting basic needs, such as medical expenses, food, and housing. In general, they are administered and guaranteed by insurance programs and federal, state, and local government agencies.

Employment Earnings

These are of course guaranteed by an employer via an employment contract. An example of this would be if you decided to work part-time or maybe transition into being a contract employee, consultant, or freelancer upon retirement. As such, earnings could be reported via a W-2 or 1099. More people are choosing supplemental employment income nowadays to supplement their retirement income and/or to acquire health care benefits prior to qualifying for Medicare at age 65. I also have many wealthy clients who choose to work in retirement simply because they enjoy it.

Potential Benefits of Working Part-Time—

- Additional guaranteed cash flow
- Personal fulfillment (making a contribution)
- Mental engagement
- Physical engagement/exercise
- Health care benefits
- Experiencing a low-stress work environment (versus one's actual vocation)
- Getting out of the house
- Maintaining a healthy routine

Rental Income

This income is guaranteed by a rental or lease agreement, and the lessee is obligated to pay so long as you don't violate your end of the rental agreement. Like all the other guaranteed income options listed here, it isn't directly affected by investment market risk or volatility. However, since the reliability of rental income may vary widely, the degree to which you are confident you can rely on it as a source of income should dictate whether you include it in the guaranteed (base) level of your pyramid or the second (stable) level.

Trust Payments

Trust payments are as varied as trusts themselves, which are virtually infinite. There are family trusts, marital trusts, charitable trusts, and legal settlement trusts, just to name a few. The list goes on, as does the variety and structure of trust income. Suffice it to say, these types of income payments only qualify for the base level of the pyramid if they are truly guaranteed and unaffected by market conditions. Otherwise, trust payments may fall into the stable or variable levels of your Income Stability Pyramid rather than the guaranteed base level. For instance, payments from a trust that is invested in traditional stocks and bonds is by no means guaranteed, unless the income produced is truly miniscule compared to the underlying principal, because the source of the income is still affected by the broad markets.

Guaranteed Life Insurance Income

Payments from certain types of permanent, cash-value life insurance contracts are not only guaranteed by the underlying insurer but may also be tax favored or even tax-free. This topic could fill another book altogether. However, for this discussion, I submit that these types of income resources are less common than others I've described, since they typically require establishment and dedicated funding over a long period of time, well in advance of retirement; and relatively few people outside of the highly wealthy are sufficiently aware of these types of retirement income funding options to have done so.

Annuity Payments

Annuity payments are guaranteed by the issuing entity, typically an insurance company in the case of a commercial annuity; but this can also be a charity, a pension fund, a trust fund, or any other entity issuing a guarantee to make payments over a period of time.

There are a wide variety of types of annuities and guarantors. They can be a flat amount for life or they can have cost-of-living adjustments or other increase provisions. They may or may not include spousal benefits. I will discuss guaranteed retirement income annuities in much greater detail in chapter 11. For our purposes here, it is sufficient to understand these payments are guaranteed by the issuing entity and can be structured so as to not be negatively affected by market fluctuations.

Legal Settlements

Legal settlement payments are financial compensations awarded to individuals or parties as a result of a legal agreement or resolution. These payments typically arise from lawsuits, negotiations, or settlements reached outside of court. They are intended to resolve disputes or compensate for damages, losses, or injuries incurred, and can cover a wide range of situations such as personal injury, employment disputes, or contract breaches. They come in a wide variety of forms and time horizons. They are typically prefunded and/or guaranteed by the party making the payments.

Royalty Payments

Royalty payments are regular payments made to individuals or entities for the use of their intellectual property, such as patents, copyrights, trademarks, or real property such as real estate or mineral rights. These payments are typically based on a percentage of the revenue generated from the use of the underlying property. The structure, characteristics, and duration of such royalties can vary greatly and only pertain to the base of the pyramid to the extent they are generally free from common market volatility that would affect most variable income resources.

Savings Vehicles

These are likely the most familiar base income resources for most readers. These are assets like checking, savings, money market accounts, CDs, and so on, commonly referred to as cash equivalents. They are typically guaranteed by a bank, credit union, or other similar issuing organization. Income is typically in the form of interest payments, which tend to be based on prevailing interest rates.

Guaranteed Home Equity Conversion Mortgage (HECM) Income Payments

These "reverse mortgages" are now highly regulated by the federal government and can provide tax-free, lifetime income for the homeowner(s). Suffice it to say this is another category of guaranteed income that is greatly misunderstood. In much the same way as annuities are misunderstood due to ignorance, bad press, and the fact that they have changed so much over the years, HECM income is also misunderstood for largely the same reasons.

HECMs are issued and income payments guaranteed by Federal Housing Administration-approved lender and are also insured by the US government. Although the complexities of this type of retirement income are beyond the scope of this book, two unique advantages of this type of income are:

1. You can "have your cake and eat it too." Meaning, you can spend the equity in your primary residence, and even if

you live long enough to exhaust that equity, you can still occupy the home as long as you are able, leaving your other resources intact.

2. Income generated by an HECM is tax free.

One of the greatest fallacies of HECMs is that they are solely a "last resort" source of income, because you must surrender ownership of your home to the bank. It's due to misconceptions like this that most people erroneously view them as a last resort. (Although we don't provide access to HECMs in our practice, we do strive to educate our clients who wish to learn more about them.)

Once again, the preceding list is not intended to be exhaustive, but to be representative of some of the most common forms of guaranteed income you might include in the guaranteed level—the base—of your pyramid. It's important not to assume that every instance of the previously listed income sources is automatically guaranteed. Some of the sources listed here may not actually be guaranteed. For instance, if someone's trust income is dependent on the performance of traditional investments, that is no more guaranteed than other investment accounts and should be positioned at the top of their pyramid, not the bottom. The devil is always in the details.

DETERMINING YOUR
INCOME STABILITY RATIO (ISR)

Moving on from the various forms of income options you may have at the base of your Income Stability Pyramid, it's time to transition to the second and third levels of the pyramid. Once you believe you have identified all of your currently available base-level guaranteed income resources (without having yet optimized every single one, since that's a separate process requiring coordination of all your income sources), you can now identify one of the most important metrics of your retirement income planning process—your Income Stability Ratio (ISR).

Einstein once said, "Not everything that counts can be counted, and not everything that can be counted counts." But some things that can be counted *do* count. And one of those is your ISR. I believe it is one of the most important concepts we use to predict the success of any given retirement income plan. And since I have proposed that the most important aspect of retirement planning is cash flow, or income, it follows that the most important single measure of success relates directly to it.

In my 25 years as a retirement specialist, I have always found one thing to be true: Regardless of how much money a retiree has, they always want as much of their income as possible to be stable and predictable, just like when they were working. Identifying your ISR enables you to determine how stable and predictable your retirement income will be throughout the remainder of your lifetime, regardless of how much your income needs might vary over time.

Your ISR is the amount of your retirement income that is guaranteed as a proportion of the total retirement income that you require. (See the "How Much Will You Need in Retirement?" text box in the previous chapter for how to calculate your retirement income need.) This is measured on an annual basis, as well as over the course of your entire lifetime. In other words, your ISR answers the question, "How much of my total required income is guaranteed, or coming from the base section of the pyramid?" Said another way, "How much of my retirement income is not directly affected by market volatility?" That is your ISR. The simple mathematical equation is as follows:

$$\frac{\textbf{Guaranteed Income}}{\textbf{Total Income Need}} = \textbf{ISR}$$

To illustrate quickly with a hypothetical retiree: Let's say the Johnsons know they need $6,000 per month to meet their needs in retirement. They have identified that $4,000/month will be coming to them from the bottom segment of their pyramid (via Social Security and a pension), and they will need to take out another $2,000/month from their IRAs (his old 403(b) and her old 401(k)). To figure the Johnsons' current ISR, the math looks like this:

$$\frac{\$4{,}000 \text{ [guaranteed income]}}{\$6{,}000 \text{ [total income needed]}} = 66\% \text{ ISR}$$

Targeting Your Optimal ISR

Once you calculate your current ISR, it's time to evaluate that number by asking yourself, "How does that feel?" If it feels good, then great; you're likely all set. If not, then you'll need to give some thought to where you'd like it to be.

When it comes to ISR, I like to target 80%, but everyone has their own unique comfort level. To understand why I target 80%, think of it this way: What if I told you your ISR was 50%, which meant if we have a terrible market crash or another Great Depression or Great Recession, 50% of your retirement income would be in jeopardy of dropping significantly or even going away. You'd probably be pretty troubled if that were to actually happen. But imagine if I instead told you, "You've got an 80% ISR, so if that same scenario were to play out, 80% of your income would still be there and only 20% of your income would likely be in serious jeopardy, having the potential to be significantly reduced or go away altogether." You wouldn't be thrilled, but my experience tells me you'd be fairly comfortable dealing with a 20% income reduction as a potential worst-case scenario. That's why I like to target 80%. But again, that target is unique to every individual.

For instance, I have some clients who desire a 100% ISR, meaning all of their required income is from the base of their pyramid, and other clients who are comfortable with a 70% ISR, leaving 30% of their income subject to investment performance. In the earlier example, the Johnsons are starting out with an ISR of 66%, which they might want to try to increase to a higher number in order to feel more secure and less at the whims of investment markets. It's completely up to them.

Of course, your ISR is highly dependent on your monthly income need. For instance, a married couple that requires $15,000 total net monthly income will need $12,000 in net guaranteed monthly income to attain an ISR of 80%, while another couple may require only $6,000 per month, meaning they need only $4,800 in guaranteed income to attain the same 80% ISR. As you can see, your income need is critical to your ISR.

Your ISR target gives a whole new meaning to the phrase "sleep number," as it is the portion of your retirement income you'd like to have guaranteed so that you can sleep well at night, not worrying about how the performance of your investments might affect your required monthly income. At the end of this chapter, I'll ask you to identify your own personal sleep number. That is, what ISR do you need in order to sleep well at night?

Why Not Always 100%?

You may be wondering why you wouldn't automatically always target an ISR of 100% so that all of your income is guaranteed. In a perfect world, most people would certainly like all their income to be guaranteed, coming from the base of their pyramid. After all, wouldn't you want all your retirement income to be guaranteed for the rest of your life if you had the wherewithal to do so without compromising your other long-term objectives? I have a number of clients whose ISR is indeed 100%. However, this is not always possible. And in some cases where it is possible, it may not always be desirable. Let's take a quick look at the two main reasons you might not want to target a 100% ISR:

1. The first reason is pretty straightforward—it's not always possible. Not everyone has sufficient resources that can be converted to guaranteed income to meet all of their income needs. In such a case, the best you can do is the best you can do.

2. The second reason is that even if you do have sufficient resources to do so, guaranteeing 100% of your income may not be the wisest option, since doing so might come at the cost of another of your retirement objectives. In many cases, resources that offer guaranteed income may come at the cost of some other feature or benefit, most often liquidity. Liquidity is important due to the need for flexibility in your plan, since your plan is necessarily based on educated guesses about the future—a future that undoubtedly contains many unknowns. When it comes to retirement income planning, obtaining income guarantees may mean losing some amount of flexibility to address future uncertainties.

There are no free lunches. Therefore, it is always prudent to consider all the costs and benefits of any particular strategy. An easy-to-understand example of this is Social Security. While we've demonstrated that Social Security is a tremendous source of guaranteed income with many features and benefits not available through other potential income sources, there's no liquidity, per se. You can't call up the Social Security Administration and say, "I've changed my mind, I don't want it paid out over the next 30 years, just give it all to me now." They won't do that. In the same way, many assets that provide guaranteed lifetime income have reduced liquidity options— an obvious problem, should you need it unexpectedly down the road.

I believe you should always seek to balance guaranteed income with all of your other objectives, including liquidity. As wonderful as it may be to secure a 100% ISR, you may be left with little flexibility to adjust your plan when or if life throws you a curve. Or perhaps you simply change your mind about your personal goals and objectives. Thirty years is a long time to have no flexibility.

Typically, the resources at the base of the pyramid provide the longest and strongest guarantees, sometimes at the expense of liquidity. As you move up the pyramid, liquidity typically increases in return for greater risk exposure, since the funds are accompanied by fewer guarantees. Depending on your specific income needs, and all things being equal (which they never are), the more resources you have, the more likely you'll be able to successfully target a high level of income stability while also maintaining sufficient liquidity. The bottom line is that it's important to have a clear understanding of all those issues before making any decisions.

GUARANTEED INCOME   **LIQUIDITY**

Figure 4.1: The goal is to strike a balance between guaranteed income and liquidity.

YOUR RETIREMENT INCOME GAP

If your ISR is 70%, then 30% has to come from somewhere else, right? This leads us to another function of your ISR, called your retirement income gap (RIG). Your RIG is the difference between your guaranteed income and your required income, measured on a monthly, annual, and ultimately lifetime basis. Whereas your ISR is stated as a percentage of your overall income, your RIG is stated in terms of actual dollars.

So if you need $10,000/month but only have $7,000 in the form of guaranteed income, your ISR is 70% and your income gap is $3,000/month. That is, the difference between what is guaranteed that you know you're going to get and what you really need/want is $3,000. This $3,000 is the amount of income you'll need to generate at the stable and variable levels of your Income Stability Pyramid in order to make ends meet with respect to your required monthly income, which I'll address in chapter 6.

Once you reach an acceptable ISR so you can sleep comfortably at night, the next step is to turn your attention toward eliminating your retirement income gap, such that you always have all the income you need in one form or fashion. This will either be accomplished by increasing your guaranteed income and thereby raising your ISR and shrinking your RIG, or by relying on nonguaranteed sources of income to fill your income gap, if you've already exhausted all opportunities to optimize your guaranteed income in order to achieve your acceptable ISR level, or by a combination of the two. This process is the focus of chapters 5 and 6.

The Real Deal: Needs versus Wants

A quick aside about needs versus wants. I've seen numerous advisors and planning software solutions utilize the concept of "income

(continued)

needs versus wants" to attempt to design retirement income plans. The idea is to differentiate your basic needs (needs) from your desires (wants), then build a plan that attempts to ensure all your "needs" are met, while providing somewhat less assurance that all your "wants" are met. In other words, needs are nonnegotiable but wants are more like icing on your cake. One way to address that concept is to ensure all your "needs" are covered by guaranteed income and your "wants" are covered by your stable and/or variable income. This is easier said than done, as most retirees have a hard time discerning the difference between needs and wants. For example, is traveling to visit your grand-children a need or a want? I generally encourage my clients to begin the planning process with their preferred future in mind. That is, assume your preferred retirement lifestyle is 100% necessary, or "needed." If the result is an unacceptable outcome, then you can begin to evaluate what, if any, needs are really wants.

TOP DOWN VERSUS BOTTOM UP

Unfortunately, most financial advisors work from the top of the pyramid instead of the base, because that's how they've been trained and how they get paid. They're not paid to do Social Security or pension planning. They're not paid to do tax planning. They're not paid to evaluate income through wages, pensions, guaranteed annuities, rental income or life insurance, just to name a few. Most advisors don't get paid for any of that.

As a result, they tend to "live" at the top of the pyramid, and they tend to recommend most, if not all, your money be invested that way, via stocks, bonds, mutual funds, and ETFs. Risk is "managed" solely by a passive asset allocation and diversification strategy. Risk is almost never transferred away, like it is in the guaranteed income assets at the base of the pyramid. More often than not, asset allocation and diversification, which have proven to be insufficient in many retirement scenarios, are the only tools used to manage portfolio risk. As a result, the most common Income Stability Pyramid shape I see for individuals seeking our help, regardless of whether they already have an advisor or not, is not a pyramid at all but rather more of an inverted pyramid (see Figure 4.2). As you can imagine, this leads to a very low ISR percentage.

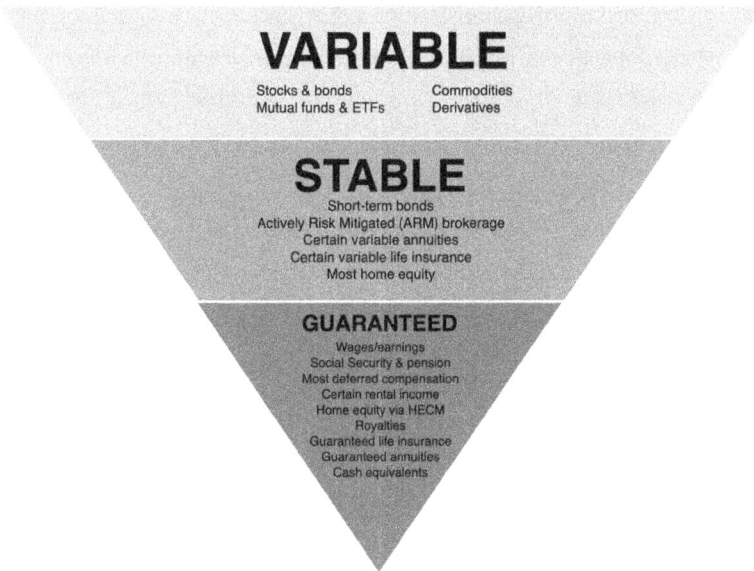

Figure 4.2: Income Instability Pyramid

Of course, most advisors aren't even familiar with the concept of income stability, much less your unique Income Stability Pyramid or Income Stability Ratio. So they're likely not going to view your retirement income–generating resources through this lens in the first place. Nonetheless, a key part of your planning process should be to create your own unique Income Stability Pyramid, starting at the base and working your way up until your planning process is complete. In this way, you will not only optimize your retirement income, but you'll also avail yourself of all the possible solutions that exist within the insurance, banking, and securities industries, rather than just one of those worlds—that is, the securities industry.

Most retirement planning ignores the concept of income stability altogether, therefore employing a top-only approach by default, only giving cursory attention to things like Social Security and pension income, which reside at the base of the pyramid. In contrast, by focusing on the base of your Income Stability Pyramid, you will create a more secure retirement income plan. Once you've determined your income need, your ISR, and your RIG, you are well on your way.

Next you'll need to determine if your current ISR is acceptable, and if not, whether you have the wherewithal and desire to increase your ISR to an acceptable level, which I'll discuss in detail in chapter 5. Thereafter, it's as simple as determining how you're going to proceed to fill your retirement income gap each year.

Taking Action

Before moving on to the next chapter, use the QR code (page 9) to access the chapter 4 resources, then:

1. Determine approximately how much annual income you expect to receive from all your **guaranteed** income sources combined, based on current assumptions. (We'll discuss optimizing these resources a bit later.)

   a. When in doubt, be conservative.

2. Divide that number by your annual income need from the last chapter to determine your current ISR percentage.

3. How do you feel about that ISR number?

   a. Can you sleep well at night knowing that's your number?

   b. If not, what is your actual "sleep number"?

4. Next, calculate your retirement income gap by subtracting your guaranteed annual income ($) from your total annual income need ($).

   a. Assuming no changes to your ISR, this is the amount you'll need to make up with nonguaranteed income.

   b. How do you feel about that number?

CHAPTER 5

REINFORCE THE FOUNDATION

The rain came down, the streams rose,
and the winds blew and beat against that house;
yet it did not fall, because it had its foundation on the rock.

—MATTHEW 7:25, NIV

Now that we've established the importance of the base level of our Income Stability Pyramid in creating secure, increasing, tax-efficient lifetime income—the primary objective of your retirement income plan—let's turn our attention to the next step of the process. By now, you have—

- Identified your monthly retirement income need ($)
- Identified your desired income stability ratio (%)
- Identified all your current, base-level, non-asset-based, guaranteed income resources ($)
- Identified your actual, current income stability ratio (%)
- Identified your retirement income gap ($)

The next step in the process is to eliminate your income gap, thus providing for all the monthly income you require. There are basically two ways to do this—

1. Increase your guaranteed base-level income in order to shrink the gap (via guarantees).

2. Generate nonguaranteed income to fill the gap (via expertise).

In either case, you want to create the safest, most predictable income achievable, without sacrificing other important objectives such as liquidity and overall flexibility. Doing so means identifying solutions that mitigate as many of the risks to that income as possible.

ELIMINATING THE INCOME GAP

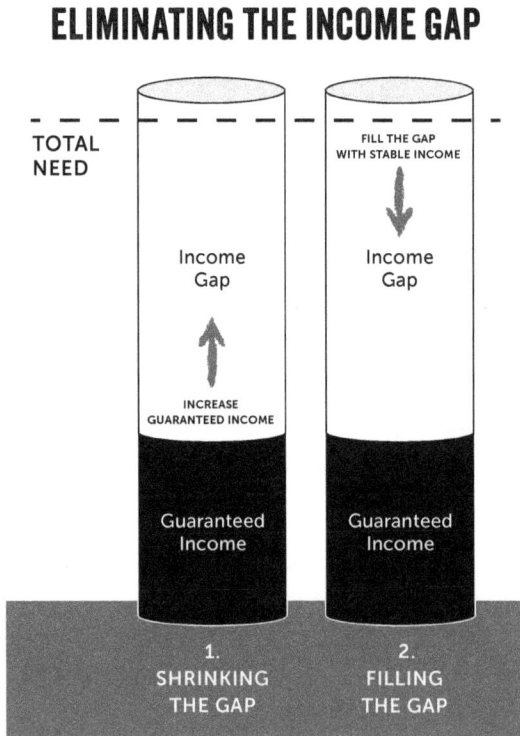

TOTAL NEED

FILL THE GAP WITH STABLE INCOME

Income Gap

Income Gap

INCREASE GUARANTEED INCOME

Guaranteed Income

Guaranteed Income

1. SHRINKING THE GAP

2. FILLING THE GAP

Figure 5.1: Eliminating the Income Gap

RISK MITIGATION

When it comes right down to it, there are just two primary ways to mitigate risk in life:

- **Guarantees.** This is someone's promise to you. Essentially, you transfer the risk to someone else. Think insurance.

- **Expertise.** This is someone's (your own or another's) ability to help you reduce or mitigate the risk in the first place, typically in the form of their unique ability to do so.

To illustrate the difference between the two, consider the example of operating a motor vehicle. Within that context, a guarantee would be like buying an auto insurance policy to transfer the liability of any losses you might experience to the insurance company, should you be involved in an accident or other loss. Gaining expertise, on the other hand, would be learning how to operate the motor vehicle more safely in order to reduce your likelihood of an adverse event occurring in the first place.

SHRINKING THE INCOME GAP

Whenever you utilize a guaranteed strategy to create additional income, you are increasing your base-level, guaranteed income, thereby increasing your ISR and reducing your income gap. When you employ the expertise of another party to generate additional income, on the other hand, you are increasing your stable or variable income, thereby filling a portion of your remaining income gap.

In this chapter we will focus on the first option—that is, increasing your guaranteed, base-level income in order to increase your ISR and reduce your income gap. The next chapter will focus on utilizing the second option, expertise, to fill the gap once you've optimized your personal ISR.

TYPES OF GUARANTEED INCOME SOURCES

Guaranteed income sources all have two things in common:

- The guarantor is contractually obligated and highly capable of paying income to you.
- Payments are not directly affected by investment market volatility, in the purest sense.

There are generally five primary ways you can increase your guaranteed income once you've reached retirement:

1. Optimizing non-asset-based income resources (SS, pensions, etc.).
    a. This is the first and typically most effective.

2. Generating income from cash and cash equivalents.
    a. This can be greatly affected, for better or worse, by prevailing interest rates.

3. Working part time (generating earnings).
    a. So long as you do your job, the employer is contractually obligated to pay you.

4. Implementing an HECM strategy.
    a. As stated previously, the devil is in the details, and most people have limited knowledge/understanding of this type of strategy.

5. Generating income from guaranteed annuities.
    a. As with HECM strategies, most people know little about these strategies, such that they, too, are greatly misunderstood.

Technically speaking, there are many other ways to accomplish this objective, but many of the other options not listed here tend to require advance planning. One example would be utilizing cash value life insurance to generate tax-free monthly income. Although that's a powerful option, with certain exceptions, it is most effective when planned for and funded well in advance of actual retirement.

It's also important to note that dividend and interest income generated from stocks, bonds, mutual funds and ETFs are not guaranteed income sources. Despite the fact that many people view these sources of income as stable and predictable, they are not guaranteed. So regardless of how stable they might have been in the past, unless they are literally guaranteed, they do not qualify as guaranteed. Corporate boards can vote to reduce dividends at will and the underlying stock value can drop precipitously. I've seen many retirees who considered their dividend-and-interest-yielding stock and bond accounts their retirement income nest egg, only to have it eventually turn into a retirement income goose egg! (Not the golden kind.)

Optimizing Non-Asset-Based Resources

As I detailed in chapter 4, for most people in the US, Social Security is by far the most common source of guaranteed and increasing lifetime income, forming the core of the base of the pyramid, with pension income a distant second. Optimizing these benefits as the core component of your guaranteed income base is critical, as they affect every other piece of your retirement income in myriad ways. Since Social Security income is likely the core component of the foundation of your pyramid, optimizing it is so important that I've dedicated all of chapter 7 to explaining how and why most people fail to optimize their SS income.

The second most common source of guaranteed retirement income for most Americans, pension income, is a distant second. And that margin is growing yearly as pensions are becoming a dying breed. Most have been replaced with retirement plans that place the onus of saving and investing for retirement on the employee rather than the employer or other sponsoring organization. It is, however, equally critical for anyone with a pension to understand all the various claiming options available to them and how each might integrate with all their other income sources to best optimize their entire lifelong retirement income stream.

Once you've anchored your foundation by optimizing your Social Security and/or pension options, you can then turn your attention to the other guaranteed resources currently available at the base of your pyramid. The potential sources of guaranteed income are endless, and unlike Social Security, the rules pertaining to each are highly unique to your personal situation. For that reason, I won't address each of these in detail.

For now, I'll simply remind you that optimizing these benefits is the number one way to increase your Income Stability Ratio and reduce your income gap throughout the entirety of your life. I say "the entirety of your life" because optimizing your income and its related taxation over the course of your lifetime doesn't necessarily equate to maximization in the present or immediate future, a mistake often made if you focus too squarely on the present at the expense of the long term. In the end, remember, retirement income planning is all about the long term. It is a marathon, not a sprint.

The Real Deal: A Note about Pension Planning

Unlike Social Security, when it comes to pensions, there are far too few commonalities or rules of thumb from which to draw generalized conclusions. I will, however, say three things about pension planning, which tend to be common themes for those with pension benefits:

1. Much like Social Security, when dealing with pension options, you should highly prioritize survivorship planning. In essence, this means you ought to place great value on the various survivorship options, relative to your overall retirement income plan.

One of the greatest dangers in retirement income planning is what happens when one spouse dies—especially if that death is premature. The surviving spouse typically loses one Social Security check and also becomes exposed to higher tax rates, since they're no longer married, filing jointly. That's a double whammy that can be exacerbated by not optimizing a spousal pension benefit when it's available.

Again, there are exceptions to every rule, so every situation needs to be examined thoroughly. But generally speaking, I encourage most people to seriously weigh any spousal pension benefit options available to them.

2. When and if you consider a "pension maximization" strategy utilizing permanent life insurance for survivorship planning, I strongly recommend utilizing a guaranteed, fixed-premium, no-lapse contract as a basis for evaluating the effectiveness of the strategy.

I learned this the hard way, long before I was practicing retirement income planning. My own father was encouraged to take the life-only pension option and to use the excess monthly income he would have given up had he chosen the spousal benefit option to pay for a permanent insurance policy. The idea was that when he eventually dies, the life insurance contract would pay a lump-sum death benefit to generate sufficient income to replace the spousal pension benefit my mother would have received from the survivorship option.

Unfortunately, the unprecedentedly low interest rates we've experienced over the past couple decades caused that life insurance policy to implode, such that it no longer exists. Because the historical assumptions within the illustrated policy did not pan out, my mom is out of luck should my father pass first. (Thankfully, as I write, my father, now 88 years old, is still going strong!)

There is no substitute for a good guarantee. It's simply not worth the risk.

3. This brings me to my third suggestion regarding pensions, but in actuality, it applies to all things retirement income planning: Always think big mistake/little mistake. If you miss out on a little monthly income, that's a little mistake, so long as you can still live comfortably.

But if a surviving spouse loses an entire SS check and/or a pension check, and also experiences higher taxes as a result of no longer being married, the result may be a very difficult standard-of-living adjustment for the remainder of their life. That's a big mistake.

The same can be said for managing investment assets for income, which I'll cover in chapter 6.

Cash and Equivalents

Cash alternatives such as savings accounts, money market accounts, and CDs are excellent means of reducing your income gap, so long as they provide sufficient income to not only meet your present needs but also keep up with inflation. Otherwise, the income provided by these resources will diminish and eventually disappear over time. Unfortunately, low interest rates have made this approach less than appealing over the past decade. More recently, rising interest rates have provided promise, but atypically high inflation has largely mitigated the benefit of increasing rates.

Another consideration for the cash alternative approach is the fact that cash alternatives are typically rather short-term, highly liquid vehicles. Therefore, any strategy incorporating these vehicles to reduce your income gap will require regular, ongoing oversight and management, which is generally contrary to the concept of automatic or "worry-free" retirement income. And the need to constantly "reload" your cash equivalent income arsenal means you are forever at the mercy of prevailing interest rates. Doing it yourself may be more laborious than you want. On the other hand, a good retirement income advisor can help make this process as automatic as anything else.

Many of you might be wondering why bonds or long-term CDs don't fit into this category, since they provide fixed income that can be guaranteed for longer periods of time. The answer is twofold:

1. As we were reminded in 2022, bond values are inversely correlated with interest rates. The sharp rise in rates in 2022, therefore, caused bond values to drop precipitously. The longer term the bond, the further the drop in its underlying value. This is completely contrary to the idea of stability when it comes to designing a retirement income portfolio.

2. The second reason is an extension of the first. You may be thinking that as long as you don't sell your long-term

bond or CD, you'll retain your principal and earn income. While that's true, it also means that as inflation occurs and interest rates rise, you'll be stuck with your lower interest payment, which you can't afford to "upgrade" because it would mean selling your lower-yielding asset at a steep discount or incurring a significant early withdrawal penalty. This means that over time, your income and principal will be unlikely to keep pace with inflation. Once again, this runs contrary to the fundamental premise of building a stable, increasing, tax-efficient retirement income portfolio.

Working Part-time (Earnings)

Although part-time employment is usually viewed as one of the least appealing options for increasing your ISR, no conversation about retirement income planning would be complete without addressing it. So long as you show up to work and do your job, your employer has a contractual obligation to pay you. That makes part-time income a viable way to increase your base-level guaranteed retirement income. One other benefit to this approach is that the right job can also provide valuable health care insurance coverage in the event you retire early and are not yet eligible for Medicare.

Many of our affluent clients have chosen to take a part-time job simply because they want to remain active, and they enjoy working in a relatively stress-free environment, unlike the way they had to shoulder so much responsibility back when they were working full time. I could say much more about the potential merits of working part time during your early retirement years, but I'll leave it at that for now. By virtue of being ready to retire, most of you reading this book are quite familiar with the idea of employment!

Home Equity Conversion Mortgages (HECMs)

As stated in the last chapter, HECMs are very poorly understood by the masses. As such, most think of them as an option of last resort. In reality, however, they can be extremely effective tools for providing guaranteed, lifetime, tax-free retirement income. As such, more and more wealthy people are using this approach in order to generate additional, guaranteed, tax-free income while preserving their other, more liquid assets.

I could easily dedicate an entire chapter to the concept, but for now, suffice it to say they are a viable means of reinforcing your foundation and can also play an effective role in your survivorship and estate planning strategies.

Commercial Annuities

This brings us to "the A word." That's right, *annuity*. I saved this one for last in our topic of guaranteed income since annuities are quite complex. In the next several paragraphs, I'm going to focus on and provide a broad overview of commercial annuities. Commercial annuities—those made available to the general public via a life insurance company—are not the only type of annuities you can utilize to reduce your income gap. As mentioned previously, there are many kinds of annuities, including private and charitable annuities, just to name a couple. But those tend to require a much more advanced level of planning. They also tend to be irrevocable in nature, meaning they have little to no flexibility once initiated, so they are not likely suitable for the typical reader of this book. Therefore, for the purposes of this chapter, I will focus on commercial annuities, which are much more likely appropriate for most retirees.

I'll take a deeper dive in chapter 11, but for purposes of this chapter, I'll touch on the annuity option in a broad sense for the following reasons:

- It's the simplest and most easily accessible way to enhance your ISR—putting more income at the bottom of your pyramid—if you wish to do so. Many of the other guaranteed income sources we've discussed are more or less black-and-white, that is, they either exist or they don't. A pension or Social Security benefit isn't something you can create once you retire, and life insurance requires underwriting and is most effective when funded well in advance of retirement. But an annuity can be secured at virtually any time, by anybody. For that reason, it's by far the most common and effective way you can enhance your base-level guaranteed income, thus increasing your ISR and decreasing your income gap, should you desire to do so.

- An annuity is one of the only vehicles that can be instantly turned into guaranteed lifetime income in a way that helps protect against the cash equivalent shortcomings I previously outlined, while also preserving ownership and access to your funds, which I'll elaborate on later in the chapter.

- Annuities are often misunderstood and therefore misused. Much of the reason for this is that in the general marketplace there's a tremendous amount of misinformation, both good and bad, about annuities. The unfortunate truth is that most advisors don't truly understand them very well at all, certainly not enough to provide the level of advice needed to effectively recommend their appropriateness for a given situation.

Ignorance Is Bliss . . .

If there were one topic that could be its own book, it would be annuities. There is so much information and misinformation about annuities, the companies that issue them, the people who sell them, and the people who utilize them—both good and bad—that I couldn't possibly do the topic justice within this single chapter. There are also so many different applications for annuities, each of which require their own unique approach and type of annuity, that it can all be tremendously confusing.

For example, not all annuities are optimal for increasing your guaranteed retirement income, for a number of reasons.

I'll start with my single best piece of advice related to annuities: If you run across someone who says that annuities are always good and everyone should own one, run, don't walk, away from that individual. In the same way, if you come across anyone who says that annuities are always bad and no one should ever use one or own one, do the same. Both of these statements are extreme and incorrect, born out of greed, ignorance, or both.

There's ignorance everywhere when it comes to annuities, even among so-called experts in the financial industry, where a severe lack of understanding about annuities is extremely prevalent. Most of these people simply don't know what they don't know. I personally know many highly intelligent financial advisors, money managers, accountants, and attorneys who know next to nothing about annuities. Some of them are aware of their lack of knowledge and are quick to confess it, while others are not. But this doesn't stop them from offering their opinions and advice, which is often blatantly incorrect. Even more unfortunate, the average uninformed person will take that advice because they assume it to be coming from an expert.

One example from my own experience that illustrates this point is that of a man I'll call "Bill," who's an accountant. This is a true story, although I've changed the name. Bill is a well-educated, experienced, highly knowledgeable individual—when it comes to tax preparation. One day we were discussing the balance sheet of a mutual client when he came across an entry and asked the following question: "Is this asset an annuity or an IRA?"

Suffice it to say I was flabbergasted, and I responded, "Um, Bill, you know those aren't mutually exclusive, right?" He was silent. Clearly he had no clue. I went on to "remind" him that an IRA is a particular type of account that is entitled to special tax treatment, which he well knew. An annuity, on the other hand, is a specific type of insurance vehicle that can be purchased with various types of funds, including those within an IRA.

An IRA can hold many different types of assets, including stocks, bonds, mutual funds, or real estate, and it can *also* hold an annuity, which he was clearly unaware of.

Even after we hung up, I wasn't convinced he understood the concept. He had probably learned about annuities decades ago and likely only dealt with them in a limited capacity, since he was completely unaware of one of the most basic fundamentals of what an annuity actually is. And this person is advising people on taxes and general finances every single day, holding himself out as a financial expert, as many accountants do. In fact, many people view their accountants as financial advisors. It is extremely common. And many accountants view themselves as financial advisors as well.

But just as I'm not a licensed accountant, few accountants are licensed financial advisors. Even in the case of someone who is both, there's a huge difference between holding a license and practicing the discipline all day, every day. Being a jack of all trades, as the saying goes, oftentimes makes you a master of none. That of course is another subject altogether, but it's an important distinction.

I'm a big believer that as you go down the path of retirement, you should have a strong team of retirement-focused advisors, including a financial advisor specializing in retirement income planning, an accountant, an attorney, and a property and casualty agent, at a minimum. If your financial advisor truly specializes in holistic retirement services, they should also be able to guide you with respect to tax, health care, asset protection, and survivor and estate planning as well. The financial advisor's job should be, among other things, to introduce you to such experts as needed and to coordinate the efforts of the entire group with your overall plan.

A second example of ignorance regarding annuities within the financial industry is my friend Sam (also a pseudonym), a money manager for a local firm that professes to offer comprehensive financial planning and advice. One day over casual conversation, I asked him what he knew about annuities, and he simply responded, "I know next to nothing about them, but what I've heard isn't very good, although I'd like to learn more." I was shocked, not that his opinion was borderline negative, since his firm only got paid to manage securities like stocks, bonds, mutual funds, and ETFs, but that as an advisor he was so content with his lack of knowledge. How can you provide anything close to comprehensive financial advice when you know nothing about such a popular financial vehicle?

According to the Insured Retirement Institute and the National Association of Insurance Commissioners, Americans currently have over $2.7 trillion invested in annuities and add almost $250 billion annually. So why the ignorance? Annuities have changed tremendously over the years, and many advisors have failed to keep up with these changes because there's little incentive to do so, as I'll explain shortly. Instead, most rely on outdated information or misinformation that remains extremely prevalent today.

Follow the Money

As with most any product or service, annuities are often promoted or rejected based on someone's vested interests. In fact, whenever you hear or read something expressing an extremely strong opinion for or against just about anything, it's a good exercise to try and follow the money. More often than not, that opinion emanates from someone who has a vested interest in that opinion.

Annuities are insurance products. So securities dealers would prefer that you don't purchase them but rather invest in securities products like stocks, bonds, and mutual funds for which they get paid. In fact, a tremendous amount of money has been and still is being spent by the securities industry to campaign against annuities. Most negative press, in my experience, emanates from the securities industry or those who have been heavily influenced by that industry.

As insurance products, there's an equal and obvious incentive for insurance agents to sell annuities, because that's how they get paid. As in any industry, there'll always be some unscrupulous individuals who promote their products based solely on a profit motive. There is, in fact, a long history of turf wars between the securities and insurance industries when it comes to annuities, but that's another subject altogether. Suffice it to say that over time, annuities have gone from being public enemy number one of the securities industry to the point where the securities industry has developed their own version, variable annuities. These qualify as securities and thus inure to their benefit. There are also many instances where securities firms now actively acquire or develop their own insurance companies, through which they capture annuity and other insurance market share. As the old saying goes, if you can't beat 'em, join 'em—which they certainly have.

The Value of Expertise

Like any financial vehicle, annuities are simply a tool, just like a hammer. They're great for specific purposes, but don't try to use one to turn a screw. As Abraham Maslow once famously said, "To the person with only a hammer, every problem looks like a nail." Also, even if the specific job requires an annuity, or in this example, a hammer, there are many different kinds: claw hammers, sledgehammers, rubber mallets, ball-peen hammers . . . you get the idea. In the hands of a skilled craftsman, each specific tool is invaluable, but in the hands of someone who lacks the necessary skills, the result can be ugly.

So if you're considering an annuity as part of your retirement income plan or for any other reason, it's essential you seek out and work with an expert who is also a fiduciary, meaning they are held to the highest standard of placing your best interests above all else, including theirs. They should also regularly deal with all types of financial products—securities, savings, and insurance instruments—and understand how to utilize the best of all those worlds in combination, for your benefit.

I'll elaborate more on finding the right financial advisor in chapter 16, but for now, suffice it to say that you want someone with the expertise to know whether an annuity or any other financial product is right for you based on your unique situation and objectives, but who doesn't have a vested interest in whether you actually purchase an annuity versus some other solution—and if you do, which one you might utilize.

I've encountered many people who own annuities that were at best not optimal, and at worst completely inappropriate for them, either because they were poorly advised or they made the mistake of trying to figure it out themselves and then simply called an annuity salesperson to execute the transaction.

Don't get me wrong, outside of your non-asset retirement income sources such as SS and pensions, a well-designed, guaranteed retirement income annuity is oftentimes one of the best ways to convert assets into additional guaranteed income, thus increasing your ISR and thereby reducing your income gap. But as I've said before, the devil is always in the details.

In chapter 11, I'll take a much deeper dive into this topic and do my best to cut through all the myths, hype, and propaganda surrounding the subject of annuities to give you a strong basic understanding that you can apply to your own situation. I will also address some of the most prevalent misconceptions that may have clouded your perspective of annuities as potentially being an appropriate piece of your retirement income planning puzzle.

ONE LAST OPTION

Many would say the only less desirable solution than working part time in early retirement to increase your ISR is the idea of reducing your monthly retirement income need. That is, lowering your household budget. However, it is necessary to acknowledge this option, if indeed your ISR is unacceptably low and you don't have the wherewithal to increase it by any other means. Lowering your monthly income need reduces the denominator in your ISR equation, thus increasing your ISR percentage.

Oftentimes a little extra monthly income, or a slightly lower need, goes a long way when it comes to increasing one's ISR. In the case of our friends the Johnsons, whose ISR was 66% ($4,000/$6,000), as little as $200 additional monthly income increases their ISR to 70%, and an additional $800 secures an 80% ISR. On the other hand, a decrease in their monthly need from $6,000 to $5,000 also equates to an ISR of 80%. As you can see, there are many ways to achieve a specific ISR objective without completely reinventing the wheel. Sometimes a small tweak here or there is all that's needed. For that reason a robust, interactive modeling software is priceless in ascertaining one's options.

Although this is not an exhaustive list of all the things you can do to increase your ISR, they are the most likely candidates. In the event you are one of the few that have other options at your disposal, an advisor who truly specializes in retirement income planning should be able to help you model the impact of those options.

Once you've evaluated all your options for increasing your guaranteed income sources and hopefully reaching an acceptable ISR, the next step is to turn your attention toward filling your income gap, such that you always have all the income you need. This will be accomplished with nonguaranteed sources of income, those at the middle and/or top of the pyramid, since you should now have exhausted all your options for creating additional guaranteed income to achieve your acceptable ISR.

Taking Action

Before moving on to the next chapter, use the QR code (page 9) to access the chapter 5 resources, then ask yourself the following questions:

1. Are you satisfied with your current ISR? If so, great. If not:

a. Are you confident you have optimized your
    non-asset-based income resources?

    i. Where specifically do you think there may be
        opportunity for improvement?

b. Are there additional resources you could reposition
    to any of the guaranteed options covered within this
    chapter, while maintaining sufficient liquidity for
    unforeseen future needs?

    i. If so, what are they?

c. Are you willing to work part time?

    i. If so, take a few minutes to imagine what that
        might look like. What would be your personal
        preferences for part-time work?

d. Can you realistically reduce your monthly retirement
    income need—lower your household budget?

    i. If so, what expenses represent the largest
        opportunity?

e. Do you have any significant debt payments that could
    be retired?

    i. If so, list them.

Any combination of these options may help you reach your ISR goal.

CHAPTER 6

FILL THE GAP

Expertise is the ultimate currency.

—TONY ROBBINS

On January 15, 2009, at 3:24 p.m., Captain Chesley "Sully" Sullenberger was piloting US Airways Flight 1549, an Airbus A320, en route to Charlotte Douglas International Airport in Charlotte, North Carolina. Shortly after takeoff from New York's LaGuardia Airport, the aircraft encountered a flock of Canada geese, which caused both engines to lose power. With limited time and altitude, Captain Sullenberger made a quick decision to ditch the plane in the Hudson River, aiming for a controlled water landing.

Sullenberger skillfully maneuvered the plane and executed the water landing with remarkable precision and composure. The successful landing allowed the passengers and crew to evacuate onto the wings and be rescued by nearby boats and ferries. Everyone on board survived. It was an incredible feat of skill and quick thinking under immense pressure.

The event garnered international attention and became known as the "Miracle on the Hudson." Captain Sullenberger was hailed as a hero for his actions, and his professionalism and ability to remain calm in a crisis were widely praised.

In chapter 5, I introduced you to the concept of guarantees as being one of the two main ways to mitigate risk. I characterized them as being insurance policies of sorts. In Sully's case, his expertise resulted in an outcome where everyone on his flight lived, but that expertise was never a guarantee of life or safety for the passengers. I also reviewed a variety of retirement cash flow resources, such as Social Security, pensions, deferred compensation, guaranteed insurance and annuity payments, income from guaranteed savings vehicles, and the like that incorporate guarantees of one kind or another. These guaranteed sources of retirement cash flow fall into the bottom level of the Income Stability Pyramid and make up the foundation of your retirement income plan. As I explained, they also represent the numerator in your ISR calculation, which means that increasing this number will increase your ISR and thus reduce your retirement income gap.

LESSEN RISK WITH EXPERTISE

Now let's turn our attention to the second way to mitigate risk associated with your retirement income: expertise. Webster's defines expertise as "having, involving, or displaying special skills or knowledge derived from training or experience." In thinking of the middle, stable section of your Income Stability Pyramid, you can think of expertise as hiring someone to actively manage the risk related to your traditional investment resources (stocks, bonds, mutual funds, etc.), as opposed to transferring that risk to another party as you would to get guaranteed income from the base of the pyramid.

As illustrated in chapter 5, expertise in a motor vehicle is akin to operating your vehicle safely, obeying the traffic laws, wearing your seat belt, and refraining from texting while driving. In other words, anything you might do to reduce the likelihood of an accident in the first place. In the story about Sully, expertise is everything he had to draw on from his training and experience to determine the best course of action in order to minimize the likelihood of a negative outcome.

The Difference between Expertise and Guarantees

When it comes to retirement income planning, the big difference between guarantees and expertise is that guarantees are the means by which you increase your base-level guaranteed income, which in turn elevates your ISR, thereby reducing your retirement income gap. An example might be our friends the Johnsons, a couple we introduced in the previous chapter that had an ISR of 66%. They might choose to defer claiming one or more of their Social Security benefits for a couple of years, thereby increasing their guaranteed income over the course of their remaining lifetimes.

Expertise, on the other hand, is used to fill the remaining income gap with nonguaranteed but highly stable and highly liquid income. The need for stability is reflected in the name, but the need for liquidity is equally important. Appropriate investment strategies at this middle, stable level should require little to no long-term commitment but instead allow for maximum flexibility and access to your funds. The key is to balance guaranteed income (the base) with ample liquidity (stable middle), since you never know what the future will hold.

Active Risk Mitigation

Warren Buffett has often been credited with saying, "The number one rule of investing is don't lose money." Some add that rule number two is, "See rule number one."

Managing the risk associated with the middle, stable portion of your Income Stability Pyramid is absolutely critical. As such, the only strategies appropriate for this portion of your pyramid are those that *have proven effective in mitigating risk in a significant way through diverse market conditions while still outperforming inflation over time.* I define *significant* as being any strategy that reduces the volatility of an equivalent, risk-weighted stock and bond portfolio by at least 50%, and preferably more, over time. I call this active risk mitigation (ARM), as opposed to the much more common passive risk management approaches like asset allocation and diversification, which are insufficient to this task. How can you achieve this?

As you might imagine, truly effective ARM is much easier said than done.

Passive Risk Mitigation

The traditional approach to risk management is passive; it relies on asset allocation and diversification as the primary strategies to mitigate market risk—chiefly, deciding how to divide money between stocks and bonds. As mentioned previously, today the vast majority of investment advisors and money managers rely on this approach, based on Modern Portfolio Theory.

An extremely simple example of this approach is the advice to invest your age as a percentage into bonds or bond funds, and the rest into stocks or stock funds. So a 60-year-old would put 60% in bonds and 40% in stocks. In other instances, the overall allocation might be determined by taking a risk-tolerance test, which is said to indicate the appropriate amount of stocks and bonds.

Regardless of the actual allocation methodology, the underlying assumption of MPT is that asset allocation (which kinds) and diversification (how many) are in and of themselves sufficient to mitigate risk over time. I'll take a much deeper dive into MPT in chapter 10. For now, just know it's likely how your own retirement savings portfolio is currently being managed, regardless of whether you are working with an investment advisor or you're a do-it-yourselfer who's relying on guidance from the financial industry and popular media.

I liken MPT to the Palmolive of the investment world. Why? Because although you may or may not have any idea what MPT is, you're likely soaking in it right now. (If you're within the intended age demographic for this book, you'll understand that reference.) That is to say, the vast majority of investment advisors, robo-advisors, and mainstream financial media religiously adhere to this approach to investing as the primary tool for risk management and portfolio optimization. It's the entire premise behind Target Date Funds, which are wildly popular these days. So whether you know it or not, your portfolio's entire risk-mitigation strategy is likely based on this concept, which in my opinion is one of the main reasons for the high rate of failure of so many retirement plans today.

One reason this passive approach has been so appealing and so prevalent with do-it-yourselfers and advisors alike goes back to the point I made in chapter 2 about appealing to the masses in the simplest terms possible. In this case, the appeal is low cost. Passive risk management enables you to hold relatively cheap index funds, since individual investment choice is not purported to be as important as asset allocation and diversification. This provides a false sense of security in a "penny wise, pound foolish" sort of way, as I'll demonstrate in chapter 8. It's kind of like buying the cheapest car on the lot for your 16-year-old child, when safety should be your number one priority. Of course, some advisors and money managers try to differentiate themselves from one another by making their own investment selections versus "buying the indexes," but most are no more than veiled attempts to appear more sophisticated than the index itself. Beneath the layers, however, the difference in outcome is nominal at best, especially since any MPT-based strategy, by definition, ignores the most important determining factor for retirees—that is, active risk mitigation.

Figure 6.1: Passive versus Active Risk Mitigation

To be clear, the number one goal of any risk-mitigation strategy suit-able for the stable portion of the Income Stability Pyramid must be to minimize losses during down markets. Pursuing gains is a distant second objective. After all, it is foolish to expect that you can produce highly stable income over a long period of time from anything less than a highly stable, risk-mitigated strategy. Moreover, managing volatility is not only more effective than the traditional model of investing for avoiding unnecessary losses, it's also more favorable for predictably growing one's assets throughout retirement, as I'll demonstrate in chapter 8, due to the power of compounding. Figure 6.2 illustrates this concept. In a perfect world of constantly rising markets with low volatility, passive risk management may actually provide a superior result. However, it also dramatically increases the likelihood of failure in all other markets. Active risk mitigation, on the other hand, greatly reduces the likelihood of failure in all markets.

For those of you who may be skeptical about the value of this approach, having been inundated with the idea that generating big returns in good years is more important than avoiding big losses in down years, I have dedicated all of chapter 8, The Flaw of Averages, to laying out and explaining the logic and mathematical justification for my position. For now, however, suspend your disbelief for the remainder of this chapter. If you absolutely cannot bring yourself to proceed without first understanding the logic behind the critical importance of loss mitigation as the primary objective of any stable income strategy, then by all means proceed to chapter 8 and return here once you've finished.

The Proof Is in the Pudding

The past 25 years have taught me that most active risk mitigation strategies look much better on paper than in real life. I have literally evaluated hundreds of money managers and perhaps thousands of risk-mitigation strategies, only to find that when the rubber actually meets the road, they simply don't achieve the objective of significantly reducing downside volatility, based on my previous definition.

Active Risk Mitigation Leads to More Predictable Results

Traditional/Passive Risk Management
Produces a Wide Variety of Outcomes

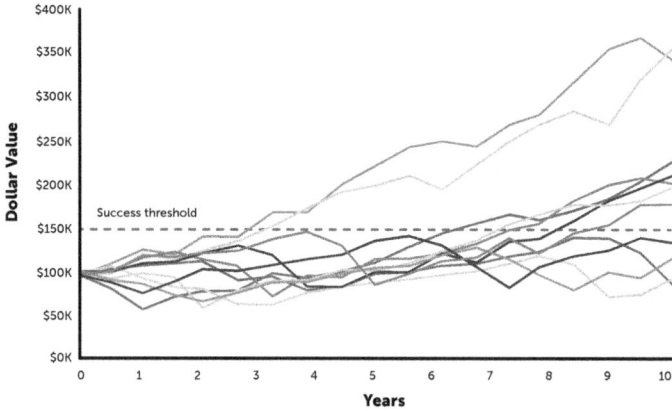

Active Risk Mitigation Produces More Consistent Outcomes

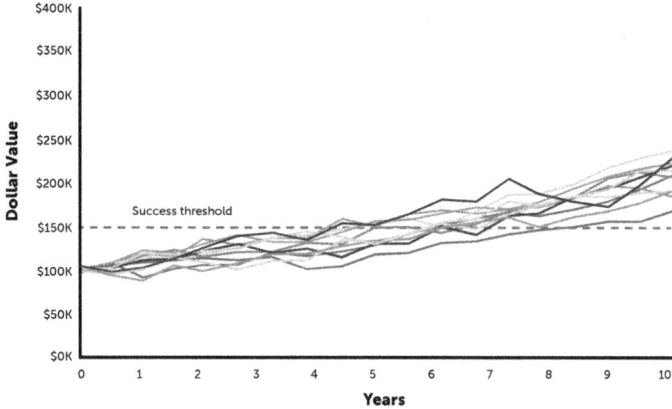

Figure 6.2: Active risk mitigation strategies enhance your likelihood of success.

The proliferation of risk-managed strategies since 2008 has made it even more difficult to evaluate the field of options, since the vast majority of strategies don't have a sufficient track record of navigating the difficulties of the past three decades.

The good news, however, is that there are indeed excellent money managers dedicated to the science of risk mitigation who have successfully navigated the unprecedented volatility of the past three decades. Most of these risk-mitigated strategies utilize many of the same traditional investments you are likely familiar with such as stocks, bonds, commodities, mutual funds, exchange-traded funds, cash, and so on. They just do so within the context of a much more active risk management focus than the mostly passive approaches of asset allocation and diversification, which recent history has shown to be inadequate, especially for retirees.[1] Simply think of these strategies as employing an additional level of risk management over and above the more passive asset allocation and diversification referenced previously.

The proof, of course, is in the pudding. Making risk mitigation the primary focus for these midlevel assets has served our clients well during these increasingly turbulent past few decades. In fact, we often affectionately refer to the managers we employ to execute our risk-mitigated strategies as our "Sullys," since they routinely go unnoticed until the proverbial geese hit the fan.

Identifying acceptable active risk-mitigation strategies is critical to building a retirement income plan based on the Income Stability Pyramid concept. It requires employing an effective process by which to identify, filter, and evaluate strategies that effectively meet the objectives of the stable midsection of your pyramid. The following are the criteria we use for sifting through the universe of options:

For starters, acceptable investment strategies must be unconstrained relative to their overall asset allocation. In other words, they go wherever they need to go, based on prevailing market conditions.

1   For recent discussions about the shortcomings of MPT for retirees, see Mark Arnold, "How Modern Portfolio Theory Has Failed Investors," Money Management, January 21, 2011, https://www.moneymanagement.com.au/features/editorial/how-modern-portfolio-theory-has-failed-investors; and John Manganaro, "Modern Portfolio Theory Is Not for Retirement Income Planning: New Paper," Think Advisor, January 12, 2023, https://www.thinkadvisor.com/2023/01/12/modern-portfolio-theory-is-not-for-retirement-income-planning-new-paper/.

They're not tethered to a specific asset allocation, as is the case with MPT-based strategies.

Second, these strategies must be primarily defensive. A defensive strategy protects principal first. Then and only then, it pursues reasonable, risk-appropriate gains, as opposed to many who pursue gains first with the protection of principal merely as an afterthought.

Third, they are responsive versus predictive. Trying to predict the future of markets is dangerous. If there's one thing we all should have learned over the past two and a half decades, it's that markets are largely unpredictable. I've yet to find anyone who can predict with consistency. Instead, we've found that the best strategies identify and defensively adjust to mid- to long-term trends. (This is not the same as trend following, which focuses more on chasing short-term gains than protecting principal. And it's not day-trading, which focuses on very short-term movements.)

A good analogy for this is the fact that I don't try to predict the weather, since I'm not a meteorologist. But when it's raining outside, I open my umbrella, wear a raincoat, or stay inside altogether to avoid getting wet. I'm not predicting. I'm just responding. And most importantly, I'm accomplishing my goal of not getting soaked.

Fourth, they are rules-based, or algorithmic. Human emotions can destroy any good strategy. Therefore, a truly reliable strategy must be process-driven and response agnostic. That is, the algorithm will automatically drive a certain and specific response to a particular stimulus or combination of stimuli. In other words, there is a clear and specific cause-and-effect relationship devoid of situational human emotion.

I don't care what the precipitating events are, and neither do you. So long as the cause-and-effect algorithms are intact, we know the process will work, regardless of whether it's a dot-com bubble bursting, a subprime debt crisis, a pandemic, or a geopolitical threat.

Fifth, acceptable investment strategies have a strong track record of proven success. This must extend over many years and many market cycles, through various extreme or unprecedented market conditions, like those previously mentioned. The years 2000, 2001, 2002, 2008, 2018, and 2020 are great litmus tests for ARM strategies. How did they pan out? Many strategies boast of "beating the market" or "beating their benchmark" year after year. But if the strategy lost only 40% when the market was down 50%, that does not constitute victory to me. Not when managing portfolios for retirement income.

This may be the most difficult hurdle in assessing various strategies, as many new strategies tend to emerge in the wake of every "unprecedented" new market event, only to lack any real track record of effectively navigating the very types of markets for which they're most needed.

Unfortunately, attaining poor results from strategies that appear to check all the boxes is common. For that reason, extensive, ongoing due diligence is a must. This process is summarized in the following chart.

ACTIVE RISK MITIGATION
STRATEGY SELECTION PROCESS

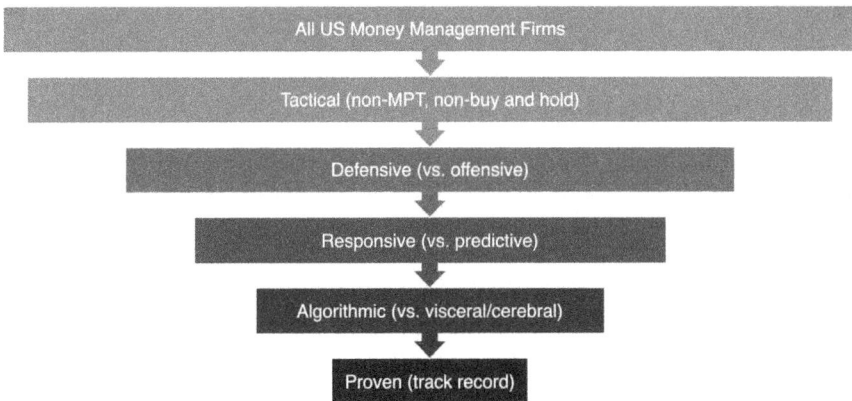

All US Money Management Firms

Tactical (non-MPT, non-buy and hold)

Defensive (vs. offensive)

Responsive (vs. predictive)

Algorithmic (vs. visceral/cerebral)

Proven (track record)

Figure 6.3: Active Risk Mitigation Strategy Selection Process

The Real Deal:
Active Risk Mitigation versus Active Management

ARM is sometimes confused with *active management*, but they are truly quite different. Active management usually exists within the context of MPT, which simply means that certain investments may be purchased, sold, or exchanged for one another from time to time but the overall asset allocation remains largely intact and unchanged. Oftentimes, advisors or money managers will suggest that they're providing "active management," which is a far cry from active risk mitigation. In fact they're typically just "massaging" the underlying holdings within an MPT strategy from time to time, which, by definition, is not active risk mitigation at all.

Neither does ARM rely on a single tactic, like always moving from stocks to bonds when there is perceived volatility in stock markets. In my mind, this does not qualify as true ARM because it is monolithic. As soon as stocks and bonds both move in the same direction, like they did in 2022, this approach becomes completely impotent. This is why a truly ARM approach should be open-ended, within reason, and focused on risk tolerance versus asset allocation.

ARM VERSUS MPT

In chapter 8, I'll explain the mathematical reasoning behind the critical importance of managing losses above all else when it comes to designing retirement income strategies aimed at supplying truly stable, long-term retirement income. Then, as mentioned previously, I'll take a deep dive into MPT in chapter 10, explaining in detail why I find it insufficient for managing investments within the stable section of your pyramid.

For now, however, I want to provide a brief visual comparison between ARM and MPT. This will help you understand the fundamental differences in the two philosophies as you seek to understand the rationale behind utilizing this approach to fill your income gap with truly stable retirement income.

Addressing Risk Tolerance

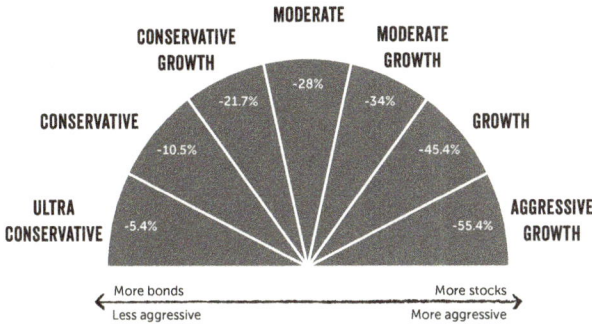

- Overall allocation is fixed
- Doesn't react to market volatility
- Portfolio goes wherever market takes it

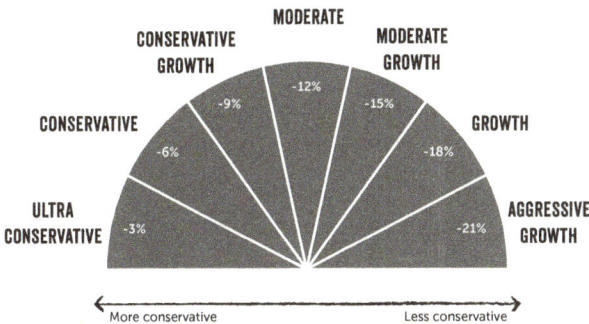

- Overall allocation is variable
- Does react to market volatility
- Primary focus is defense, second is growth

Figure 6.4: Speedometers of Risk

Think of figure 6.4 as your "speedometers of risk." On the top, you'll see the speedometer of risk representing MPT. On the bottom is the speedometer of risk representing an ARM approach. Both approaches attempt to identify the investor's risk tolerance. The far left side of each speedometer represents the most conservative type of investor. Toward the far right represents the most aggressive type of investor. In between is the entire spectrum of investor profiles, which identify the particular risk tolerances of any given individual. That is, how much can you tolerate your account or portfolio dropping during particularly volatile markets? (Think of the losses in 2008.)

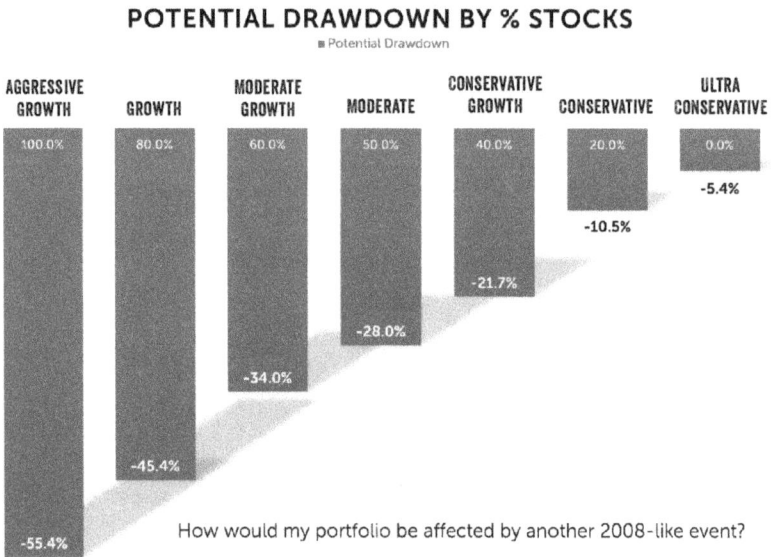

POTENTIAL DRAWDOWN BY % STOCKS

■ Potential Drawdown

AGGRESSIVE GROWTH	GROWTH	MODERATE GROWTH	MODERATE	CONSERVATIVE GROWTH	CONSERVATIVE	ULTRA CONSERVATIVE
100.0%	80.0%	60.0%	50.0%	40.0%	20.0%	0.0%
						-5.4%
					-10.5%	
				-21.7%		
			-28.0%			
		-34.0%				
	-45.4%					
-55.4%						

How would my portfolio be affected by another 2008-like event?

Figure 6.5: Maximum Drawdown by Percentage of Stocks in Portfolio, Based on MPT

MPT says that the more conservative investor should hold more bonds and cash, while the more aggressive investor should hold more stocks, as represented in the diagram. According to MPT, this overall allocation should remain fixed. Although there can and will be many underlying nuances differentiating one MPT-oriented strategy from another, the general concept is that the overall allocation is relatively fixed. The investor or investment manager never reacts to market volatility by adjusting the overall allocation. As a result, the account or portfolio will go wherever the market takes it.

This approach is often characterized by the attitude that, based on history, if you identify and stick to an appropriate allocation, everything will work out in the long run despite the roller coaster ride in between.

ARM investing, however, doesn't equate each level of risk tolerance directly with a particular asset allocation. Instead, the overall allocation is always variable. In this case, the ARM approach *does* react to market volatility, according to whatever process or strategy the particular manager utilizes. Once again, the primary focus is defense, while the secondary focus is growth.

Within each section of these speedometers, I've indicated the degree of potential loss that an investor might historically expect to experience, based on their stated risk tolerance, during a particularly volatile market. For example, according to the chart, a growth-oriented MPT investor whose portfolio is essentially 80% stocks and 20% bonds likely experienced a loss of approximately 40% or more during the 2008 market crisis. A growth-oriented ARM investor, on the other hand, would have been more likely to experience a loss in the neighborhood of 18% or less. Generally speaking, by my definition of an *effective* ARM strategy, the goal is always to mitigate losses during down markets by 50% or more, whenever possible, over the long term. (Historically speaking, we have done much better than this. However, I believe it is better to under-promise and over-deliver than vice versa.)

As discussed in chapter 2, historical averages rarely occur. They are simply the average of what actually does occur. As such, there are going to be times in history where the rules of thumb don't hold up. For instance, there may be times when holding bonds isn't an appropriately conservative approach. A great example of this is 2022, when interest rates and inflation rose dramatically. As a result, bond volatility was unusually extreme. At the same time, the S&P 500 also experienced significant volatility in 2022, dropping approximately 20% for the year. Many investors following the MPT approach experienced the worst calendar year of combined stock and bond losses since the 1960s.

An effectively managed ARM approach, on the other hand, designed to move freely between stocks, bonds, cash, or other asset classes in response to market volatility, might have reallocated to extremely short-term bonds, commodities, and/or cash, resulting in significantly lower losses. Alternatively, another ARM approach might have used futures and/or options contracts or some other mechanism to provide a buffer against stock volatility. Either way, the desired outcome is to significantly reduce drawdown of the underlying assets during a time of extreme volatility.

The secondary objective of ARM strategies is to pursue reasonable risk-sensitive or risk-adjusted returns during times of relative calm. We sometimes refer to these types of gains as "low-hanging fruit." ARM strategies are not interested in reaching for the fruit at the top of the trees. That's what gets people into trouble. That's why it's critical during the planning process for you to determine the minimum required level of risk necessary for the purpose of achieving the success of your overall retirement plan, then make a commitment to not exceed it, regardless of how you might feel about current market conditions. Otherwise, you'll be tempted to reach for the fruit at the top of the trees.

One of my main jobs as an advisor/coach is to demonstrate to our clients what minimum level of risk is required in order for them to achieve their defined outcomes, and then help them refrain from exceeding that level of risk when they are occasionally tempted. After all, it's human nature to underestimate the level of most risks in our pursuit of keeping up with the Joneses. We all have a higher level of risk tolerance in theory than we do in actuality. For this reason, the best ARM strategies are not driven by emotion or market perception, but rather by emotionless, tried-and-tested algorithms. Otherwise, you're back to where you started, taking on inappropriate levels of risk, not so much based on your own market assessments but on someone else's.

If you can adequately mitigate volatility, you don't need particularly high rates of return to achieve success, thanks to the power of compounding. This means you don't need to concern yourself with what might appear to be "missed opportunities," because reducing your level of risk exposure by using ARM investing will more than offset those potential gains over the long run, as I'll explain in chapter 8.

IN SUMMATION

By now you've learned not only how to build your retirement income base with an acceptable level of guaranteed, increasing, tax-efficient lifetime income, but also how to fill your remaining retirement income gap with income generated from the stable midsection of your income pyramid. This income, by definition, is not guaranteed, but it is highly stable and reliable.

In addition to any type of stable income you might generate from nontraditional investment assets, such as certain rental or royalty income, actively risk-mitigated strategies are your most accessible, reliable, and liquid option. This necessitates an extremely high level of expertise to achieve, which means hiring the best firms you can find, but it can absolutely be done. It just requires a renewed mindset when it comes to your investment priorities. As I said in the introduction, you've been trained to think of pursuing growth as paramount and risk management as simply an afterthought. But during retirement, risk management *must* become the primary driver, with achieving reasonable gains an important but distant second.

In a perfect world, it is best to generate all your retirement income at the first and second levels of your ISP. Any income need that isn't met within the first two levels of your ISP will need to come from the top, from the variable level of your pyramid, including stocks, bonds, mutual funds, ETFs, and other traditional investments managed—or not managed—in the more traditional manner, without prioritizing active risk mitigation. As such, they rely mainly on asset allocation and diversification for their risk management capabilities. For this reason, income generated from this level of your ISP can be highly unpredictable.

The planning I've described thus far is just the tip of the iceberg when it comes to a comprehensive retirement income plan. It's what we call the "Happily Ever After" version of your plan, where you and your spouse live a long, healthy life and die quietly in your sleep. It's all about lifetime income stability. It's the goal. But a truly comprehensive plan must also deal with the less optimistic potentialities of life, which we call the "What-Ifs." We'll review some of those in chapter 13.

Taking Action

Before moving on to the next chapter, use the QR code (page 9) to access the chapter 6 resources, then ask yourself:

1. What, if any, active risk-mitigating strategies (expertise) does your current retirement portfolio include, over and above basic asset allocation and diversification?

2. Do these strategies have proven, verifiable track records of successfully mitigating losses during the most volatile periods of time over the past three decades? (Think 2000, 2001, 2002, 2008, 2018, 2020, 2022.)

3. What were their actual track records during those specific years?

4. Would you be okay with those levels of volatility now?

    a. If so, great. You're not losing sleep. Make a copy of this worksheet and save it for the next major market correction. (Many people have a much higher risk tolerance in theory than in reality.)

    b. If not, what steps could you take in the short term to alleviate the risk to your investments in the immediate future?

5. Longer term, are you open to taking the steps necessary to rectify the situation permanently?

    a. What if that means changing advisors?

    b. If the answer is yes, consider establishing a plan of action to move to a more suitable, retirement-appropriate, actively risk-mitigated approach to portfolio management before the next major market correction.

        i. Create a timeline for identifying, interviewing, and hiring the right professional.

        ii. Don't procrastinate.

        iii. See chapter 16, "Finding the Right Advisor."

PART 3

Myths, Hype, and Propaganda

CHAPTER 7

SOCIAL SECURITY MISTAKES

Guaranteed income is the best kind of income.

—ROBERT KIYOSAKI

T he typical Social Security planning process leaves much to be desired. More often than not, the "planning" is limited to a discussion that goes something like this: "If you're concerned that Social Security might be going away or you might have a short life expectancy, you should take Social Security at age 62. This will allow you to get as much as possible during the first years just in case. It will also help preserve your retirement savings. If you think you'll live a long time, you can delay taking Social Security and you will receive a higher benefit over time, but you'll have to live to about 80 before you reach the break-even point. So what would you like to do?"

To suggest this is an extremely inadequate approach is an egregious understatement. It leaves the most important retirement income issues concerning Social Security untouched. And good luck if you call the Social Security Administration looking for help. Not only are they technically prohibited from providing advice, but any advice they do choose to provide is, as often as not, incorrect.

TOO MANY ADVISORS LACK EXPERTISE IN SOCIAL SECURITY

Since most of our new clients come to us from other advisors, we see a fair amount of the financial industry's typical approach to Social Security planning. And it seems that a lot of advisors don't give much thought to Social Security (SS). Certainly not proportionate to its contribution to and effect on your overall retirement income plan.

One of the first questions I ask prospective clients who currently have an advisor is, "If you already have an advisor, why are you here? Do they not specialize in retirement?" Oftentimes I get an answer like, "Oh, yes. They do. And they are excellent. But they don't do Social Security planning, or Medicare planning, or tax planning, or . . ." You get the picture. How can you be a retirement specialist and not do advanced Social Security or tax planning?

The problem, it seems, is that most advisors have little to no high-level knowledge or expertise regarding Social Security benefits and how they affect every other aspect of retirement income planning. Perhaps this is because, for the average advisor, there is little to no incentive to spend a lot of time learning about and advising on the intricacies of SS. This is especially true if they don't specialize in working only with retirees. If you think about it, advisors are actually disincentivized to recommend any sort of delayed approach to claiming SS. This is because advisors get paid to manage assets. So the sooner you take Social Security, the longer you delay spending those assets they are being paid to oversee.

This is particularly problematic because delaying one or more of a couple's SS benefits is, as often as not, the better long-term strategy for a number of reasons, not the least of which are tax planning, survivorship planning, investment risk mitigation, and inflation hedging—issues that are rarely considered central to a SS-claiming discussion, but should be. The fact is, your SS-claiming strategy directly and indirectly affects all your other forms of income throughout your lifetime. So if that decision isn't made wisely, your entire retirement income plan will be built on a less-than-optimal foundation.

As illustrated in Figure 7.1, our software analyzes thousands of claiming strategies in order to identify, isolate, and compare any number

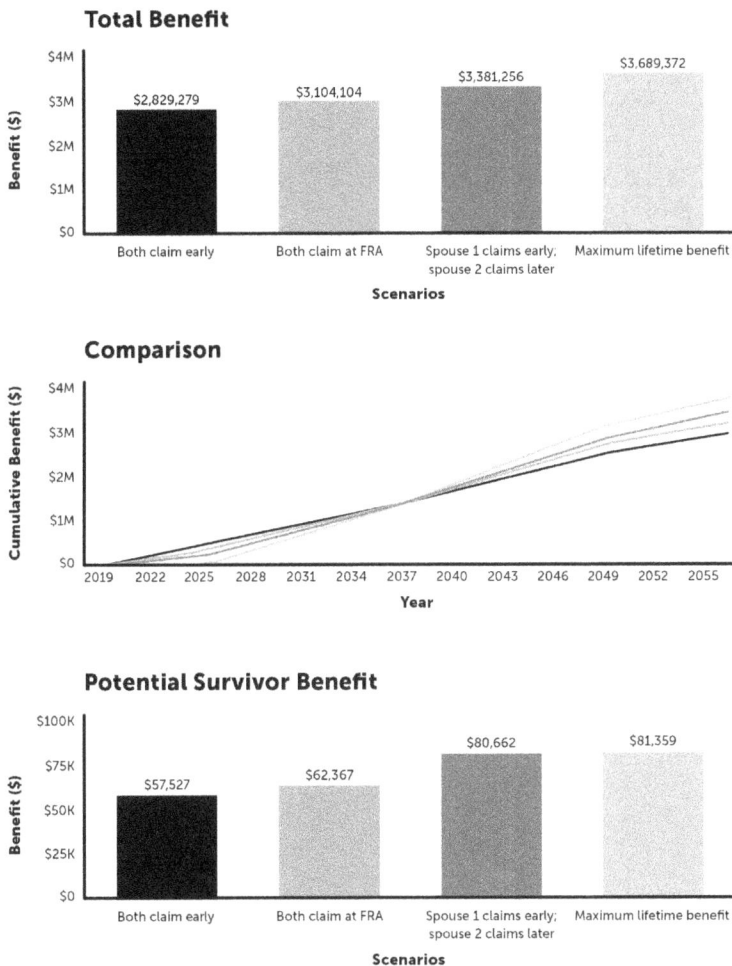

Figure 7.1: Cumulative Benefits

of the most likely scenarios for consideration. Some of the key metrics we consider are total lifetime living benefits, time to breakeven, and lifetime survivor benefits. Once we've successfully identified the most likely scenarios, we can then test each approach within our comprehensive retirement income planning software; the goal of which is to create stable, increasing, tax efficient, lifetime income and to maximize the projected residual estate. This enables us to consider the many effects each unique strategy has on the effectiveness and efficiency of every other retirement resource.

THE TRUE VALUE OF YOUR SOCIAL SECURITY BENEFITS

Regardless of what you personally think of the Social Security system in our country, in the vast majority of cases it represents a significant piece of the puzzle when it comes to retirement cash flow. In fact, studies indicate Social Security currently provides approximately 40% of the average retired couple's annual income.[2] In terms of our Johnson example, the couple with an ISR of 66%, this might mean Social Security payments account for some $2,400 of their $6,000 monthly income need.

---

2   Social Security Administration, "Social Security: Understanding the Benefits," SSA publication no. 05-10024, ICN 454930, January 2006, https://www.dol.gov/sites/dolgov/files/ebsa/about-ebsa/our-activities/resource-center/publications/10024.pdf.

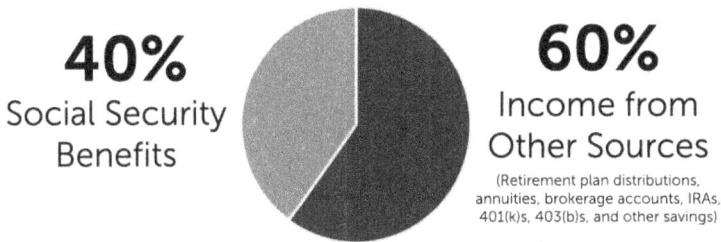

40%
Social Security
Benefits

60%
Income from
Other Sources

(Retirement plan distributions,
annuities, brokerage accounts, IRAs,
401(k)s, 403(b)s, and other savings)

Figure 7.2: What is Social Security to the average retiree?

In addition to its proportionate significance as an income source for most retirees, SS comes with numerous additional benefits: it's guaranteed by the US government, it includes spousal benefits, cost-of-living adjustments, disability benefits, survivor benefits, and is tax favored in that at most, only 85% of it is currently subject to income taxation, and that percentage can be as low as 0% depending on your other income sources. Most other types of retirement income lack some or all of these benefits.

On average, I find properly optimized SS benefits are likely to provide a typical married couple more than $2 million over the course of their expected lifetimes. In some cases, that number may exceed $3 million. That's serious income, and certainly well worth taking the time to get right. If that's not enough motivation for you, then how about this: You've contributed to SS your entire working life. Don't you owe it to yourself to optimize your benefit?

One impactful way I like to help people understand the value of their SS check is to think of replacing it in terms of cash flow. After all, retirement is a cash flow problem, remember?

Let's say you have a $2,500 monthly Social Security check. That doesn't include cost-of-living adjustments or any increases for deferring. It's just your basic benefit. If you multiply that by 12 months, that means you get $30,000 a year from Social Security. For comparison purposes, if you assume you could take 4% out of a theoretical investment portfolio for spending each year in retirement without jeopardizing the principal, that means that you would have to have $750,000 of investments generating a 4% income in order to provide the equivalent $30,000 a year. That means your $2,500 monthly Social Security check is roughly equivalent to three quarters of $1 million dollars, generating a constant 4% income stream.

And for that to happen as consistently as your SS check, you'd have to get 4%, guaranteed, every single year for the rest of your life. With zero volatility in your principal. Ever. And of course, that doesn't account for any inflation adjustment. That's just that $30,000 forever.

Having guaranteed income of a certain amount today is one thing. Having guaranteed income of that same amount 20 years from now is another. Without any cost-of-living adjustments, that could be quite problematic. But the only way to account for inflation would be to get an additional return over and above your guaranteed 4%, equivalent to the annual rate of inflation. For 2021, the Social Security cost-of-living adjustment was a healthy 5.9%, and for 2022, a whopping 8.7%. That means you'd have had to get a 12.7% return on your investment portfolio without exposing yourself to any risk.

Hopefully that description helps give you some perspective on how valuable Social Security cash flow is and what you'd have to do to replace it with another asset-based income stream if you didn't have it. It would be extremely hard to replicate, especially in times of low interest rates such as we've had for the past decade or so. So although many people undervalue SS benefits and therefore spend a proportionately small amount of time identifying the optimal claiming strategy, I suggest the opposite approach.

Social Security income is by far the most common piece of the puzzle in the guaranteed-income base level of the pyramid, so it's only natural when thinking in terms of creating guaranteed, increasing lifetime income that this is the place to start. If you qualify for an SS benefit, I believe job one of your retirement income plan is to optimize your SS-claiming strategy.

WHY MOST PEOPLE GET IT WRONG

The unfortunate truth of the matter is that most people get their Social Security claiming option wrong in that they fail to truly optimize their benefits. There are four main reasons this happens, but all four come down to the same underlying issue—fear. Fear of missing out, to be precise. In my experience, the four most common reasons you might fail to optimize your SS benefits are—

- Fear you may not live long

- Fear of spending your nest egg

- Fear of SS going bankrupt and leaving you without benefits

- Fear of paying higher taxes in the short term

I will address each of these arguments and describe why these lines of reasoning are faulty.

Fear You Might Not Live Long

This is by far the most common argument I hear for claiming SS benefits earlier than might be optimal. Perhaps you're concerned about premature death. If you die young and you start Social Security later than, say, age 62, you may feel you're not going to get much.

I always ask this question when I teach a Social Security class: "If you believed you were going to die prematurely, how would that affect your SS claiming option?" Without a single exception, the answer is always, "I would begin taking it as soon as possible." This, of course, is a reasonable response and makes a ton of sense on the surface. Then I go on to ask the students to think about other ramifications of that decision. I ask: "What would happen if you claim this strategy and then you actually do die prematurely? What would be the impact on your surviving spouse?"

If you die young, by definition, your spouse will be single for a longer period of time with only one SS check, since they will lose the other one upon your death. If yours is the larger of the two SS checks coming into the household, and if you choose to claim early, this is especially detrimental because you have now doomed your spouse to that longer lifetime not only with just one check, but a much *smaller* check. You failed to maximize the one SS check they will be receiving for the remainder of their life. This will be compounded by the fact that they will also be taxed at a much higher rate since they'll no longer be claiming married, filing jointly (I'll revisit this idea in chapter 13).

So if you take the time to do the math, the idea that you might die prematurely should motivate you to want to defer your Social Security longer, if you can afford to do so. Of course, this decision must be incorporated with the entirety of your retirement income plan, but the point stands.

You should always base your initial plan on living a long, healthy life and then dying peacefully in your sleep—together, if you're married. That's what we call the Happily Ever After part of the plan. That's the goal, right? That's what you're hoping for.

But then you need to circle back and ask what happens if certain things don't go as planned—one of those being the premature death of one spouse. We call this the What If part of the plan. Rules of thumb are dangerous because there are often as many exceptions to those rules as not. But the general rule of thumb you should at least consider is the idea of having the higher earner of any given couple try to defer SS as long as possible. This is not only due to the survivorship issues I just explained, but it is also typically the most tax-favorable approach over the long term, which I'll elaborate more on in chapter 13.

As a side note, this same process generally pertains to pension optimization as well. Once you clearly understand your benefit options in a vacuum, you must also consider them outside of that vacuum, both as a component of your Happily Ever After scenario and also your What If scenario.

Fear of Spending Your Nest Egg

This is the second most common reason that people tend to fail to optimize their SS claiming strategy. Let's face it—you've spent your entire working lifetime saving for retirement, so the last thing you're inclined to do is spend it down any sooner than absolutely necessary. It's human nature to treat that asset as your security blanket, of sorts. It's your nest egg. And you've spent the last 40 years trying to grow it as large as you possibly can.

However, there are three main reasons delaying withdrawals from your retirement savings can be a bad idea.

1. **Tax planning**—For reasons I'll elaborate on in chapter 13 (taxes), it is often in your best interest to begin spending your tax-deferred retirement savings immediately upon retirement. Stated simply, the years immediately following your retirement are likely the lowest tax bracket you'll see for the rest of your life—and that assumes tax rates remain the same, which I highly doubt they will. Think about it. You're no longer earning a full-time income, but you're not yet required to collect Social Security or take required minimum distributions (RMDs) from your retirement accounts. You are fully in control of your tax liability— likely for the last time. Once you hit your 70s, there is a tax time bomb waiting for you in those Social Security payments and RMDs.

   In addition to your being in a particularly tax-favored time of life, spending your tax-deferred dollars first provides another tax advantage down the road—it reduces the size of your required minimum distributions once you reach the age at which you are required to make fully taxable withdrawals from these accounts, whether you need the funds or not.

This is just the tip of the iceberg when it comes to retirement income tax planning. The time immediately after your retirement is rich with tax-planning opportunities, but it means coordinating all your income planning with the clear intention of minimizing taxes over the remainder of your life. There's much more I'd like to say here, but I'll save it for chapter 13. For now, you'll just have to trust me. (If you can't wait, jump ahead and then come back.)

2. **Managing investment risk**—Remember, your investments are exposed to market risk. Social Security is not. If you choose to take Social Security early and defer taking money out of your investments, you are unwittingly placing more of those assets at greater risk of exposure to a major negative market event at some point during your retirement. If, upon your retirement, you knew another 2008 was coming down the pike, you would likely choose to spend some of those assets now, right?

   Time exacerbates all risks, as it simply increases the odds of the risk eventually occurring. If markets are favorable when you retire, spending some of your funds early on will reduce the exposure of your investments to that next big market sell-off.

3. **Enhancing your financial legacy**—This may seem counterintuitive, given the fact that I'm suggesting you spend more of your nest egg early on in retirement. However, even if you initially spend down your retirement accounts more quickly during the first few years by deferring Social Security, once your higher Social Security income kicks in, you ultimately slow the rate of attrition for those retirement savings assets to such a degree that they will end up being preserved to a greater extent over your remaining years.

In other words, more often than not, spending more of your retirement savings first while deferring Social Security to some degree will make your retirement savings last longer in the end. Most people are astonished to see this with their own eyes, which is why we always model every scenario in our retirement income planning software. Remember, a picture is worth a thousand words.

Fear of SS Going Bankrupt

Although I often hear this reasoning for why you might want to initiate your SS benefits payments sooner than later, it's not a big concern for those of you who are within five to 10 years of retirement. Any action taken by Congress to shore up Social Security is not likely to greatly impact those of us who have already been contributing for decades. Of course, I could be wrong, but this has always been the modus operandi of those looking to keep their elected positions.

The warnings about the trust fund having insufficient funds to pay all its liabilities as of 2037 seems to me a bit of a show. Quite frankly, Social Security has been essentially bankrupt for years now. That is to say, there's no actual money sitting in the Social Security trust fund. At best, there's a bunch of IOUs, and at worst, just like down the street at your local bank, it's nothing more than a bunch of numbers on a computer. Those funds were spent long ago.

If Congress wants to fund the shortfall, it will. It has proven it's willing and able to tax and borrow ad infinitum. Higher taxes are always just one vote away, and debt limits are no more than a procedural technicality anymore. Since politicians are largely motivated by self-preservation, any reduction in benefits is far more likely to affect our children and our children's children than us. So if the government ever comes after our Social Security benefits in earnest it will be because of a much broader government default, and Social Security will be the least of our concerns.

My belief is that most everyone reading this book will retain their Social Security benefits largely intact. My children, on the other hand, are liable to have to foot the entire bill for their own retirement, not unlike the current generation is having to do without a pension in every household, which much of our parents' generation had.

In looking for a silver lining to all the potentialities, I wonder if perhaps it would necessitate families drawing closer together once again in order to leverage the benefits of multigenerational living, as was the case before everyone became so financially independent. In my book, that wouldn't be such a bad thing. (No pun intended.)

All waxing philosophical aside, I believe you have to plan for those things that you have the ability to control. There are far too many possible futures, all beyond our ability to control, to reasonably incorporate them all into our planning in any realistic manner. For that reason, I encourage you to base your Social Security claiming decisions on a future with Social Security as we know it.

Fear of Paying Higher Taxes in the Short Term

The last of the four most common reasons people fail to optimize their Social Security–claiming strategy is short-sightedness. This is a common problem when it comes to taxes. It is a major reason the vast majority of retirees face a ticking tax time bomb of their own making. So as to not steal too much of my own thunder from chapter 13, I'll simply say that many people choose to defer spending their tax-deferred nest egg immediately upon retirement, in favor of initiating their Social Security benefit payment in order to keep their tax bill as low as possible because Social Security payments are more tax efficient than are payments from tax-deferred retirement savings. The idea is to defer spending the least tax-efficient assets as long as possible. This is extremely short-sighted in that it simply exacerbates the tax time bomb issue, kicking the proverbial can—the growing nest egg that will ultimately be taxed—further down the road. But the tax liability never goes away. It just gets bigger and bigger.

DON'T NEGLECT YOUR SOCIAL SECURITY-CLAIMING STRATEGY

Many retirees—and advisors—fail to fully comprehend the ramifications of their Social Security–claiming strategy. As a result, many retirees fail to optimize their benefits and unwittingly open themselves up to unnecessary risks related to their retirement income. As you can see, just determining the optimal Social Security–claiming strategy involves numerous considerations. And this is only the first piece of solving the retirement income puzzle. But it's a critically important one nonetheless, because it sets the entire stage for all the remaining pieces to come together and work like a well-oiled retirement income machine.

Everyone's Situation Is Unique

Optimizing your Social Security benefits in light of your entire financial situation depends on your unique personal circumstances—

- Marital status
- Tax status
- Health/life expectancy
- Monthly budget
- Other assets
- Other income sources
- Estate planning considerations

Unfortunately, many retirees lack the information needed to make an informed decision about how to make the most of this key benefit. Hopefully the information in this chapter has given you a better understanding of how to think about this underestimated retirement benefit and how it integrates with your other retirement resources to help you make the most of your retirement years.

Taking Action

Before moving on to the next chapter, use the QR code (page 9) to access the chapter 7 resources, then:

1. Log in to SSA.com and access and print/save your Social Security benefits statement.

    a. If married do the same for both spouses.

    b. Do the same for your pension benefits, if any.

2. Before picking up this book, at what age were you planning to initiate your Social Security benefits?

3. If applicable, what pension option were you planning to choose?

4. As of this moment, has your thinking changed?

    a. If so, why?

    b. If not, why not?

CHAPTER 8

THE FLAW OF AVERAGES

There are three kinds of lies:
lies, damned lies, and statistics.

—BENJAMIN DISRAELI

I magine you gave your advisor $100,000 to invest and then you left the country for two years. During that two years, there was a major stock market crash causing the S&P 500 to fall 50%. Then, the following year, there was an equally robust rebound of 50%. When you return, you anxiously ask your advisor for an accounting of your funds over the past two years. To your surprise, his reply is, "Your average rate of return over the past two years was 0%." Relieved, you thank him for taking such good care of your money amid all the turmoil. Later that week, you receive an account statement reflecting an account balance of a mere $75,000. You are beside yourself wondering how your advisor could have misled you like that. What happened?

Upon closer inspection of the historical performance, you see the following: Line one states your initial deposit of $100,000. Line two shows the first-year loss of 50%, or $50,000, leaving a $50,000 balance. Line three shows the second-year gain of 50%, or $25,000, for a total of $75,000. At the bottom of the statement, your average rate of return for the two-year period is calculated as follows: a -50% loss in year one, and a +50% gain in year two, divided by the two-year period of time equals an average return of 0%.

$$\$100,000 - 50\% = \$50,000$$
$$\$50,000 + 50\% = \$75,000$$
$$\text{Two-year average rate of return} = 0\%$$
$$\text{Actual two-year loss} = \$25,000$$

Indeed, your advisor was correct. You did earn an average rate of return of 0% over the course of the two years. But your account still lost 25% of the original principal! Suddenly it dawns on you—your advisor didn't lie. You simply asked the wrong question.

You see, the concept of average rate of return completely disregards how much money is involved from year to year. It only considers percentages. In this case, your 50% loss was on $100,000. But your 50% gain was only on $50,000. (In case you're wondering, the outcome would be identical if we reversed the order and experienced the 50% gain first, then the 50% loss. Try it for yourself.)

THE BIG LIE

This is the big lie of average rates of return and why for the average investor, in my opinion, it's your worst enemy. I call it the *flaw of averages*.

The flaw of averages is a concept that highlights the limitations of using historical average returns to make decisions, particularly when it comes to investing. The problem is that averages can be misleading because they fail to take into account the underlying distribution of data. For example, when evaluating the performance of an investment, it is common to use the average rate of return as a measure of success. However, this ignores the fact that there may be a wide range of returns within that average. A high average return may be the result of a few large gains, while a low average return may be the result of many small losses. A more accurate indicator of investment success is volatility, or the degree of variation in returns. A low-volatility investment is one that has a stable and consistent return, while a high-volatility investment is one that has a wide range of returns. Low-volatility investments are generally considered to be less risky and more stable than high-volatility investments.

Volatility Is a Better Indicator than Average Rate of Return

The reason volatility is a more important indicator of investment success than average rate of return is that it better captures the underlying risk of the investment. A high average return may be the result of a few large gains, but it also may be the result of taking on a lot of risk. Low-volatility investments, on the other hand, are less likely to experience large losses, which means that they are less risky and more stable. Additionally, volatility is a better indicator of long-term performance. A high average return may be the result of luck or temporary market conditions, but a low-volatility investment is likely to have consistent returns over time.

Another factor to consider is the impact of compounding. The power of compounding lies in the way it allows an investor to earn returns on their returns. A low-volatility investment with a consistent return will compound over time, allowing the investor to earn more over time than a high-volatility investment with a similar average return.

The Arithmetic of Loss

Understanding the flaw of averages is critical as you move up the Income Stability Pyramid, away from the relative safety of your guaranteed income sources—those that are promise based—to those sources of income that begin to have some level of exposure to the various types of investment risk.

The example at the start of the chapter, of course, is hypothetical—greatly oversimplified for illustrative purposes. But as you'll soon understand, the mathematical concept holds true regardless of the specific underlying numbers. Because average rate of return completely disregards the underlying amount of money in play, it's always the case that a certain percentage of loss has a greater negative impact on your investment success than an equivalent positive gain has a positive impact. Said another way, *losses always hurt more than gains help.* I call this the arithmetic of loss.

That's why a certain percentage of loss always requires a greater percentage of gain to recover that loss.

Percentage Loss	Gain Necessary to Recover Loss
10%	11%
20%	25%
30%	42%
40%	66%
50%	100%
60%	150%
90%	900%

Table 8.1: The Arithmetic of Loss

Imagine you have a plan that calls for a 6% average annual rate of return. If you experience a 20% decline in your portfolio in a given year, coupled with a 5% income distribution, you now require a 33% return in the following year just to replace the lost funds. But even that's not enough, because during that "break-even" year, you still need to earn your 6%, which is now greater than 6% because you have less principal! So you actually need to earn 40.5% to recover from last year and be where you planned to be at the end of next year, as Table 8.1 illustrates.

This phenomenon becomes greatly exacerbated once you begin taking withdrawals from your portfolio. That's because, in addition to the need to overcome the losses you experienced, you must also replace whatever withdrawals you took and continue to make withdrawals while doing so. The result is that you would need almost a 50% return the following year to be made whole and catch up to where you initially planned to be after year 2. And even if you are patient and take five to 10 years to catch up, you'd still need between 10% and 15% every single year in order to do so.

Decline in Year 1	Portfolio Value after Year 1	Gain Needed to Break Even in Year 2	Gain Needed to Earn Original Goal: Compounded 6% (Based on $100,000 Investment)		
Original Investment: $100,000			Year 2: $112,360	Year 5: $133,823	Year 10: $179,085
-10%	$90,000	11.1%	24.8%	10.4%	7.9%
-15%	$85,000	17.6%	32.2%	12.0%	8.6%
-20%	$80,000	25.0%	40.5%	13.7%	9.4%
-25%	$75,000	33.3%	49.8%	15.6%	10.2%
-30%	$70,000	42.9%	60.5%	17.6%	11.0%

Table 8.2

For a client in or approaching retirement, the recovery from a 20% loss may be long and difficult to achieve. The new portfolio value of $80,000 puts significant pressure on the ability to grow and maintain risk parameters, even before considering any withdrawals.

Do you see where this is going? Once you've retired, you no longer have a seemingly endless time horizon before you will need to tap into your investments. Nor are you saving and investing new money on a regular basis (buying low when the market's down). Once you start taking withdrawals, the rules change completely. Just one significantly bad year can completely change your long-term outcome.

WHAT REALLY MATTERS

This next example will help bring the concept closer to home. It's one I review with every prospective new client, since it is central to all we do.

The Flaw of Averages: How to invest $100,000 for five years

	Year 1	Year 2	Year 3	Year 4	Year 5
PORTFOLIO A	+12%	−16%	+21%	+11%	−15%
PORTFOLIO B	+4%	+7%	−3%	+6%	0%
PORTFOLIO C	+21%	+16%	−20%	−18%	+22%
PORTFOLIO D	−30%	+22%	−22%	+41%	+21%

Table 8.3: The Flaw of Averages

Imagine you're an investor with $100,000, which you give me to invest for the next five years. Now imagine I have four different investment options for you to choose from: A, B, C, and D, each with a $100,000 minimum, and you must place all your money in just one of those options. Next, imagine I have a crystal ball so I can tell you exactly what's going to happen with each of the four investment options over the next five years on a year-by-year basis. Portfolio A, for example, will grow 12% in year one, and in year two, it's going to lose 16%, and so on.

Now imagine I say to you, as an investor, "Which of these portfolios would you like your money invested in for the next five years?" For obvious reasons, almost everyone gravitates to those with the biggest returns. But then once you've made your choice, I will give you one additional piece of information and allow you to change your mind if you wish. That additional piece of information is the average rate of return for each investment over the coming five-year period.

	Year 1	Year 2	Year 3	Year 4	Year 5	Average RoR
PORTFOLIO A	+12%	−16%	+21%	+11%	−15%	2.60%
PORTFOLIO B	+4%	+7%	−3%	+6%	0%	2.80%
PORTFOLIO C	+21%	+16%	−20%	−18%	+22%	4.20%
PORTFOLIO D	−30%	+22%	−22%	+41%	+21%	6.40%

Table 8.4

Now, without exception (unless you suspect a trick), you're likely gravitating to option D. If you think it's a trick, then your likely choice is C, with the slightly lower average rate of return. But only one thing really matters, right? So let's reveal what matters—in this case, how much money will you actually have at the end of five years?

	Year 1	Year 2	Year 3	Year 4	Year 5	Average RoR	End Value
PORTFOLIO A	+12%	−16%	+21%	+11%	−15%	2.60%	$107,405.02
PORTFOLIO B	+4%	+7%	−3%	+6%	0%	2.80%	$114,418.10
PORTFOLIO C	+21%	+16%	−20%	−18%	+22%	4.20%	$112,332.92
PORTFOLIO D	−30%	+22%	−22%	+41%	+21%	6.40%	$113,646.73

Table 8.5

Of course, now, without exception, every single person chooses portfolio B because it's got the most money. That's because when push comes to shove, the only measure that really matters for an investment account is the value of the account, right? So despite the fact that portfolio B has the second lowest average rate of return, and portfolio B never once delivers the best annual return, and the average returns of portfolios C and D are two to three times greater than portfolio B, portfolio B results in the most money at the end of five years.

If you're fairly shocked by this example, you're not alone. That's the typical reaction I get from most everyone I review this with. It's completely counterintuitive and exactly the opposite of how you've been trained to think about your investments.

Avoiding Losses Should Be the Retiree's Primary Goal

The math behind this example is the exact same as the first two; average rates of return ignore how much money is at play. But when actual money is involved, losses hurt more than gains help. So when it comes to measuring long-term success, average rate of return is meaningless in and of itself, in the absence of volatility measures. And it becomes less and less valuable as more time passes. So now you can begin to see why avoiding losses becomes so much more important once you're retired: Income stability and asset preservation should now be your core objectives since they will have the biggest impact on your success. In other words, volatility, not average rate of return, is the key.

Think about it. If you were evaluating your own investment performance over a period of time during your own retirement and were told you'd earned an average of 6.4%, you'd likely feel quite satisfied. Even seeing the ending value of your investment probably wouldn't change your feelings about it, in the absence of any other information. And if I told you that I only averaged 2.8%, you'd feel even better, assuming you'd done really well by comparison. That is, unless you saw my account balance, which would likely never happen. That's the crux of the problem. Most people are diligently measuring something that simply doesn't matter. And they have no idea because they have no true basis for comparison. You never see the end result of the alternative.

TO COMPOUND OR NOT TO COMPOUND

You may have heard the famous quote attributed to Thomas Edison, "Compound interest is the eighth wonder of the world. He who understands it, earns it. He who doesn't, pays it." But you may not realize that volatility, or experiencing losses, completely defeats the concept of compounding. If an investment has higher volatility, it means you will spend more time losing money and more time recovering from those losses versus actually compounding your positive returns. Less volatility, on the other hand, enables compounding because you're spending less time losing money, less time having to recover from those losses, and more time compounding your returns (even if small). The compounding issue is made worse once you begin to take withdrawals from your investments. Why? Because those funds are no longer in the account to compound.

That means you don't need a particularly high average rate of return once you've solved the problem of volatility. And that's why I can average 2.8% over time, as described earlier, and have more money than you who averaged 6.4%. So the moral of the story here is that focusing on rate of return is both extremely deceptive and very counterproductive.

This explains why one of the main jobs of any advisor who truly specializes in retirement income planning should be to help you understand how much risk is absolutely necessary for you to take in order for you to accomplish your stated objectives, then help to ensure you don't take any more than that. Even when your investments are down and you're tempted to be more aggressive to try and recover your losses or withdrawals, don't. Minimizing losses is always the key. Always.

Returns will eventually happen. Low-hanging fruit will eventually present itself. You just need to be patient. Small losses will only kill you slowly over time if they are endless, which they never are. But large losses will kill you quickly. And an empty account has no chance to recover. That's why impatience kills so many investment accounts. Inappropriate measures of success, even over a short period of time, can get you into trouble, because you're likely to become impatient and feel the need to boost your returns by taking on more risk. And that is a recipe for failure over the long term, which is what matters most.

Not only will focusing on volatility enhance your financial outcome, but it may well lead to a better quality of life along the way. How? By reducing stress. Stress kills, and investment volatility is a major cause of stress for many retirees. Effective risk management is the key to a stress-free retirement income plan. You should strive to be the tortoise, not the hare.

Figure 8.1: Be the Tortoise

The million-dollar question, of course, is how to accomplish this, which I've covered in previous chapters under the concepts of "guarantees" and "expertise." If you have sufficient guaranteed income complemented by strong, proven risk mitigation strategies for your liquid investment portfolio, you'll maximize your chances of success. This is true whether you have more money than you'll ever need or you're just trying to make what you have last a lifetime.

STINKIN' THINKIN'

Thanks in large part to decades of reinforcement of wrong thinking from the financial industry and mainstream media, average rate of return is by far the most common metric used by investors to both select and evaluate the performance of their investments. In reality, however, as these examples demonstrate, average rate of return is extremely misleading and ineffective at predicting and measuring your actual investment success over time.

Unfortunately, the industry has trained us all to focus almost exclusively on average rates of return as the standard measure of investment and portfolio success. As a result, most people believe they have to accept unnecessary levels of risk in order to boost their average annual return over time. And it's true. If your only goal is to have a high average annual return over time, you should take more risk, and you will need to take more risk. The problem is that it's counterproductive to the objective of having more money, more consistently, in your account over time.

And if you follow this line of thinking to its likely conclusion, by the time you realize that it's not working, it will be too late. If you have one really bad year like 2000 or 2008 shortly before or early into your retirement, it's likely to be unrecoverable. Now that doesn't necessarily mean you'll run out of money. Maybe you have more money than you'll ever need. But what it does mean is that your long-term outcome is going to be significantly inferior to what it could have been had you taken less risk and focused on managing volatility and compounding returns instead of maximizing your average rate of return.

One of the most common examples of the misuse of the average rate of return, which most readers will be able to relate to, is when you choose your investment options within your 401(k) or other qualified retirement plan. If you think back to the last time you did so, you'll recall you were probably given a list of investment options to choose from, accompanied by a list of trailing historical average rates of return for each option. Not only are these charts conveniently provided, but ironically they are *required* to be provided, thanks to regulations governing both securities and the Employee Retirement Income Security Act of 1974 (ERISA).

An example might be the hypothetical XYZ Fund. Let's say it's an option within your 401(k), and its description includes the one-, three-, five-, and 10-year average rates of return. Most people simply pick the investment options with the highest average rates of return, mistakenly thinking that means those investments performed the best over those periods of time. Not only do we all know that "past performance is no guarantee of future results," but as you just learned, the average rate of return for a given period of time may have little to do with the actual performance of your account as measured in dollars, which is what matters most to the average investor.

In similar fashion, when it comes to reviewing investment performance—whether it's in your 401(k) or any other type of investment account—most investors, and even most advisors, behave in the exact same way. They review the average rate of return for whatever period of time they're interested in. Think of how often you've wondered or asked, "What's my average rate of return over the last five years?" or "What's my average rate of return over the life of my investment?" And based on the answers to those questions, you decide to either be happy or not, right?

But again, the answers to those questions don't tell you what you really want to know. Nevertheless, average rate of return is the financial industry's standard for measuring and evaluating investment performance. It's literally required to be listed on prospectuses and alongside investment options within qualified retirement plans.

DON'T OVERTHINK IT

The problem with encouraging reliance on such a metric is that it leads to either a false sense of confidence or a false sense of insecurity. This phenomenon is exacerbated by the fact that the same flawed statistic that's used to choose the investments is also used to measure their success. That's one of the main reasons your retirement income plan should be your litmus test of progress versus some arbitrary metric. And it's also why you should never compare your returns to an index or benchmark, something I'll elaborate on in chapter 9.

There will always be good years and there will always be bad years. Thinking back to my AAA TripTik analogy, even with detailed maps for our vacations, there will always be delays and detours. The true measure of success isn't your average rate of speed. It's whether you're still on track to accomplish your original objective. If you focus solely on your average rate of return over time, there will be some years where you're really happy and some where you'll be really disappointed, but that won't tell you if you're on track to achieve your long-term objectives.

This also describes the example of the two coworkers in the introduction, whose average rates of return were both far in excess of their expectations, yet one of them still failed miserably. By the time you realize something's wrong, it's too late.

I am reminded of a prospective client who recently showed me an investment statement from a well-known mutual fund and then proudly said, "If I had followed your advice, I wouldn't have earned anywhere near the 11% return I got over the past 12 months." So I entered the ticker for the fund in question into a simple online quote engine and said, "You're right, you wouldn't have, but that fund appears to have lost far more than 11% in the 12 months prior to the report you're holding. In fact, it still hasn't recovered to where it was two years ago." He responded with, "Yeah, but it's coming back."

My responsibility is to educate and inform you. It is your responsibility to decide what to do with that information.

NOW WHAT?

The obvious question is what you should do with this information. I believe the answer is similarly obvious: Stop focusing on maximizing your rate of return and instead focus on minimizing volatility. The goal isn't to maximize your average rate of return over time, it's to maximize the likelihood of your success, which means minimizing the odds of failure. In this case, it means minimizing volatility without sacrificing a reasonable return such that you can keep pace with inflation over time.

The Threefold Approach

When designing your retirement *investment* plan, I encourage you take a threefold approach:

1. Start with your income plan. Let your investment strategy flow from your plan, not vice versa.

    a. Your retirement income plan should help you clearly identify the minimum acceptable level of risk that will allow you to maximize the likelihood of your desired outcome, which we've defined by optimized cash flow and maximized residual estate value. Make a commitment to not exceed that level of risk, no matter what. As soon as you do, you're falling into the trap, and one really bad year can alter your entire plan.

2. Figure out a way to remind yourself of this principle when you forget (because you will).

   a. You will get feedback in terms of rates of return that you won't like or that you feel are disappointing or not as good as they should be because stinkin' thinkin' has been ingrained. You'll be disappointed. You're going to feel that you're missing out.

   b. Remember, there will be good years and there will be bad ones. You can't control markets. You can only control your level of risk exposure. That's when you need to remind yourself not to focus on those arbitrary metrics, but instead return to your plan, your stated objectives and risk tolerance, and ask yourself, "Am I still on track?"

   c. The exception would be if you have "extra" investment resources that you can afford to completely lose without jeopardizing your retirement goals. If so, and if you enjoy taking a little more risk with some of your funds, then go for it. (I call these "play" accounts). But never take risks with assets you will rely on to maintain your standard of living.

3. Utilize your Income Stability Pyramid to identify strategies that will allow you to effectively attain your objective by taking the least amount of risk possible. The name of the game is risk mitigation. Your goal is to minimize the risk exposure of your retirement income streams. Remember, there are just two ways to do this: guarantees and expertise.

Taking Action

Before moving on to the next chapter, use the QR code (page 9) to access the chapter 8 resources, then answer this question:

1. What is the maximum amount of loss you are willing to tolerate in a very bad market year (% or $)?

   a. Don't think about or look at your answer to the questions at the end of the last chapter. Just answer this question in a vacuum.

   b. Don't worry how much you want to *make*, on average. That's a trap. Just focus on how much you can tolerate *losing*.

2. What assurance do you have that your current investment strategy will protect you from experiencing greater levels of loss than this in a bad market year?

3. Based on your answers to questions one and two, are you comfortable with your current investment strategy, or do you feel you need to make a change?

   a. If no, then great. You are still sleeping well at night.

   b. If yes, then once again, what if that change means finding a new advisor? Would you be willing to do that? If not, keep reading. We'll deal with this issue in a later chapter. If so, commit to a specific plan to identify, interview, and hire your new advisor by a specific date.

      i. Don't procrastinate.

      ii. See chapter 16, "Finding the Right Advisor."

CHAPTER 9

THE JONESES DON'T EXIST

Trying to keep up with the Joneses when the Joneses aren't real,
is the silliest game you can play.

—NAVAL RAVIKANT

M uch like average rates of return, indexes and benchmarks are misleading. They encourage poor investment decisions and provide
either a false sense of achievement or a false sense of failure. Yet we're constantly bombarded with information about the performance of certain
key indexes. Some of the most common examples are the S&P 500, the
Dow Jones Industrial Average, the NASDAQ, and the total bond market
index. We're constantly told "the index is up," "the index is down," or "the
index is flat" for the day, week, month, or year. Almost every financial
radio or TV program starts or ends their broadcast with a summary of
what "the major indexes" have done for the day. We're also constantly told
"this or that investment has beaten its benchmark," as if it's an appropriate way to evaluate the performance of a particular investment. In reality

however, benchmarks, much like average rates of return, are completely irrelevant when it comes to evaluating your investments.

Just like average rates of return, the financial industry strongly reinforces this misdirected focus on benchmarks and indexes. Much like it requires the reporting of trailing average rates of return, it often requires the reporting of certain benchmarks alongside investment results. We've been therefore conditioned to believe that benchmarks must serve as an appropriate frame of reference for how our own investments are doing.

But the truth is they're completely inappropriate as a means of comparison, and using them is deeply flawed. Thinking differently about benchmarks may be especially challenging for the average investor, since we've been practically brainwashed by the media's reliance on them as a frame of reference. I encourage you to open your mind and think outside the box that's been painted for you as you read the rest of this chapter.

THE MYTHICAL INDEX

Now that I've poked your sacred cow, I'd like to turn your attention to the core issue: What is an index, anyway? All you need to do is read the fine print under any reference to an index. What does it say? It says you cannot invest directly in an index. It simply isn't possible. That's because an index is just an idea, not real and not constrained by reality. Even if you invest in an index fund or other index surrogate that seeks to replicate the performance of an index, it won't ever perform like the index itself. It can't.

Here's why:

- **An index has no actual capital invested, but you do.** Why does that matter? Remember the flaw of averages? If an index loses 50% one year and gains 50% the next, its average rate of return for that two-year period is 0%. But your investment would be down 25%. That's an enormous difference—one the index can tolerate, but you can't.

- **An index has no time constraints.** Indexes go on forever, but you don't. You don't have forever for your investments to "average out," so you can't afford a "lost decade." You don't care about forever. You only care about the period of time for which you are invested.

- **An index never needs money.** Indexes don't care what the market does from day to day, month to month, or year to year, because they never need to make a withdrawal. But you do, especially if you're retired. And in the case of an IRA, distributions are required whether you need them or not. So managing volatility is far more important to you than it is to an index.

- **An index contains no cash.** Indexes constantly add or subtract certain investments or shares of investments, and they distribute and reinvest dividends or interest magically, without any cash whatsoever. You don't have that luxury. You must hold and utilize cash to execute all these transactions. This greatly alters your performance versus the index itself.

- **An index has no time lag.** Every transaction is accomplished instantly within an index, but your investments encounter significant time lags to complete each of these actions. If you sell one security and buy another, there are two separate transactions that take place, and each one takes time to finalize and settle. And time is money, but not for an index.

- **An index has no costs associated with it.** You have to pay fees and taxes. These may represent a significant drag on your investments and may alter buy and sell decisions based on their tax ramifications, which don't apply to an index.

- **An index is not impacted by inflation.** I would argue that the main reason for the rise in most equity indexes over the past 50 years is not due to the increased intrinsic value of the underlying index components, but rather due to inflation. The US dollar has lost almost 80% of its purchasing power over the past 50 years. So if the value of all the components of an index are priced in dollars, and if it takes more dollars to buy the same amount of those components, the price of the index will increase. But if the rise in the value of our investment is simply the result of the devaluation of the currency in which it's priced, the degree to which we've become enriched depends solely on the rate of inflation over that same period of time.

The index, on the other hand, doesn't care about inflation because it has no expenses. So the performance of an index isn't relative to anything else, like the cost of living. But your investments must take this into account since it's the very reason for their existence.

- **An index has no objectives.** In my option, this is the most important issue of all. Your entire investment strategy should be built around your personal financial objectives. For retirees, minimizing losses in bad market years is paramount to long-term success. By definition, that means deviating from monolithic indexes and/ or combinations of indexes and embracing a much more fluid investment strategy. There is no benchmark that equates to your unique personal financial objectives. So comparing your investments to a benchmark with no objective other than to track itself is fruitless.

So why would you ever use an index as a basis for comparison? To do so means you're likely to either be routinely disappointed and frustrated, or you're likely to routinely take on far too much risk trying to keep up with the mythical index. As you can see, there is simply no rational, valid basis for comparison between the performance of an index or benchmark and that of an actual investment. So in my mind, there should be no comparison. The only valid use of a benchmark or index might be for purposes of generalized market insight, such as understanding how a certain market sector did on a particular day. For anything longer than a day, and especially for purposes of evaluating your own results over any significant period of time, benchmarks and indexes are highly irrelevant.

CAVEAT EMPTOR

One last thought on indexes. We've all heard certain money managers boast about beating their index or benchmark over a certain period of time. A typical claim sounds something like, "We've beaten our benchmark for the last 20 consecutive years."

It sure sounds good, but here's the problem: If you had purchased an investment like this and held it throughout 2008, and if your investment lost 40% but the index lost 41%, then your investment would have beaten the index, right? But the more important question is, would you be okay with losing 40%? Probably not, especially if you're retired. So even if you do compare favorably to an index, the question remains as to whether it's even a relevant issue.

In summary, indexes and benchmarks, which ignore all constraints of reality and have little to nothing to do with your personal long-term objectives, are completely irrelevant when it comes to evaluating your investment success. Instead, your success should be measured by your unique personal goals and objectives, including your time horizons, your tolerance for volatility, your cash flow needs, and your need to keep pace with inflation, which occur within the context of your actual life.

There will always be good years and bad years. That's unavoidable. Your goal should be to understand whether, despite those, you are still on track to achieve your goals. That's why your only measure of ongoing success should be your retirement income plan. You should review it annually and simply ask yourself, "Am I still on track despite whatever has happened over the past year?"

Remember the example from chapter 8, The Flaw of Averages? If you were invested in portfolio B and were able to compare your returns each year with the other three portfolios, every single year you would have been disappointed. Someone else would have fared far better than you. But in the end, you would have had the most money.

Remember, benchmarks and indexes are not real. They're misleading. They encourage poor investment decisions, as they are not constrained by reality. They have nothing to do with your personal objectives, so it would be wise to stop comparing yourself to them. What really matters to you in retirement is creating predictable, increasing, tax-efficient lifetime income. If you're able to do that, your plan will succeed. And quite frankly, your plan will be blissfully boring. It will provide everything you need and enable you to sleep well at night.

Taking Action

Before moving on to the next chapter, use the QR code (page 9) to access the chapter 9 resources, then ask yourself:

1. What are the primary statistics, benchmarks, or people you have historically used to evaluate your personal investment success, that you believe may be inappropriate/unhelpful/erroneous?

   a. Short term?

   b. Long term?

2. Make a personal commitment to do the following:

   a. Stop ingesting popular financial media, including television, radio, and periodicals.

   b. Stop watching indexes over time (glance at them only to see what the market did *today*).

    c. Stop comparing yourself to any/all benchmarks —including the Joneses (that is, anyone else).

3. Resolve to make losses the only performance metric you will pay attention to going forward.

    a. Just like golf, a lower (absolute) number is better.

    b. That is, the smaller the loss in a bad year, the better.

4. Start utilizing your retirement income plan as your sole litmus test for success.

    a. And if you don't have one, get one.

CHAPTER 10

T IS FOR THEORY

If it's not broken, don't fix it.
—UNKNOWN

If it's broken, fix it.
—JOHN VANWEELDEN

S o now that we've identified and hopefully freed you from some of the
biggest fallacies prevalent in the financial industry and particularly in
retirement planning in the form of rates of return and benchmarks, it's time
to examine the elephant in the room: Modern Portfolio Theory (MPT).

MPT is a widely used investment philosophy that emphasizes the
importance of asset allocation, the process of dividing an investment portfolio among different asset classes such as stocks, bonds, and cash; and
diversification, which means holding a sufficiently large number of investments in order to spread out the underlying risk. The theory suggests
that by allocating assets among a sufficient number of different types of

investments with varying types of risk exposure, investors can create a portfolio that matches their desired level of risk and return over time.

While this has often been true over very long periods of time, between 50 and 100 years, it's rarely true within shorter periods of time. And as I've previously stated, as a retiree you don't have infinitely long time horizons. Only the next 20 to 30 years are relevant, and my experience suggests the next five to 10 years are the most critical, as they will dictate your longer-term outcomes.

The year 2022 is a great example of this approach backfiring over the short term, as bonds had one of their worst years in decades, while stocks also suffered major losses. As stated previously, 2022 was the worst combined year of stock and bond returns since the 1960s.

UNDERLYING ASSUMPTIONS OF MPT

For simplicity's sake, the theory also purports that stocks always equate to both higher levels of risk and higher returns over time, while bonds equate to lower levels of risk and lower returns over time. It follows, then, that more conservative investors should hold more bonds, and less conservative investors should hold more stocks. This is because the primary assumption underlying MPT is that stocks and bonds are inversely correlated. That is, they tend to move in opposite directions. In other words, stocks are your engine and bonds are your shock absorber. Once again, 2022 blew that assumption out of the water, as bonds experienced stock-like losses not seen in over half a century.

The term Modern Portfolio Theory is ironic, as it's anything but modern. It's actually an idea based on research that was conducted many decades ago.[3] The research was insightful, concluding that asset allocation and diversification tend to have a greater influence over long-term

3   Harry Markowitz is credited with developing the Modern Portfolio Theory in 1952.

average rates of return than does individual investment selection. But it was never meant to suggest that asset allocation and diversification were sufficient, in and of themselves, to mitigate risk. That wasn't a conclusion of the research.

Nevertheless, two key tenets of this theory as universally adopted by the financial industry are that 1) asset allocation and diversification are the primary drivers of investment performance over time, and 2) that they are sufficient, in and of themselves, to manage risk. The industry has taken the theory and run with it, most likely because it serves the industry quite well.

The biggest problem with MPT is that it's invisible to most investors, although the vast majority are beholden to it whether they know it or not. To say that MPT is widely used is a major understatement. The vast majority of investment advisors and portfolio managers utilize this approach, as the industry has unilaterally endorsed and adopted it. This is likely due to the fact that by definition, MPT promotes certain investor behaviors that greatly benefit the financial industry itself for three reasons:

1. It's easy to implement.

2. It's defensible, regardless of outcome.

3. It keeps you, the investor, always invested.

Ease of Implementation

A fixed allocation or mix of investments that changes only based on the investor's time horizon, rather than market trends, is quite easy to manage. If you think about it, this requires two fairly simple, even automated, processes to take place. First, the portfolio needs to be rebalanced from time to time in order to maintain the overall asset allocation. There is no decision-making here. It's simply a matter of rebalancing the underlying investments back to their originally defined proportions. Second, usually on an annual basis, the allocation itself may or may not be adjusted to reflect a slightly shorter time horizon for the investor. This too is a fairly simple, often automated process, involving nothing more than a slight adjustment of underlying quantities of all the current holdings.

Defensible

As an advisor, following a "proven and industry-endorsed" process like MPT means the investment management process is defensible regardless of the outcome. For instance, if a conservative retired investor experiences large losses because an advisor takes unnecessary and inappropriate risks with the investor's money, say by investing only in internet growth stocks in the late 1990s, that advisor's process would understandably be subject to scrutiny. However, if that same investor experienced similarly bad results during the 2008 market crash despite having a "risk-appropriate" portfolio built on MPT, the advisor's process would be much more defensible, despite the same disappointing outcome.

Always Invested

MPT suggests you should always be invested in whatever underlying asset allocation you have deemed appropriate. Thus, it argues you should not reallocate or otherwise respond to market movements. The underlying rationale for this is what we discussed in the previous chapter on average rates of return, the idea being that if you just stick with a particular asset allocation over time, eventually your average rate of return will approximate the historical average. But of course, you now understand that while this may indeed be true, the historical average rate of return is highly irrelevant to the actual outcome you are pursuing.

If you follow MPT to its logical conclusion, you will always be invested. You will always hold some combination of stocks and bonds, along with some nominal amount of commodities and cash equivalents. This is good for the financial industry, as it ensures everyone who adheres to this paradigm is always invested—and not sitting on the sidelines with their cash or using it to pay down debt.

MPT is not wholly dissimilar to the concept of *dollar cost averaging*, which ultimately says you should always be buying more, regardless of the underlying price movement. The math is valid, in that if you're always buying into a volatile market regardless of price movement, you will likely lower your average cost per share over time. But it also means you will always be acquiring more of a particular investment, even if the price is plunging and may or may not ever recover. It is not surprising that an industry built on selling investments largely endorses such concepts.

Like MPT, dollar cost averaging assumes the underlying investment will always appreciate over the long term—and in the case of retirement income planning, it must also outpace inflation. But this is not always the case.

THE MPT MOUSETRAP

It's important to note that your advisor probably utilizes Modern Portfolio Theory, whether you realize it or not. I would venture to estimate that 95% of investment advisors rely on it. Since most advisors use this approach, the majority are simply trying to convince you that their version of MPT is better than the next advisor's. The problem is, "a better mousetrap" isn't the solution to your problem, especially during retirement. To the contrary, I would argue that you don't need a mousetrap at all.

To better understand the limitations of Modern Portfolio Theory, you must take a slightly deeper dive into its underpinnings, including the following:

- Asset allocation and diversification are sufficient to manage risk.

- You must commit to (and retain) a specific asset allocation over time.

- History will always repeat itself.

- MPT ignores sequence of returns risk.

- Investors have an unlimited amount of time to invest.

- Investors never withdraw funds.

- MPT only incorporates traditional securities.

Asset Allocation and Diversification Are Sufficient to Manage Risk

History suggests this supposition to be inadequate. Recent examples are 2000, 2001, 2002, 2008, 2018, 2020, and 2022. In 2000–2002, the dot-com bubble burst. In 2008, the subprime debt bubble burst. We had another mini-crisis at the end of 2018. In 2020, of course, the pandemic hit. And most recently, the market crash in 2022 was a result of dramatically rising interest rates and inflation, which caused the worst combined stock and bond market returns since 1969.

So, just since the turn of the century, we've seen at least five examples of where asset allocation and diversification were clearly insufficient to manage risk in such a way as to allow the average retirement investor to recover from their losses and achieve their original cash flow objectives in anything remotely resembling short order. Remember, in the wake of the dot-com bubble, the S&P 500 took some 14 years to meaningfully exceed its pre-crash highs. As discussed in the flaw of averages, this kind of portfolio volatility is unacceptable and likely unrecoverable for most retirees.

You Must Commit to and Retain a Specific Asset Allocation over Time

In other words, most advisors and mainstream financial media talking heads tell you not to change your allocation in response to market conditions. So, MPT assumes that you're going to choose an allocation and you're going to stick with it indefinitely (with the exception, again, of very small tweaks as you age). This is evidenced by such common phrases from investment advisors and the media as:

- "Just hold on. It will all come back eventually."
- "Don't worry, it will all average out over time."
- "Don't let your emotions get in the way."
- "Just stay the course."
- "Whatever you do, don't get out of the market or you'll miss the recovery."

The theory advocates that you take on slightly more bonds and slightly fewer stocks as you age, but otherwise do nothing. The idea of committing to and retaining a certain asset allocation over time is due in large part to the flawed assumption that the relationship between various asset classes will always be the same.

In other words, bonds will always be a good shock absorber for stocks because they generally have been. You don't need to look any further than 2022 to see how flawed this assumption is. As mentioned previously, the S&P 500 was down 20%, and simultaneously the most broadly accepted bond indexes were down approximately 15%. This was the worst combined year for stocks and bonds since the 1960s. So, clearly, just because there has been a certain correlation between certain asset classes in the past doesn't guarantee that correlation will continue in the future.

My final thought about this "buy and hold" approach to investing is that I recall meeting with many retirees back in 2009 who had lost a lot of money during the 2008 crash. When asked, many of them stated they had a strong hunch to get out of the market in early 2008 when things began to turn really ugly. Without exception, however, these investors were encouraged to "stay the course" by their advisors. That was MPT talking. And we all know how that turned out. Many retirees were forced to completely redefine their retirement standard of living or go back to work part-time due to losses they sustained during the Great Recession of 2008.

History Will Always Repeat Itself

Modern portfolio theory doesn't account for what are called *unprecedented aberrations*, which seem to have happened frequently now. As referenced earlier, almost every major correction since 2000 has been attributed to something "unprecedented." Often retirees would come into our office and say that one of these events had thrown their entire plan off because their advisor said that 2008, for instance, was unprecedented and couldn't have been accounted for in their modeling. As a result, they were going to have to make significant adjustments in their expectations for retirement cash flow. The obvious problem is that most everything is unprecedented. Aberrations will always happen, so they need to be expected.

When markets are good, with nothing more than normal, cyclical fluctuations, staying the course appears to make sense and work. But like everything else, when times are most difficult, that's when the cream rises to the top. That's when you can see which strategies will actually weather the storm. This is why I believe all planning—and all investing—should assume that the toughest times lie ahead, and they should be designed to weather those storms. MPT alone is inadequate.

MPT Ignores Sequence of Returns Risk

If you think of a market crash as an acute occurrence, then sequence of returns can be characterized as a chronic but less discernible cancer to your investment success—one that occurs more slowly and discreetly over time.

In the introduction I gave the example of the two coworkers with the exact same plan and exact same investments, based on Modern Portfolio Theory. One of them had tremendous success and the other one failed miserably. The reason for the disparity in their outcomes was that one coworker experienced their best returns early in retirement while the other coworker experienced their best returns later in retirement. But both of their metrics were good—far beyond their expectations, in fact. But the one who experienced their best returns later in retirement failed altogether. They ran completely out of money.

Coworker number one's plan didn't fail because of a market aberration like what happened in 2008. It simply failed because their returns—despite resulting in a higher average rate of return, one that was far in excess of what they were expecting—didn't come in a favorable order. This is what is meant by sequence, or order, of returns. Their unfavorable sequence of returns caused them to run out of money, even without major market turmoil.

At least when 2008 happened, people realized they were in trouble. But in a situation like coworker number one (you) experienced in the example, people usually don't even see what's happening until it's too late, when they realize their entire plan is in jeopardy.

Investors Have an Unlimited Amount of Time to Invest

Just as we discussed in the last chapter, the historical averages that Modern Portfolio Theory relies upon are derived from ultra-long-term time frames. They may go back 50, 70, or even 100 years or more. That is not an appropriate frame of reference for an investor, especially a retiree, because no one has that long of a time frame. And once you're retired, your time frame is virtually imminent, meaning you're going to need your money—or the government is going to require you take distributions—very soon.

S&P 500 Index

Figure 10.1: Proponents of MPT want you to view the stock market like this: a somewhat bumpy but always increasing line.

But you don't have 150 years. So zoom in, because with traditional investing, the first 10 years of your retirement will likely dictate your success or failure.

S&P 500 Index

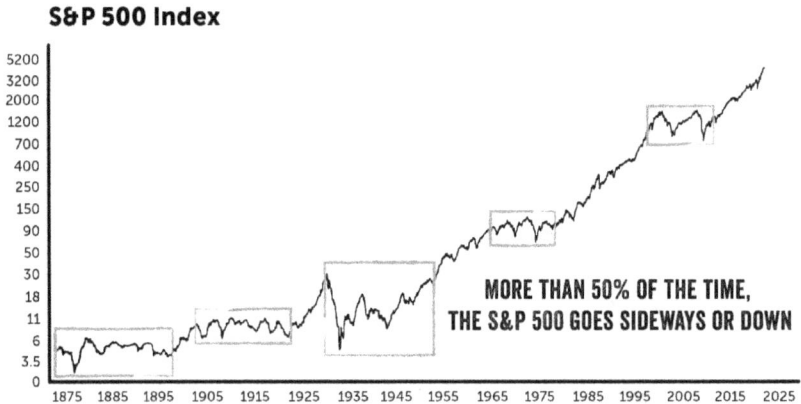

MORE THAN 50% OF THE TIME, THE S&P 500 GOES SIDEWAYS OR DOWN

Figure 10.2: In reality, it's a series of much shorter increasing, decreasing, and sideways lines. If the market isn't in an uptrend when you retire (indicated by the boxes), the traditional MPT approach will likely prove insufficient.

Investors Never Withdraw Funds

MPT also assumes you will never need to withdraw funds. Therefore, a completely separate planning process is required for managing income. Oddly enough, many retirement income plans are built upon an MPT investment approach. The irony in this is that Modern Portfolio Theory itself exists in a vacuum. It gives no thought to withdrawals. Building an income plan on a theory that assumes there will be no withdrawals is like building a swimming pool where you have no access to water; it's pointless. As soon as you introduce a withdrawal from the investment, the underlying tenets of MPT are destroyed. The money you take out is gone. The average rates of return metric may well hold up, but the cash flow will not.

One way MPT has failed is because we have had such dramatic declines in the market that it simply throws off the plan, especially for the retiree. And unfortunately, it doesn't help for an advisor to simply shrug and say there was an "aberration." A good retirement income plan should assume and be the antidote to the aberration.

Compare tables 10.3 and 10.4, which illustrate this point. You've already learned about how sequence of returns can affect the outcome of your retirement income plan. In other words, depending on the order of your returns, your plan may or may not be successful. But as you'll see in this example, even a relatively benign sequence of returns can prove lethal to your retirement income plan once you begin making withdrawals.

Assume you hold a portfolio for 20 years, during which time the market is up and down and sideways. Twenty years from now, your outcome will be as stated in Figure 10.3. You don't really care about the sequence of your returns. The outcome is the same regardless. But if you have the exact same portfolio over the exact same number of years, yet you need to pull money out of it over time (either because you need it or the government requires you do it), what changes? The exact same sequence of returns doesn't work out so well. See Table 10.4.

DURING ACCUMULATION

Deposit $100,000 | 10-year average rate of return: 6% | No withdrawals

Year	Ms. Lucky			Mr. Unlucky		
	Rate of Return	Annual Gain/Loss	Ending Value	Rate of Return	Annual Gain/Loss	Ending Value
			$100,000			$100,000
1	30%	$30,000	$130,000	-30%	-$30,000	$70,000
2	20%	$26,000	$156,000	-20%	-$14,000	$56,000
3	10%	$15,600	$171,600	-10%	-$5,600	$50,400
4	15%	$25,740	$197,340	15%	$7,560	$57,960
5	15%	$29,601	$226,941	15%	$8,694	$66,654
6	15%	$34,041	$260,982	15%	$9,998	$76,652
7	15%	$39,147	$300,129	15%	$11,498	$88,150
8	-10%	-$30,013	$270,116	30%	$26,445	$114,595
9	-20%	-$54,023	$216,093	20%	$22,919	$137,513
10	-30%	-$64,828	$151,265	10%	$13,751	$151,265

Table 10.3

DURING DISTRIBUTION

Deposit $100,000 | 10-year average rate of return: 6%
Withdrawal rate per year: 6% of initial value

Year	Ms. Lucky				Mr. Unlucky			
	Rate of Return	Beginning Value	Withdrawal	Ending Value	Rate of Return	Beginning Value	Withdrawal	Ending Value
		$100,000				$100,000		
1	30%	$130,000	$6,000	$124,000	-30%	$70,000	$6,000	$64,000
2	20%	$148,800	$6,000	$142,800	-20%	$51,200	$6,000	$45,200
3	10%	$157,080	$6,000	$151,080	-10%	$40,680	$6,000	$34,680
4	15%	$173,742	$6,000	$167,742	15%	$39,882	$6,000	$33,882
5	15%	$192,903	$6,000	$186,903	15%	$38,964	$6,000	$32,964
6	15%	$214,939	$6,000	$208,939	15%	$37,909	$6,000	$31,909
7	15%	$240,280	$6,000	$234,280	15%	$36,695	$6,000	$30,695
8	-10%	$210,852	$6,000	$204,852	10%	$33,765	$6,000	$27,765
9	-20%	$163,881	$6,000	$157,881	20%	$33,318	$6,000	$27,318
10	-30%	$110,517	$6,000	$104,517	30%	$35,513	$6,000	$29,513

Table 10.4

MPT Only Incorporates Traditional Securities

The typical MPT portfolio is constructed with stocks, bonds, and cash, whether individually or in the form of mutual funds or exchange-traded funds. In other words, Modern Portfolio Theory doesn't consider any of the modern alternatives to traditional securities. These include hybrid securities, hybrid savings vehicles, insurance, annuities, hedge funds, derivatives, options, futures, or any number of active risk-mitigation strategies. Therefore, most of today's retirees are unwittingly using an antiquated investment approach to solve their modern-day cash flow problem. It's no surprise that that approach so often results in underperformance, and even failure.

One last word about MPT: Many firms suggest the use of a tool called *Monte Carlo simulation* as a way of trying to circumvent the main shortcoming of MPT, that is, failing to protect from sequence-of-returns risk. In a nutshell, this type of simulation runs thousands of hypothetical sequences of return, based on a particular asset allocation, in order to come up with a likelihood of success. But don't be fooled. A Monte Carlo simulation doesn't do a thing to change any of the shortcomings of MPT, because all the hypothetical scenarios are still based on all the aforementioned flawed assumptions. In addition to the fact that the faulty assumptions are baked into the analysis, knowing your statistical likelihood of success is not very helpful. To the contrary, statistical probabilities can create a false sense of security. After all, the two coworkers in the opening scenario had the exact same high probability of success, right? And everyone who retired just before or shortly after 2000 or 2008 became a statistical anomaly because those scenarios hadn't ever happened before. It didn't matter if their probability of success was 90%. It's like saying, "There's a 90% chance you'll make it across this bridge." By that logic, 10% of the people crossing it will be doomed. And that doesn't account for things that "never happened before." Are you willing to take that chance?

A TIGER CAN'T CHANGE ITS STRIPES

If this chapter sounds all too familiar to you, then I suggest you seriously consider making a change. Unfortunately, that means finding a new advisor, not asking your current advisor to change their approach. In my experience, you can't just educate your advisor and expect him or her to change. Their modus operandi is in their blood, for better or worse. Any advisor remotely worth their salt has a strong conviction about what they do, why they do it, and how they do it. So getting them to change isn't the answer. It would be like saying, "My advisor's a wonderful person, but I think I'm a square peg and they're a round hole. I'll ask them if they can become a square hole for me."

It has taken me 25 years to come to these conclusions I have about retirement. I always tell prospective clients, "If this doesn't resonate with you, then we shouldn't work together. And that's okay. Because a tiger can't change its stripes. This is who we are. If you love it, we'll have a great relationship. If you don't, there are plenty of other advisors that you can choose from. No hard feelings."

It's the same with your advisor. If you try to educate them about these concepts, one of two things will likely happen:

1. They will tell you that yes, they can do that, when they really don't know how. The question then becomes whether you, the investor, have the wherewithal to discern the difference before it's too late.

2. They will try to dissuade you from making that "mistake," because they operate at the top of the Income Stability Pyramid with only MPT to guide them. And that's where they want to stay. It's their universe, and you are asking them to create a new one for you. It's simply not going to work.

My advice is not to ask your advisor to change. It's much easier for you to change advisors. Find someone who truly understands the nuances

that matter most to you, who is on your same page, and who truly specializes in retirement. They are out there. See chapter 16 on tips for finding
the right advisor.

MPT Comes Up Short for Retirees

Modern Portfolio Theory is almost universally used or endorsed
throughout the financial services industry—particularly with respect to
retirement planning and the do-it-yourself investment community—
to construct retirement portfolios. In fact, most advisors, retirement
calculators, and/or robo-advisors use MPT as the framework to help
construct investment portfolios. Despite this prevalence, MPT has
proven time and time again to be a highly insufficient approach to
managing risk and ensuring investment success, especially for retirees
and especially in light of today's new normal of increasingly elevated
market volatility.

CONCLUSION

Hopefully you now understand Modern Portfolio Theory a little better
and why it is an insufficient tool to manage investment risk, especially in
retirement. Whether you have an advisor or are a do-it-yourselfer, MPT
is likely the core of your investment plan. Today's new normal necessitates a more comprehensive approach to risk management, including
alternative solutions involving securities, insurance, savings, and even
hybrid strategies for protecting wealth and generating stable, increasing,
tax-advantaged lifetime income.

In the end, I believe MPT is an important investment concept, worthy
of your understanding. But the name says it all . . . *theory.* And it's far from
sufficient to navigate today's new normal, especially in retirement.

Taking Action

Before moving on to the next chapter, use the QR code (page 9) to access the chapter 10 resources, then answer the following questions about your own retirement portfolio:

1. Does your investment strategy appear to be based solely on MPT for its risk management?

    a. What, if any, active risk-mitigation strategies are incorporated into your portfolio? (Remember, actively trading securities within an overall MPT-based strategy does not qualify as active risk mitigation. It's just lipstick on the same old pig.)

2. Do you have strategies in place to mitigate the effect of major market events such as the crash of 2008 on your retirement portfolio?

    a. If not, what steps can you take to ensure you do?

3. Do you understand sequence-of-returns risk?

    a. Do you have strategies in place to mitigate the effect of an unfavorable sequence of returns on the outcome of your retirement income plan?

    b. If not, what steps can you take to ensure you do?

4. Knowing what you know now, what steps can you take, if any are needed, to course-correct?

5. Make a commitment to address both acute and chronic risk exposure in your investment portfolio within a specific period of time (preferably before the next market crash).

CHAPTER 11

THE TRUTH ABOUT ANNUITIES

It ain't what you don't know that gets you into trouble.
It's what you know for sure that just ain't so.

—MARK TWAIN

As mentioned in chapter 5, annuities are probably one of the most misunderstood yet incredibly popular financial vehicles in existence today. Over $200 billion was placed in annuities in 2021 alone, and that number continues to grow annually as the growing number of retirees look to replace the vanishing pension plan with secure retirement income for life. Employer-sponsored retirement plans such as 401(k)s are also considering ways to incorporate commercial annuities into their plans for the exact same reasons.

My goal for this chapter isn't to provide you with a comprehensive education about annuities. That would be impossible. I have spent 25 years learning about retirement-appropriate financial vehicles, including annuities. Not only am I still learning every day, but there also seem to be new product innovations every day. So my goal is simply to provide you with a solid general understanding of annuities and how they work, cutting through the myths, hype, and propaganda to teach you the truth.

I will also spend some extra time explaining how to use an annuity to increase your own ISR, should you desire to do so. I will approach this tutorial in three steps:

1. First, I'll provide a broad overview of some of the most helpful ways to categorize annuities, along with the most common features and benefits of each.

2. Second, I'll explain some of the most common uses of annuities.

3. Finally, I'll present the most prevalent criticisms of annuities, and will separate fact from fiction.

By the end of the chapter, you should have a strong basic understanding of the various types of annuities and an improved ability to evaluate their place, if any, in your own personal retirement income plan. So let's start at the beginning.

WHAT'S AN ANNUITY?

At its core, an annuity is a contract with an insurance company, just like a CD is with a bank, or a stock or bond is with the issuing entity. Both parties have certain rights and certain obligations. The history of annuities is deep, which I'm going to avoid for the purposes of this book. But it's worth understanding that the history of annuities is one of the main reasons they are so misunderstood.

Dictionaries define *annuity* as "a series of payments over a specified period of time, often for a lifetime." And this is indeed how annuities originated. Although this definition still applies in certain circumstances today, annuities can also be quite different from that definition, so much so that the actual definition barely applies to some and is practically irrelevant to others.

Think of it like Scotch tape or Kleenex facial tissues. Originally these were specific products with certain features and benefits, but now each has become a generic term. Scotch and Kleenex brands now produce many varieties of products, many of which have nothing to do with tape or facial tissues. In the same way, many annuities' specific uses have little or nothing to do with the original definition of an annuity.

Since there are currently so many different types of annuities with many different features and characteristics designed to address a multitude of needs, some of which have little or nothing to do with a series of payments, the word annuity itself is oftentimes a complete misnomer.

CATEGORIES OF ANNUITIES

For the simplified purposes of this book, annuities can be classified in the following basic ways—

- Qualified or nonqualified
- Fixed, indexed, or variable
- Immediate or deferred

Qualified or Nonqualified

A *qualified annuity* has been funded with tax-deferred funds from an IRA or other similar type of retirement savings vehicle. You have not paid taxes on these funds yet but will be required to do so as you withdraw them. In contrast, a *nonqualified annuity* has been funded with monies that are not tax qualified, such as the money that's sitting in your checking or savings account. You already paid taxes on these funds.

This can seem a bit complicated at first glance, since an annuity contract is by definition tax-deferred. So regardless of what type of money you fund your annuity with, it will not be taxed again until the money is withdrawn. Exactly how those withdrawals are taxed, however, depends on whether you funded it with qualified or nonqualified funds. If funded with qualified funds, it will be taxed exactly the same as withdrawals from any other IRA. If funded with nonqualified (after-tax) funds, the gains must come out first (with few exceptions) and are taxed as regular income versus capital gains. When using nonqualified funds, there is no tax when withdrawing your principal, which was previously taxed.

Fixed, Indexed, or Variable

Fixed, *indexed*, and *variable* describe the way the principal in the contract grows. Fixed annuities operate much like a CD, with fixed interest payments of a certain guaranteed term.

Fixed indexed annuities also pay interest, but the interest rate is typically based on the performance of some unrelated index such as the S&P 500, bond index, or commodity index. However, like a fixed annuity, fixed indexed annuities cannot lose value due to the underlying performance of that specified index. They may or may not generate a return from year to year, but they cannot experience market losses. Hence, they're still considered fixed, since your principal is not at risk and you either earn or do not earn interest each year.

Variable annuities, on the other hand, operate quite differently. They are more akin to a portfolio of mutual funds or a 401(k), with direct exposure to various markets, meaning the underlying funds may grow or shrink depending on how those funds are invested within the annuity contract. A helpful way to think about a variable annuity, at its core, is that it is similar to a collection of mutual funds (but here they're called subaccounts), which are then placed into a tax-deferred wrapper. There's much more to it. But for simplicity's sake, this is a good way to think about it.

Please understand this is an extremely oversimplified explanation of these three varieties of annuities, as there are many more details related to each type. But I hope you get the general idea.

Immediate or Deferred

Immediate or *deferred* describes when, if ever, the annuity will ever be "annuitized." Think of "annuitization" as converting the principal to guaranteed payments for a certain period of time, often for the life of the owner or annuitant, in exchange for the principal. Some annuities provide this type of guaranteed income from day one. Some defer it until later. And some never do so at all. An *immediate annuity* is one that provides this type of guaranteed income from day one, similar to the original definition of an annuity. A *deferred annuity* is one that defers either the income *or* the option for the income until some later date. This type of an annuity may or may not ever be converted to an income stream via annuitization.

Complicating matters a bit more is the fact that certain annuities include riders that allow you to take guaranteed lifetime income without annuitizing, or giving up, your principal. These are often called *lifetime income riders* or some other similarly clever moniker. As you might imagine, this option is almost always my preference, since you retain all rights of ownership over your principal. However, there are certain situations where one might consider annuitization. I will not address those very limited situations in this book.

Categorizing annuities is kind of like breaking automobiles down into various groups by their size, their main purpose, or the type of fuel they use. There are many different ways to categorize annuities, and I've chosen just a few. Even determining how to begin to categorize something depends largely on what your personal objectives are and thus what features and benefits matter to you most. For example, I might want to categorize an automobile based on its fuel type, and you may be more concerned about its passenger capacity or how fast it can go. That's going to be critical as you evaluate what type of vehicle you want.

Additionally, each of these categories that I just described includes a multitude of additional features, benefits, and options within each subtype. Some annuities have death benefits like that of life insurance. Some have living income benefits without requiring "annuitization," as previously described. Some have spousal benefits, some have nursing home benefits, and some have cost-of-living adjustments. The list goes on and on.

COMMON USES FOR ANNUITIES

An annuity is only as good as the use to which it is put. After all, the best hammer fails miserably when used to drive a screw. A few examples of the most common uses for annuities are as follows.

Death Benefit

Certain annuities are designed to provide an enhanced *death benefit* to the beneficiaries, such as in cases where the principal may not be needed by the annuity owner during their lifetime and they wish to guarantee a certain amount goes to their heirs. This is especially helpful in the event the purchaser is uninsurable for life insurance purposes, as annuities do not require health-related underwriting.

Health Care Benefit

Other annuities may be used to provide enhanced, guaranteed benefits to help pay for long-term care such as home health, assisted living, or nursing care. Once again, this can be especially helpful if the owner wishes to insure against such possibilities but can't otherwise qualify for the necessary coverage. It's also a great alternative for someone who wants coverage but is worried about paying into a traditional long-term care policy and having nothing to show for it if they end up not needing the insurance.

Growth and/or Income

Some annuities are designed to provide a rate of return for a specified period of time, much like a CD. This can provide guaranteed *growth and/or income* to the owner or another person. Other annuities have the potential for growth and/or income, but it is not guaranteed.

Guaranteed Income

Some annuities have lifetime income riders that can be used to provide *guaranteed income* for the life of an individual or a married couple, without them relinquishing ownership of the underlying principal. This type of annuity tends to be the most appropriate for enhancing one's guaranteed lifetime income, like a pension, without sacrificing ownership of the principal. It can be especially useful for enhancing one's ISR. But be careful. Some annuity structures are far better at this than others, while some are outright problematic. This is a great example of where working with an independent fiduciary expert on annuities is critical to ensure you employ the best option given your unique situation. Once again, the devil is in the details..

Medicaid Planning

Certain *Medicaid-qualified annuities* can help enable a person to qualify for Medicaid benefits while simultaneously protecting the maximum amount of assets and income allowable by law.

Tax Deferral

Since all annuities are *tax-deferred* by definition, they are sometimes used to shelter assets from current taxation, deferring the tax on the underlying investment gains until funds are withdrawn from the contract. This can be attractive to someone with a high taxable income who wants to defer some of the tax until later in life. As mentioned previously, however, these gains will eventually be taxed as ordinary income versus capital gains.

IF YOU'RE CONSIDERING AN ANNUITY, FIND AN ANNUITY EXPERT

This is just the tip of the iceberg when it comes to categorizing and identifying uses for annuities. There are many more categories, subcategories, and creative uses for annuities than we can possibly address here. The point here is that each of these various applications necessitates the use of a unique kind of annuity with specific features and benefits in order to effectively achieve your stated objectives.

Hopefully you're beginning to comprehend the many types of annuities that exist, the wide variety of features and benefits available, and their myriad applications. I believe it's critically important to work with a knowledgeable expert when deciding if an annuity is appropriate for your particular situation, and if so, in determining the appropriate product to use.

One example that comes to mind is a couple who asked me to review an annuity they had previously funded at the recommendation of another advisor. They were exceptionally conservative, and guaranteed income was high on their list of priorities. Upon reviewing their annuity, however, it turned out to be a nonqualified variable annuity with no income rider. It was also invested very aggressively, such that it was exposed to a great deal of volatility. In their particular case, there was no real benefit to owning the annuity over that of a portfolio of mutual funds, and the fees for the annuity were significantly higher. Moreover, the majority of their funds were less liquid inside the annuity than they would have been in traditional mutual funds. It wasn't that an annuity couldn't have met their retirement income planning needs. It was just that the particular one they owned didn't fit the bill. It wasn't even close.

Why was this particular contract recommended by their previous advisor? Who knows? But it clearly wasn't in their best interest based on their stated objectives.

COMMON CRITICISMS OF ANNUITIES

Now that we've shed a little light on annuities in general, let's turn our attention to some of the most common criticisms of annuities, some of which are valid and some of which are not.

As I've demonstrated, the topic of annuities is quite broad. There are many types of annuities. There are applications and misapplications. It's taken me 25 years to accumulate the knowledge I have. There's no way I can possibly transfer that knowledge to you in a short or even long chapter of a book or conversation. For that reason, whenever the topic of annuities comes up, whether it be with a current or prospective client or in social settings, which is often the case, I always start by asking these four questions:

1. How do you feel about annuities?

2. Why do you feel that way?

3. Who told you that?

4. What potential application for an annuity are you asking about, relative to your personal situation?

This allows me to frame the conversation in a way that laser focuses our time and attention on the crux of the matter at hand and bypasses everything else we might be tempted to discuss that's not particularly relevant to their question, based on their specific situation. Again, the most important point is to focus on the intended use and then back in to the questions, "What is your need?," "What are you trying to accomplish?," and "Is an annuity the best way to achieve that outcome?" If so, using my proper tool analogy, I ask: "What would be the best tool [specific annuity contract] for that specific job?"

In my experience, misunderstandings (good or bad) about annuities typically arise out of an extreme overgeneralization pertaining to some underlying truth that simply doesn't apply universally to all annuities. As many times as I can think of a scenario where the perception might be accurate, I can usually also think of just as many scenarios where it is not. With that in mind, the following is a high-level broad analysis of the six most common criticisms I hear about annuities.

Criticism No. 1: You Are Required to Relinquish Ownership of Your Principal

These critics say you're essentially giving away your money. This is an argument from what I would call "an annuity dinosaur." It's virtually never the case anymore. Although some annuities do exist for which this is still the case, in my experience, they're quite rare. Given the plethora of other options, this kind of annuity is only appropriate for certain limited situations. The vast majority of annuities used today do not require you to relinquish ownership of your funds, period. As such, this criticism is not valid for most annuities.

Criticism No. 2: Annuities Have High Fees

Some annuities have high fees, some have low fees, and some have zero fees. So saying annuity fees are high is a gross overgeneralization. Some are high and some aren't. Generally speaking, variable annuities tend to have the highest fees. In reviewing and/or analyzing prospective client portfolios, it's common to see variable annuities with annual fees as high as 3%, 4%, or even higher, depending on the features and benefits of the particular contract.

Most nonvariable (fixed or fixed-indexed) annuities, however, have fees that range anywhere from zero to 1.5% or so—obviously much lower than that of a variable annuity. This is largely because there are no underlying investments, per se, in which your funds are invested. Instead, these contracts simply pay interest based on current interest rates or some independent index. The index may be based on the stock market, allowing for much higher potential gains than that of current interest rates. But since your money is not actually invested in the market, it is not at risk of market losses.

Higher fees do sometimes equate to additional features and benefits, but not always. It's extremely important to know what you're getting in return for any fees you're paying so you can evaluate the underlying value proposition. That's true for most anything in life that you pay for. Suffice it to say fees are as unique as the underlying contract and should be considered on a contract-by-contract basis. There's no truth to the general rule of thumb that they're always high. They're sometimes high. And sometimes low.

Criticism No. 3: You Can't Access Your Money

This criticism is different from suggesting that you're relinquishing your money. The argument here isn't that you're relinquishing ownership but that you simply can't access your money because it's "locked up." Once again, generally speaking, this is simply not the case. More often than not, and I would go so far as to say in the extreme majority of cases, you can access your funds whenever you want. In fact, so long as you haven't "annuitized" your annuity, thus relinquishing ownership of your principal (which I already suggested is an extremely rare occurrence), you should always be able to access your funds.

The "catch" is that there may or may not be a surrender charge schedule that limits the amount of funds you can take out at any given time without incurring an "early withdrawal" penalty. Surrender charges, as they're called, are generally on a declining schedule that lasts anywhere from zero to 10 years or more, after which time there are typically no fees associated with accessing your funds. During any period of time in which there is a surrender charge, most contracts provide access to your funds through some combination of the following options:

- Penalty-free withdrawals up to a certain percentage each year, the most common percentage being 10% a year. So if you can access 10% of your money each year, after 10 years you would have essentially accessed 100% of your money.

- You can always withdraw enough to satisfy a required minimum distribution when IRA funds are involved. In other words, if you have attained the age in which you are required to take a distribution from your IRA, there will be no penalty for doing so, regardless of how long the account's been open.

- If your contract includes an income rider, you may be able to access the amount specified in that rider at any time. An income rider is simply an option that some contracts have that provide a guaranteed income of one sort or another. In the case of a contract with an income rider, all income rider payments are penalty-free.

- In the case of a death, disability, or nursing home stay, many but not all annuities allow for penalty-free withdrawals under each of these life circumstances.

- You can always access 100% of your funds subject to any remaining surrender schedule. If the penalty to withdraw is 0% or 1%, it will be a much easier decision than if it is 7% or 8%. For that reason, I encourage you to only allocate funds to an annuity to the extent you don't believe you'll need to access more than the annual free withdrawal amount during any single year for the duration of the surrender schedule period. Pulling an excessive amount of funds out during the surrender penalty period should be a last resort. But in the truest sense, the funds are indeed accessible, potentially subject to an early withdrawal penalty.

Remember, every contract is unique. Many annuities have no surrender schedule at all, or just one or two years. Some may be 10 years or more. The bottom line is it's important to understand that if there is a surrender charge schedule, you need to understand your liquidity options during that period of time and make sure the options don't conflict with your plans for those funds. A key factor in determining if an annuity is right for you and in choosing the right one is to evaluate the intended use of those funds in light of any surrender schedule that exists. When utilizing annuities with an income rider to increase a client's ISR, we take the approach of assuming those funds are "off limits" forever (even though they're not), and we only do so if there are plenty of other liquid assets to ensure those funds are never required.

Criticism No. 4: Annuities Have High Taxes

This criticism is usually aimed at using nonqualified money to fund an annuity. In doing so, the growth within the annuity is tax-deferred until withdrawn, but then it is taxed as ordinary income instead of capital gains. Assuming your ordinary income tax bracket is higher than the capital gains rate, this can be a valid concern. Of course, you would need to weigh this concern against that of your ability to defer those taxes in the first place.

This concern about taxation completely disappears, however, when funding an annuity with qualified or pretax funds like an IRA, because the tax rules governing IRAs take precedent, just as they would with any other IRA.

The Real Deal: Should You Fund an Annuity with IRA Money?

Many people assume that since annuities are already tax-deferred, that must always be the primary motivation for using one. Therefore, they sometimes argue you should never use IRA money to fund an annuity, since IRAs by definition are already tax-deferred. But as you have learned, annuities were originally designed to be retirement income vehicles, designed to be a mechanism for providing guaranteed lifetime retirement income for the owner, acting much like a private pension of sorts.

So in my opinion, the greatest value an annuity provides isn't tax-related at all, but the underlying guarantees regarding safety of principal, earnings, and income, which vary greatly from contract to contract. Therefore, I believe IRA funds are actually one of the best, most logical funding sources for an annuity, as those assets are already earmarked as a source of long-term retirement income.

If you think about it, most people already plan to spend their tax-deferred retirement savings slowly over the course of their lifetime. This is a perfect fit for certain types of annuities, whose objective is to provide you with a guaranteed lifetime income, especially if you don't already have a high level of guaranteed income sources.

Two additional reasons I suggest caution when funding an annuity with non-IRA funds:

- **Liquidity**—Your IRA funds are already somewhat illiquid unless you're willing to pay a huge tax to have complete access to all your funds at once. That's not very appealing to most people. Therefore, why would you put your non-IRA funds into a vehicle that may have a surrender schedule that would potentially reduce your ability to access those assets without a penalty, should you need them unexpectedly? It would be better to keep your non-IRA funds 100% liquid (or as liquid as possible), because you don't know what the future holds and whether you might need access to a large amount of funds.

- **Taxation**—This gets to the heart of the "high taxes" argument. Unlike long-term capital gains, which are taxed at either 15% or 20%, when you eventually take gains out of an annuity funded with non-IRA money, or non-tax-deferred money, those gains are taxed as normal income. So depending on your income tax bracket, you could potentially be taxed at a higher rate when you eventually withdraw the funds. Again, this is irrelevant if an annuity is funded with IRA funds, because by virtue of them being IRA funds, they're already subject to income tax. But with respect to utilizing nonqualified, or non-tax-deferred funds, this is a valid concern.

Criticism No. 5: Annuities Have Low Returns

Quite frankly, this idea would seem to make a lot of sense, given the fact that in many cases you're utilizing an annuity to transfer some or all the potential risk to the underlying insurance company. You should absolutely expect lower returns in exchange for this transfer of risk. It's reasonable to assume there's a cost for doing so. However, much like the discussion regarding fees, this may or may not even be true.

The best way to think of the return potential of a variable annuity is like that of a mutual fund because they're invested in subaccounts that you, the investor, choose. These subaccounts function similarly to mutual funds. And like a mutual fund, they can be comprised of any combination of securities, including stocks, bonds, commodities, and so on. The most noteworthy feature about the potential return on a variable annuity is that like a mutual fund, it can be positive or negative, which again is one of the main reasons I don't generally favor using variable annuities for retirement income planning, as it tends to defeat the purpose, which in my mind is primarily about safety and guarantees.

Fixed index annuities by definition are not exposed to market losses.

So the lowest possible annual return is 0%, but I've also seen annual returns well over 20%. On average, however, I would caution you to expect an average return of somewhere closer to 4%, give or take. Ironically, if you use this kind of annuity for generating guaranteed increasing lifetime income, the actual return is of far less importance than the structure of the underlying income benefit—which is critical, in my opinion.

Lastly, fixed annuities tend to offer a guaranteed rate commensurate with current interest rates, similar to a multiyear CD. So relatively speaking, this may be high or low, depending on the prevailing interest rate at the time.

As a side note, this is one of the few instances in which I might favor using nonretirement dollars to fund an annuity. For example, if you're looking to earn a guaranteed return of, say, 5%, (which is quite attractive as of the writing this book) for a period of two years on otherwise idle cash, you might choose to utilize a two-year fixed annuity as an alternative to a two-year CD. After the two-year period, much like with a CD, you will have the freedom to do whatever you wish with the proceeds from that contract. Either way, the interest earned will be taxable as ordinary income, regardless of whether you used a CD or an annuity.

So like most any savings or investment vehicle, you can expect your annuity returns to be unique to your specific contract, of which there are literally hundreds if not thousands, and also relative to the economic situation at the time.

Criticism No. 6: Annuities Are Too Complicated

The irony here is extreme. Most fixed and fixed-indexed annuities, when clearly explained, are much simpler to understand than most securities. When pressed, many people don't truly understand their own stocks, bonds, mutual funds, or ETFs as well as they think they do. All you need to do is compare a fixed or fixed-indexed statement of understanding to a mutual fund prospectus. The difference is dramatic.

The annuity statement of understanding is typically a fraction of the size and much simpler to understand. Once again, it really all comes down to working with someone who is able to clearly explain your investment to you. Like most foreign concepts, when well explained, they're not rocket science.

It's also important to note that annuities offer numerous guarantees that do not typically accompany securities like stocks and bonds. Not that I am, but you could argue that if you fail to fully understand what you're placing your money into, you might be better off placing it into something with a guarantee versus something that has no guarantee whatsoever. In other words, if I put my money in a security I don't understand, I face the potential of losing 100% of my money. Whereas if I put it in a fixed or fixed-indexed annuity that I don't understand, at least I don't stand the prospect of losing any of my principal.

But the truth is no one should ever place their money into something they don't fully understand, regardless of what it is. If you don't understand something and your advisor is unable to explain it to you so that you can understand it, you should at the very least not put your money in it—and perhaps even find a new advisor, one who can explain such concepts to you clearly and concisely.

A rule of thumb I have for any strategy you are contemplating is this: You should be able to explain it to someone else in about five minutes over the dinner table, were they to ask you for a high-level conceptual explanation of what it is you're doing and why.

I believe the number one job of an advisor is to teach. And your number one job is to make educated decisions. In the end, an annuity applied in the correct manner to the proper situation can be a wonderful tool for achieving an intended outcome. The wrong annuity applied incorrectly can be an equally big mistake.

BE SELECTIVE

In my daily practice, the most common use of a commercial annuity is to create supplemental guaranteed lifetime income in order to raise your Income Stability Ratio (ISR) to a comfortable level via a guaranteed retirement income annuity. However, there are certainly other scenarios in which an annuity may be the best tool for the job. Some of those include:

- To provide leveraged dollars for potential long-term care needs
- To replace CDs for short-term guaranteed returns
- To provide an enhanced death benefit for inheritance purposes

Hopefully this has been a helpful primer for you to better understand the world of annuities and whether they might make sense as a part of your retirement planning arsenal. Annuities aren't good or bad. Of course, the devil is always in the details, so you should be selective. To say that not all annuities are created equal is an enormous understatement. Choosing the correct annuity product for the intended purpose is as crucial, if not more so, than determining whether an annuity is even the correct tool for you in the first place.

Taking Action

Before moving on to the next chapter, use the QR code (page 9) to access the chapter 11 resources, then answer the following questions:

1. Do you own an annuity? If so, do you know exactly what kind of annuity it is (based on the categories listed in the chapter)?

2. What was the main reason you originally acquired it?

Based on what you've learned here, does that rationale still seem like an appropriate reason to keep it?

3. When was the last time you had the annuity's effectiveness in achieving this goal reviewed by an objective third party?

4. If you don't own an annuity, what is the main reason you don't?

5. Has reading this chapter made you think differently about annuities? Why or why not?

6. Do you believe the right annuity may enhance your retirement income plan?

PART 4

Putting It All Together

CHAPTER 12

BUCKET PLANNING

Organization is not just about being neat.
It's about creating systems that allow you to live
more effectively and efficiently.

—GRETCHEN RUBIN

Back in chapter 3, I shared how my father taught me how much easier any task becomes if you have the right tool for the job. I pointed out the value of our Income Stability Pyramid (ISR) in categorizing assets according to the reliability of their income streams. In this chapter, I will introduce you to another invaluable retirement income planning tool called *bucket planning*.

As emphasized in the previous chapters, the number one investing mistake retirees make is failing to adequately manage risk. And when it comes to investment risk, it may surprise you to learn that the number one investment-related risk to retirees isn't a market crash, such as we saw in 2008, although that's extremely important to defend against. The number one and most commonly overlooked investment risk is *sequence-of-returns risk*. I briefly addressed sequence-of-returns risk as being the core reason for coworker number one's failure back in the introduction. I also noted MPT's failure to adequately address sequence-of-returns risk in chapter 10.

One of the reasons sequence-of-returns risk is so dangerous is because most people don't know what it is, much less how to defend against it. As you think back to our coworkers from the introduction, I ask you to reflect on exactly what happened. Why was it that coworker number one had such a dismal outcome as compared to coworker number two? I've already explained that it was essentially bad luck. But more specifically, what kind of bad luck?

The specific kind of bad luck coworker number one experienced is the result of sequence-of-returns risk, which relates to the fact that the timing of your investment returns is actually more important than the returns themselves.

Sequence of Return Is Critical Once Withdraws Have Started

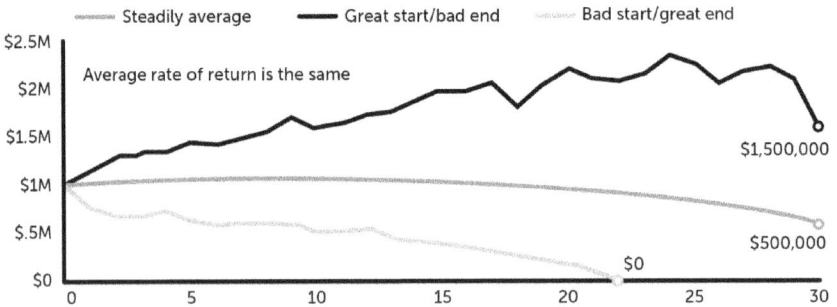

Figure 12.1: Reversed Returns

Refer to Figure 12.1 showing positive and negative sequences when taking income for a simple reminder of how the sequence of returns affects you once you're in your retirement years and, specifically, once you begin to require funds from your investments—whether to sustain your standard of living or because the government requires you to do so, as is the case with your tax-deferred retirement savings.

During your working years, which we call the acquisition and growth years (see Figure 2.2, page 40), you're generally not making withdrawals from your retirement savings investments. So, as you may recall from Table 10.3 (page 174), the order of investment returns doesn't really matter. You can completely reorder, in this case reverse, any particular series of returns over any period of time, so long as you're not making withdrawals. The end result, in terms of both your average rate of return and your actual investment value, will be identical.

However, as soon as you begin to make withdrawals from your investment account, the order of returns suddenly has a profound impact on your account value in dollar terms, as illustrated in Table 10.4, (page 174). The average rate of return is still identical regardless of the order of returns, but your ending account value is dramatically different.

As this example illustrates, the risk is that you may experience a negative sequence of returns versus a positive sequence of returns. Experiencing a negative sequence of returns can have a lasting impact on your financial security, permanently reducing the amount of money available for future expenses; on the other hand, experiencing a positive sequence of returns may result in a significant surplus down the road. The problem, of course, is that you don't know and can't control what sequence of returns you will encounter throughout your retirement.

As you'll recall from my introductory example, although all of coworker number one's traditional performance metrics were excellent and significantly better than both their own expectations and the performance metrics of coworker number two, their actual outcome was catastrophic. They ran completely out of money due to the unfortunate sequence in which their returns were realized. Put simply, coworker number one's best returns occurred later in their retirement, while coworker number two's best returns happened early in their retirement.

Given your understanding of the flaw of averages and arithmetic of loss concepts presented earlier in this book, the problem of sequence-of-returns risk should be fairly easy to comprehend, as it incorporates those same principles. Hence, if a market downturn occurs shortly before your retirement or soon thereafter, you lose the power of compounding in those early years, which is so essential to getting off to a good start. Although this downturn can be overcome, it is difficult to do without taking on excessive levels of risk in order to try to catch up or by dramatically reducing your retirement income need—spending less—in order to allow your investments to recover. The worst-case scenario occurs when you experience a negative sequence of returns early on, combined with the need to take distributions, forcing you to sell investments at a loss.

Sequence-of-returns risk highlights the importance of truly comprehensive retirement income planning—that is, the need to coordinate and optimize all your sources of retirement income and to invoke a variety of strategies aimed at mitigating the various risks you'll undoubtedly face throughout the course of your retirement. If you can successfully manage volatility, the likelihood of a truly adverse sequence of returns is much reduced.

THE BUCKET PLANNING PHILOSOPHY

One of the most effective ways to combat sequence-of-returns risk is through bucket planning. Bucket planning involves dividing or allocating one's assets into different "buckets," or categories, based on the time

---

4   Jason L. Smith, *The Bucket Plan: Protecting and Growing Your Assets for a Worry-Free Retirement* (Austin, TX: Greenleaf, 2017).

horizon, specific use, or risk tolerance for each asset. There are many different versions of bucket planning out there, with varying numbers of "buckets" involved in the planning process. Some focus more on time horizons, others on the specific intended use of each asset, and still others on the underlying degree of risk associated with each asset. Most varieties of bucket planning, however, involve some degree of each of these factors.

Most people view their retirement savings as being comprised of just two major categories: the cash reserves they hold at a bank or in their sock drawer, and the money that is invested in any number of investment accounts, viewed cumulatively as their investment portfolio. The problem with this approach is that if all of your investment resources are viewed cumulatively, your entire portfolio tends to be exposed to the same level and types of overall risk, regardless of the specific timing or purpose for when and how you plan to utilize those funds. As a result, you are either fortunate enough to experience a positive sequence of returns, which enables you to accomplish your long-term objectives, or you are unfortunate enough to experience a negative sequence of returns, which may cause you to come up short.

By dividing your savings and investments into different buckets, on the other hand, each one invested in a risk-appropriate manner that matches its intended time frame or intended use, you're able to manage various resources independently of one another in accordance with the ultimate objective they will fulfill. In this manner, you can rely on your most stable, lowest-risk assets for your more immediate income needs, while deferring the use of your less conservatively invested assets for future, less income-oriented needs. This enables you to mitigate sequence-of-returns risk by helping you avoid making withdrawals from your less conservative investment accounts at times when they may have temporarily declined in value.

In other words, the closer you get to requiring the use of a specific asset, the more conservatively it should be invested. This helps you protect against the sequence-of-returns risk, as the funds you rely on to meet your income needs will be less subject to market fluctuations. As these nearer-term, more conservatively invested assets are depleted over time, your less conservative assets can continue to grow, which will further reduce the impact of sequence of returns over the long term.

Thus, by implementing a bucket planning strategy, you can balance your need for income in the short term with your desire for growth over the long term, thereby reducing the risk of running out of money in retirement.

A UNIQUE APPROACH TO BUCKET PLANNING

My approach to bucket planning was influenced by the process found in *The Bucket Plan* by Jason Smith.[4]

My approach simply combines time horizon with the underlying role each asset plays in your overall retirement income plan. Since we work exclusively with retirees, our approach to bucket planning is a strategic approach to organizing your assets according to the three key objectives of a secure, predictable retirement. As such, we call our three buckets:

1. Peace of Mind

2. Pay the Bills

3. Plan for the Future

BUCKET PLANNING

A Strategic Approach to Organizing Your
Assets According to the Three Objectives
of a Secure, Predictable Retirement

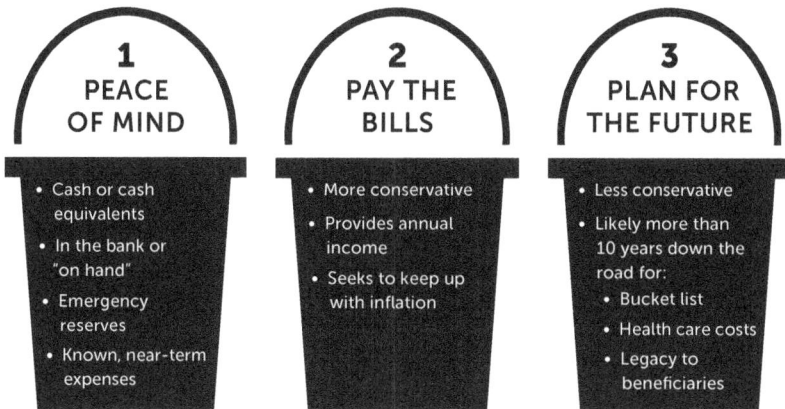

1 PEACE OF MIND

- Cash or cash equivalents
- In the bank or "on hand"
- Emergency reserves
- Known, near-term expenses

2 PAY THE BILLS

- More conservative
- Provides annual income
- Seeks to keep up with inflation

3 PLAN FOR THE FUTURE

- Less conservative
- Likely more than 10 years down the road for:
  - Bucket list
  - Health care costs
  - Legacy to beneficiaries

Figure 12.2: Retirement Bucket Planning

The first bucket, the Peace of Mind bucket, is composed of readily available cash and cash equivalents set aside for planned, near-term major expenses or emergencies. These may or may not be needed anytime soon, so time frame isn't always the main issue here, although it can be. Rather, bucket number one meets the fundamental need for you to have a certain amount of money readily available at a moment's notice—and not invested, so it's not exposed to any investment risk. Preservation and liquidity are the goals for this bucket, not growth.

Think of this as a parking spot for your cash and cash equivalents, not investments. We call it Peace of Mind because this bucket should give you the assurance—the confidence—of knowing it is always there, when and if you ever need it. Nothing will need to be liquidated or transferred. It's just there. The amount of money in your Peace of Mind bucket varies greatly from one person to another, since your need for this type of "security" is uniquely personal. I have clients who are content with $10,000 in readily accessible cash, so long as they know they have other investments that can be accessed within a couple days' time. I have other clients who need several hundred thousand dollars sitting in cash at all times in order to feel comfortable.

The second bucket, the Pay the Bills bucket, means exactly what it says. This is money you're going to use to pay bills to cover your expenses and maintain your current standard of living. It contains assets primarily focused on generating cash flow to provide for annual income needs. These funds must be invested in highly conservative vehicles and be capable of providing a stable, increasing, tax-efficient income stream.

The time frame for these Pay the Bills assets can vary greatly. Some assets may be designed and designated to provide income right now, while others may be earmarked for a specific time in the future—for example, 5–10 years down the road. Furthermore, some may be focused on providing income only for a specific period of time, and others may be designed to provide income for the remainder of your lifetime. The main issue is that the overriding focus of any asset in the Pay the Bills bucket is to generate income to meet specific retirement income needs.

The last bucket is called the Plan for the Future bucket. As the name suggests, any assets allocated to this bucket aren't anticipated to be required in the near future—generally speaking, they shouldn't be needed for at least 10 years or so. However, some may not be used until much later in retirement, and some may never be used at all. I call assets that you are unlikely to use during your lifetime *legacy assets*. Because you will be leaving these assets to your heirs, they should be invested with that objective in mind. This includes not only the underlying investment strategy but the actual investment vehicle as well. The goal for your legacy assets is to pass on the greatest amount of money, at the right time, in the most tax-efficient manner.

Of course, some assets in the Plan for the Future bucket may be tied to a specific future need, such as long-term health care costs, final expenses, leaving a legacy as I just described, or maybe your personal "bucket list" (no pun intended), while others may not be tied to any specific objective. Thus, the actual time frame for use of these assets can vary greatly. But once again, there is a strong likelihood they will not be required within the next 10 years or so. This allows these assets to be invested less conservatively, if desired, since there is more time for these investments to recover any potential short-term losses.

IT'S YOUR MONEY

Instead of labeling the investment approach for the Plan for the Future bucket as "aggressive," we prefer to say "less conservative." This is because, as you are hopefully becoming convinced, when it comes to retirement income planning, there's little to no rationale for being truly aggressive with anything. Having said that, in your own bucket number three, you can be as aggressive as you want. It's your money.

Nonetheless, as we've demonstrated repeatedly throughout this book, even with your growth-oriented investments, volatility mitigation is still, in our opinion, far more important than chasing high returns. Therefore, even though particular assets might be positioned in your later bucket and you might want to be more aggressive with them, we still recommend utilizing active risk mitigation strategies to optimize your outcome. Hence the preferred term "less aggressive." As stated previously, one of our main jobs as advisors is to help you resist the desire to take more risk than absolutely necessary. In the end, this will help maximize both the likelihood and extent of your long-term financial success.

CONCLUSION

As a retiree or soon-to-be retiree, I believe sequence-of-returns risk is one of the biggest risks facing your investment portfolios. Because of this, we encourage bucket planning as a way of organizing assets based on their intended use and to help you avoid making withdrawals from your less conservative investments during periods of increased market volatility. Bucket planning is an effective way to mitigate sequence-of-returns risk, but it won't do its job effectively if your underlying assets are still susceptible to major declines like we saw in 2000, after which the S&P 500 index took roughly 14 years to meaningfully recover. That would still be problematic, even for something in your later bucket.

S&P 500

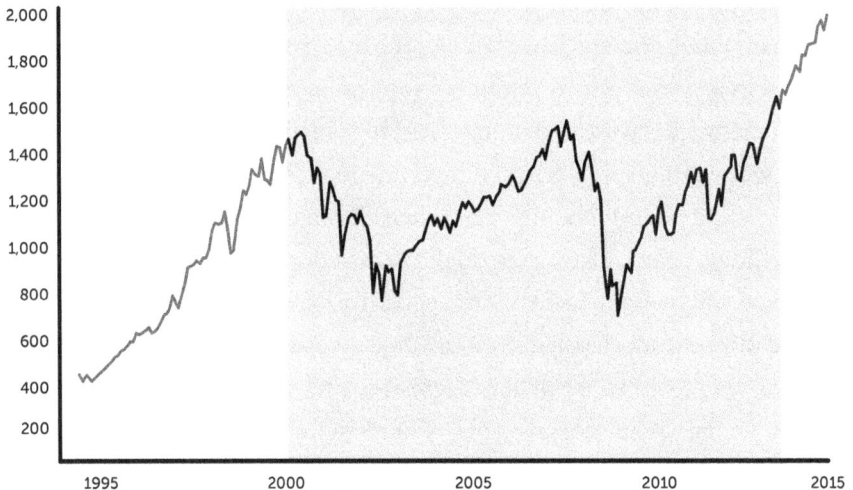

Figure 12.3: The Lost Decade

In view of this risk, we still recommend a high level of risk mitigation for all three buckets, regardless of your overall risk tolerance.

In summary:

1. Peace of Mind: How much liquidity do you need to sleep well at night?

2. Pay the Bills: How much income do you need to maintain your quality of life?

3. Plan for the Future: How much money won't be needed in the foreseeable future?

Taking Action

Before moving on to the next chapter, use the QR code (page 9) to access the chapter 12 resources, then answer the following questions:

1. How much money do you need readily available, sitting in the bank, for you to sleep well at night—your Bucket No. 1/Peace of Mind bucket?

2. Based on your current situation, which current assets do you believe belong in your Bucket No. 2/Pay the Bills bucket?

3. Based on your current situation, which assets do you believe are best spent later in life (or never) and can be allocated to your Bucket No. 3/Plan for the Future bucket?

4. Based on your current situation, which assets might be the most efficient ones to leave to your beneficiaries?

5. Use this information to create an initial draft of your own bucket plan.

CHAPTER 13

TAXES AND RETIREMENT, PART 1

In this world, nothing can be said to be certain
except death and taxes.

—BENJAMIN FRANKLIN

According to the Tax Foundation, a research group, the average American worker has to work until approximately mid-April just to earn enough money to pay their annual federal income tax bill. This means that nearly one-third of each year, or about 100 days, is spent solely fulfilling our federal income tax obligations, not to mention all the other taxes we pay. Once retired, most Americans receive a taxable monthly Social Security and/or pension benefit, in addition to the majority of their retirement savings being in taxable (tax-deferred) retirement accounts, like 401(k)s and IRAs. As a result, although retirement may signal the end of working to pay your income taxes, it's far from the end of actually having to pay them.

On the contrary, most Americans will continue to pay taxes for the remainder of their lifetimes. The average length of retirement for most of you reading this book will be 20 to 30 years, and taxes will likely be your number one expense throughout your retirement. Let that sink in. So having a formalized, long-term tax mitigation plan is essential. It can't stand alone and it can't stand apart from the rest of your retirement income planning. It must be highly integrated with the entirety of your plan. Effective tax planning can save you thousands, tens of thousands, or even hundreds of thousands of dollars over the course of your retired lifetime.

TAX PLANNING VERSUS TAX PREPARATION

Think about it. When your accountant or tax preparer sits down to prepare your taxes, they're dealing with numbers from last year. It's already over and in the books; nothing can be changed except for maybe a deduction here or credit there. Their job is to ensure you pay as little taxes as possible in accordance with the law, and no more—based primarily on things that have already happened. This is a necessary and valuable service, but it's not the same as tax planning. The typical tax preparer simply doesn't have the time or expertise to provide truly comprehensive long-term tax planning, which involves looking into the future.

What's worse is that most financial advisors don't have the expertise or inclination to provide this service. In fact, many advisors will tell you straight out that they cannot and will not provide tax-planning services, just as they likely cannot and will not provide advanced income planning, Social Security planning, Medicare planning, risk management, survivorship planning, or estate planning. It's simply not what they do and it's not how they get paid.

Unfortunately, many people fail to understand the importance of truly comprehensive planning, so they're content with an advisor who focuses almost exclusively on their investments. As a result, most retirees mistakenly believe that tax planning is the purview of their accountant.

Many advisors will happily tell you to seek the advice of your accountant regarding tax planning matters, as it removes the onus from themselves. But tax preparation and tax planning are completely different. Tax planning involves looking down the road at the next 20 or 30 years and taking proactive steps to minimize the amount of taxes you and your loved ones will pay over your remaining lifetime and perhaps into the next generation. I've yet to meet a single individual who wanted to pay more taxes than what is legally required.

Yet most people are doing, and will continue to do just that, year after year, because they don't have a proactive tax plan in place. The word "plan" should be the tip-off that this process should be an integral part of a holistic financial plan, versus a 30-minute conversation with your tax preparer. Believe it or not, in my 25 years of providing holistic retirement planning services, I've yet to see a single person walk through our door with a written, proactive, long-term tax plan in place.

So what should a retirement income tax plan look like? And what should it do? Generally speaking, it should evaluate all the critical areas of retirement planning, including investment income, health care, survivorship, estate, and risk management from a tax-sensitive perspective. It should then identify the most tax-efficient path for achieving all of your lifetime and legacy goals.

TAXING NON-ASSET-BASED (SOCIAL SECURITY & PENSION) INCOME

When it comes to taxation, not all retirement income is created equal. As you consider all the income that will be generated from all your resources, it's critically important to keep in mind the various tax treatment of each type. One of the most complex parts of this process is understanding the tax implications associated with non-asset-based income.

Most commonly, this includes Social Security and/or pension income. But it can also include things like deferred compensation, annuities, royalties, or wages.

Social Security income, for example, carries with it one of the most complex taxation schemes of all income. That should come as no surprise, given that it's a government program and the government is notorious for unnecessarily complicating things.

To begin with, the taxation of your Social Security income depends entirely on how much you earn from all other sources in the same year. It is based upon something called your "provisional income." Your provisional income consists of 50% of your Social Security income plus 100% of practically all of your income outside of Social Security, including—

- Wages

- Pension payments

- Distributions from 401(k)s and IRAs

- Interest and dividend income, including interest from municipal bonds

- Capital gains

- Any taxable portion of an inheritance—this includes income from inherited IRAs or annuities

Provisional income = 50% of SS income
+ 100% of all other income

Once you have calculated your provisional income for a given year, you can then determine the portion of your Social Security benefit that will be taxable. For example, based on your provisional income, the following amounts of Social Security income are currently subject to taxation:

Single Filing		Married Filing Jointly	
Provisional Income	Taxable Benefits	Provisional Income	Taxable Benefits
Under $25,000	0%	Under $32,000	0%
$25,000–$34,000	Up to 50%	$32,000–$44,000	Up to 50%
Over $34,000	Up to 85%	Over $44,000	Up to 85%

Table 13.1: Social Security Taxation

Once you've determined the proportion of your SS payments that will be subject to taxation, the actual amount of income tax you owe can be determined in a similar manner to all your other income, based on the current tax brackets for your specific filing status.

As you can see, the degree to which you will pay tax on your Social Security benefit payment depends on the degree to which you receive any of these other types of income at the same time. Without getting into the minutia of all these different types of income and their taxation, suffice it to say the decision of when to claim Social Security to optimize your Social Security benefits relies heavily on what other income sources it will need to be coordinated with and what the resulting tax consequences over time will be.

Determining your Social Security taxation alone is a significant undertaking, much less coordinating it with all your other forms of income. The smallest incremental increase in any form of income can transform nontaxable Social Security income into taxable Social Security income. Something as simple as making an extra IRA distribution for that new furnace or special vacation could end up incurring a whopping incremental tax, simply because it caused previously nontaxable Social Security income to become taxable.

50% Tax! How Did That Happen?

What Intuitively Should Happen:

$1,000 additional IRA withdrawal	12% bracket	$120 tax

What Actually Happens:

$1,000 additional IRA withdrawal	12% bracket	$120 tax
Causes $850 new taxable SS	12% bracket	$102 tax
Causes $1,850 capital gains to be taxable	15% bracket	$277.50 tax

TOTAL ADDITIONAL TAX BURDEN ON $1,000 WITHDRAWAL   **$499.50**

Pension income is another form of non-asset-based income that can include a wide variety of tax implications, based on the specific kind of pension income. Not all pension income is created equal. And every state has its own unique rules related to the taxation of pension income.

These are just two examples of the many complications involved in tax planning for various forms of non-asset-based retirement income. And we have only considered a single year. Stepping back once again to consider the big picture, it's critical to understand and incorporate the tax consequences of each of these types of income streams into your lifetime income plan based on your individual situation. You must also remember that whether the source of income is from an asset that you own or a non-asset-based income stream, each income stream affects the taxation of all the others—thus the need for a high level of coordination. So as you can imagine, coordinating all your various forms of non-asset-based retirement income over the next 20 to 30 years can be extremely complicated. Nonetheless, with the right tools the process can be greatly simplified, and it can be one of the biggest difference-makers in optimizing your lifetime income. Our clients love the fact that our retirement income planning software allows us to experiment by changing the amount and timing of various income sources in order to instantly generate a visual depiction of the effects over time.

TAXING ASSET-BASED INCOME

In addition to the various ways in which your non-asset-based income sources may be taxed, your asset-based income sources also vary widely in the way they're taxed. A helpful way to understand these major differences is to divide your assets into three general categories: pretax, after-tax, and tax-free.

NOT ALL MONEY IS TAXED EQUALLY

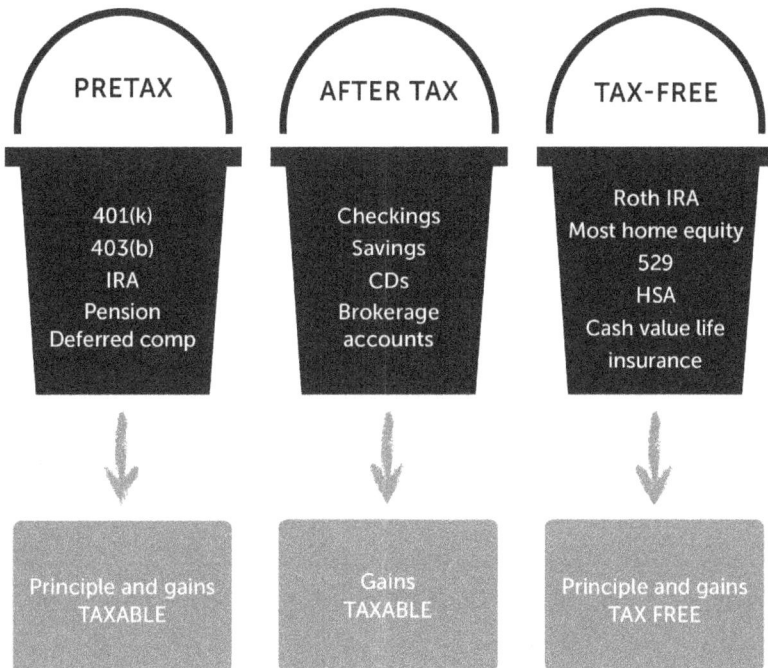

PRETAX	AFTER TAX	TAX-FREE
401(k) 403(b) IRA Pension Deferred comp	Checkings Savings CDs Brokerage accounts	Roth IRA Most home equity 529 HSA Cash value life insurance
Principle and gains TAXABLE	Gains TAXABLE	Principle and gains TAX FREE

*Restrictions may apply

Figure 13.1: Not All Money Is Taxed Equally

Pretax or Tax-Deferred Assets

The first category, as you'll see on the left side of Figure 13.1, is tax-deferred or pretax assets. These include assets or savings on which you have never before paid taxes. Most people can best relate to this with respect to an IRA, a 401(k), or 403(b) account, in which you simply agreed with your employer and the IRS to defer the realization of the receipt of these assets (income) until a later time. That's why they're called tax-deferred. The growth on these assets is also not taxable during the deferral period. All withdrawals, however—including all deposits and any increases over the years—are fully taxable as a result.

Pretax money is promoted as the most tax beneficial kind of retirement savings, since it isn't taxed when you earn it. As a result, it is typically the most prevalent type of asset for most retirees. What's not so often promoted is the fact that upon retirement, this kind of asset immediately becomes the worst, most tax-disadvantaged money, since it is always 100% taxable. In essence, the government allows you to defer paying taxes on the dollars you put in these plans so that you will pay tax on those same dollars—plus all the growth—later, at whatever tax rate Congress decides.

After-Tax

The second type of money is known as after-tax money. This is money that you've received in one manner or another, whether from a paycheck or a gift or any other receipt of funds, that has already been taxed. For instance, if you receive a paycheck and you pay taxes on it and then you place that money in your bank account, or you use it to purchase a car or real estate or investments, it is after-tax money at the time you make those deposits or acquisitions.

The growth on most of these assets will be taxable, with some exceptions, depending on the underlying asset itself. Interest and dividend income, for example, is taxable in the year in which it's earned. But capital gains are not taxed until they are realized, usually upon the sale of the underlying asset.

The withdrawal from this type of asset, on the other hand, does not trigger taxation in and of itself. An example would be a savings account that you have at the local bank. Any interest you earn on the savings account over the course of the year is taxable, but the act of actually withdrawing money from that account to go make a purchase is not a taxable event. The same could be said of capital gains. If you invest after-tax money in a particular stock, when you eventually sell that stock, you will owe capital gains tax if it has appreciated in value. However, the subsequent withdrawal of that money from your account does not trigger a taxable event.

As you can see, I think of this money as being better than pretax money because you've already paid the tax on the principal and now you are only potentially subject to taxation on the growth. And you even have some control over that taxation. For instance, if you invest after-tax dollars into a municipal bond, the interest earnings are exempt from taxes at the federal and possibly state levels.

Tax-Free

The third type of assets are tax-free assets. The most common examples of this type of asset would be a Roth IRA or your primary residence.

The money that you place into a Roth IRA has already been taxed, just like your after-tax funds. But unlike after-tax funds, any growth and subsequent withdrawals from a Roth IRA are also tax-free—forever—subject to certain parameters. This makes the income from these types of accounts extremely tax advantageous.

Likewise, the equity in your primary residence can also be accessed without taxation. Some of the popular ways to do so are through the sale of the property, once again subject to certain limitations or by initiating a home equity conversion mortgage.

As you might imagine, I consider tax-free assets like Roth IRAs to be the best type of assets to have in retirement because they will never be subject to taxation, regardless of the growth they experience. Furthermore, if you pass these on to your beneficiaries upon your death, they can be tax-free to them as well.

Hidden Taxes

There is also the issue of hidden taxes to consider. For example, the amount of taxable income you receive each year after age 65 will directly affect your Medicare premiums two years down the road. This is called your income-related monthly adjustment amount, or IRMAA. Although increased Medicare premiums aren't technically considered a tax, they certainly look and smell just like a tax. After all, you're required to pay more to the government as a direct result of having more income.

There are other hidden taxes lurking out there too, such as those related to having what the government deems an excessive amount of non-ordinary income, or those associated with your state of residence, age, or marital status. Even the fact that otherwise "tax-free" income, such as an inheritance or municipal bond income, is added back into the equation when determining how much of your Social Security income is taxable is also a kind of hidden tax.

WHAT-IF AND HAPPILY EVER AFTER PLANNING

Last, it is critical to address the effect of taxes on other-than-optimal life circumstances. The first and most important objective of any retirement income plan is to lay out what we call your Happily Ever After plan. This assumes you and your spouse will live until your full life expectancy and both die quietly in your sleep, at the same time. After all, this is what you want to happen. You need to be sure you're financially prepared for this outcome and that you won't run the risk of outliving your income.

But any conversation on long-term tax planning would be incomplete without addressing the eventual issue of the passing of one spouse. We call this survivorship planning, or more broadly, What-If planning. This second part of your plan is just as important (if not more so) because if one of you were to die prematurely or suffer a severe accident or illness, or if some other drastic life circumstance occurs, you need to be certain your plan will still work.

Loss of a Spouse

One of the simplest examples of this pertains to the premature death of a spouse. There are many implications for such a scenario that must be considered and planned for, but since this chapter is about tax planning, I will focus on and share an example of how this could throw a major wrench into a plan that has not taken into consideration such a possibility.

Tax Considerations for a Surviving Spouse
(Married couple over age 65)

BEFORE	AFTER
Married Filing Jointly	**Single Filer over 65**
• John's Social Security Income = $20,000	
• Mary's Social Security Income = $10,000	• Highest Social Security Benefit = $20,000
• IRA Distributions = $30,000	• IRA Distributions = $40,000
Total Tax Due = $615	**Total Tax Due = $4,736**
Net Income = $59,385	**Net Income = $55,264**

Increase in IRA Withdraw = 33%
Tax Increase = 770%
Net Income = $4,121 LOWER

Imagine a scenario in which John and Mary Smith, a married couple over the age of 65, are married, filing jointly. John has a Social Security income of $20,000, and Mary has a Social Security income of $10,000.

They have determined that they need a gross annual income of $60,000 to live comfortably. So they are currently taking $30,000 in distributions from their IRA in addition to their $30,000 in Social Security payments in order to generate the $60,000 gross income they need.

The total federal tax that would be due at the end of the year is $615. And the net income they would realize, which is their gross income of $60,000 minus the $615 tax due, is $59,385. That's what they have to live on.

But let's now suppose John passes away. The good news is that Mary will retain the higher of the two Social Security paychecks, in this case $20,000. The bad news is that she will lose the smaller of the two Social Security paychecks, in this case $10,000.

Assuming Mary wishes to maintain the same $60,000 gross annual income, she would need to increase their IRA distributions from $30,000 to $40,000. Simple math tells us this is an increase of 33% for their annual IRA distributions. Furthermore, since Mary is no longer married filing jointly, the total tax that will be due at the end of the year will increase to $4,736. That is a 770% increase over the $615 she was paying when her spouse was alive and they were married filing jointly. The net income after subtracting the total tax due from the $60,000 gross income is now $55,264. This means the surviving spouse gets hit with an annual net income decrease of $4,121 (see page 223).

So as you can see, something as simple as the death of one spouse, which is inevitable at some point in time, has a dramatic impact on the taxation of the surviving spouse, as well as the rate at which the surviving spouse will be required to consume their personal savings to maintain their standard of living. Thus it has a profound impact on a couple's lifetime income planning—especially if the spouse's death was premature—that is, significantly earlier than their normal life expectancy.

This is just one example of the type of What-If planning that needs to be considered with respect to a long-term retirement income plan.

The Real Deal: Retirement Income Needs

Many advisors assume retirees' income needs always decrease over time as they age, then perhaps rise again late in life as health care becomes more of an issue. This certainly puts less pressure on the plan and makes it look better on paper, but I don't agree with this approach. I always assume your current living expenses will steadily increase each year for the remainder of your lifetime. If your expenses do decrease over time, great! But if they don't, your plan will still work. Otherwise, you will be forced to reduce your spending at some predetermined time. Not fun.

Many advisors also assume a surviving spouse's living expenses will decrease after the death of the first spouse. In my 25 years' experience, however, I have NEVER seen this happen. Not only are many household/living expenses fixed, but the death of one spouse often results in the surviving spouse spending more time outside the home as they attempt to fill the void left by the death of their loved one. This usually adds to one's financial need. It doesn't decrease it. Furthermore, the surviving spouse will now be subject to much higher tax brackets since they'll no longer be filing jointly, as demonstrated in the example on page 223.

CONCLUSION

Failing to incorporate long-term tax planning into your retirement income planning would be a huge oversight, simply because taxes will likely be your largest retirement expense. As you learned in this chapter, there is a significant difference between tax preparation and tax planning. All of your retirement income sources affect one another from a standpoint of taxation; therefore, it's vital they all be coordinated. For maximum benefit, this should be overseen by your retirement specialist, possibly in coordination with your accountant, if you can find one willing and able to work as a team with your other advisors. By being mindful of the information presented in this chapter, you will both increase your net after-tax income during the course of your lifetime and also the tax efficiency of any assets you leave to beneficiaries.

Taking Action

Before moving on to the next chapter, use the QR code (page 9) to access the chapter 13 resources, then answer the following questions:

1. Who do you rely on for long-term tax planning?

2. Do you have a specific, written, long-term tax minimization plan?

3. If not, do you now better understand the importance of having one?

4. Will you consider finding an advisor who has demonstrated expertise in this area, one who can help you create a retirement income plan that incorporates tax planning?

    a. What, if any, obstacles are standing in your way?

CHAPTER 14

TAXES AND RETIREMENT, PART 2

The best time to plant a tree was 20 years ago.
The second-best time is now.

—CHINESE PROVERB

A few years back, a retired airline pilot came into my office for a second opinion on his retirement plan. He had been retired for four years but was still quite young. He had about $2 million in tax-deferred retirement savings, another $1 million in a non-tax-deferred investment account, and several hundred thousand in cash.

During our discussion I asked him what he had had been living on over these past four years. He answered that he had been living off his cash savings that he had in the bank and that he planned to continue doing so for the next few years, so long as it lasted. When I asked him why he chose to do that, his response was that he paid very little in taxes by doing it that way. He went on to say that he'd paid almost no income tax over the last four years. I could tell he was extremely proud of that fact, and he acknowledged that his advisor had concurred with him that it was the best, most tax-efficient approach to take.

I suspect he had paid more than his fair share of taxes during his working career and he was probably overjoyed to now pay next to nothing in comparison. Likewise, his advisor, who got paid to manage his investments, was strongly incentivized to endorse this approach. The advisor didn't have to do any tax planning, and the pilot wasn't spending any of the funds the advisor was being compensated on. Even his accountant probably agreed that a $0 tax bill spelled success.

PENNY WISE, POUND FOOLISH

I, on the other hand, was disappointed by his answer. I explained to him that he had missed an enormous opportunity over the last four years to spend some of his worst money first—that is, his tax-deferred savings. Instead, he had been spending his best money, that is, his least taxable money first, during the time in his life when he was in the lowest tax bracket he will ever be in. He could have instead spent some of his tax-deferred money (IRAs) and paid an extremely low tax rate, rather than deferring it until later, when he'll be paying a much higher tax rate to access those funds as his income increases, thanks to upcoming pension payments, required minimum distributions he will be forced to take from his IRAs, and two Social Security benefits payments for him and his wife. And that's not even taking into account the fact that tax rates are currently scheduled to reset higher after 2025.

Alternatively, he could have taken advantage of his current, lowest-ever tax bracket to initiate sizable Roth conversions. By converting tax-deferred funds into a Roth IRA over the past several years, he could have paid some tax now at his lowest-ever tax bracket and neither he nor his children would ever again be taxed on the converted principal or future growth of those assets. Instead, the principal and any future growth on those funds will be taxed at his much higher future tax rate. I estimate the approach he has taken will cost him many tens of thousands of dollars in taxes (if not more) over his and his family's lifetimes.

I went on to explain that, if he had been our client for the past four years, we would have suggested an alternate strategy. I laid it out for him using our tax planning software to clearly show him the math and how it would have benefited him. I also suggested it wasn't too late for him to create a long-term tax plan now in order to capitalize on his many remaining opportunities, since he still had ample amounts of various resources available. It was clear by the look on his face that he understood the mistake he'd made. He thanked me for teaching him so much and said I'd hear from him soon.

I never saw that pilot again. I can only assume he didn't have the nerve to leave his "longtime, trusted advisor," as he put it. He probably just shared my teachings with him, believing that's all there was to it, assuming that his advisor would magically become a retirement income and tax-planning specialist. Maybe he just didn't like being told that he'd missed four years of opportunity. I really don't know. They say ignorance is bliss and that you don't know what you don't know. Some people just prefer to live in ignorance and not know. I say that's an expensive way to live.

Nevertheless, the net effect on the amount of taxes he'll pay over the length of his retirement will be dramatic. In addition, there will be a day in his future, once he enters his 70s, when he'll find that he has almost no liquid funds at his disposal that aren't 100% percent taxable. His pension, Social Security, and IRA funds will all be taxable, and he will find himself paying far more taxes than would have been necessary. Eventually, he'll be at an age where he doesn't have the ability to turn off any of these income sources or to control the amount of taxes he'll be paying.

WHAT WAS THE ADVISOR THINKING?

This raises for me a second potential issue over and above the fact that most people simply don't like paying taxes before they have to. That is the question: Why didn't the advisor recommend the pilot take advantage of his extremely low and temporary tax situation? There are only two plausible answers. The first is that the advisor simply did not understand long-term tax planning. That in and of itself is extremely concerning, especially since he was advising a retiree.

The second possibility is that the advisor doesn't get paid to do tax planning, but he does get paid on assets under his management. Therefore, it would be in the advisor's financial best interest to encourage the pilot to spend the cash that he has in the bank while allowing his tax-deferred assets to continue to grow. Hopefully this was not the motivation. Regardless, it is concerning.

I will add that not only would it have been in the pilot's long-term best interest to pay some taxes now by spending his worst money first, but I believe it would also have been in the advisor's best interest over the long term. After all, it's always in an advisor's best interest to do what's in the client's best interest, because over time that will result in a healthy, robust, sustainable practice for the advisor. Short-sightedness leads to bad decisions on both sides of the relationship.

IT'S NEVER TOO LATE TO START

If I could wave a wand such that every person who walks through my door started thinking about their retirement income tax planning 20 years ago, it would make my job much easier and incredibly enjoyable to see all the millions of dollars in resultant tax savings. Nonetheless, it's never too late to initiate a long-term tax plan. There's usually still plenty of meat left on the bone—meat that's better off not being fed to the government in the form of taxes. Since all your assets and income sources are unique to you, there's no substitute for a well-thought-out, personalized, strategic tax plan.

However, for the purposes of this book, the following are some thoughts on how to begin to reprogram your mind regarding taxation.

STOP DEFERRING ALREADY

Figure 14.1

From a tax perspective, I'll go so far as to say that tax deferral is the single issue that leads to the three most expensive mistakes made by the average worker/retiree:

1. Overemphasis of tax deferral by saving as much as possible into tax-deferred accounts—that is, qualified retirement plans and IRAs

2. Being biased toward spending the wrong money first, early in retirement

3. Being reluctant to sell an investment that has appreciated in value due to fear of having to pay capital gains

Unfortunately, most people never notice these expensive mistakes and their associated costs because they're hidden in their annual tax return and spread out over time. All most people see and focus on is today's tax bill. There's never anything to compare it to because there's no way to know what would've happened had you done things differently, if no one shows you.

This is particularly true if it doesn't occur to you to even consider the notion of doing something different, which is the case for most people, because as I said previously, we are all bombarded with the idea that minimizing taxes today is the ultimate objective. However, I can tell you for a fact, having worked with retirees for the past 25 years, two things have become abundantly clear to me:

1. The most effective approach isn't minimizing your taxes today, as most would have you believe. It's minimizing taxes over the course of your lifetime. These are two very different things, and in most cases, they are mutually exclusive.

2. For the past several years and for the time being, taxes are actually on sale—in fact, historically speaking, they're cheap—making wise, long-term tax planning all the more impactful.

The implications of these two facts should be obvious. It may be beneficial to pay some taxes sooner rather than later. Of course, I've never met someone who was happy about the amount of taxes they're paying. So saying taxes are on sale and that you should pay more now is not a popular opinion, because nobody ever thinks their taxes are low and no one ever wants to pay more that absolutely necessary. However, what most people don't realize is that the top tax brackets today are among the lowest we've ever seen throughout history.

I find it humorous that over the past decade or so, the financial industry language surrounding tax-deferred retirement accounts has changed. Most literature now refers to them as "tax advantaged." It stands to reason that you'd be a fool to not maximize your right to save in a tax advantaged account, right? That's very clever if not downright misleading marketing. I haven't deferred a single dollar into a traditional, tax-deferred retirement account in over a decade. Everything I save is either in a tax-free Roth 401(k) or Roth IRA, up to the limit, or an after-tax account. I lose the up-front tax deduction by doing so, but I know that every dollar I save into my Roth can grow to infinity and I will never, ever pay tax on it. I suggest you might at least consider biting the proverbial bullet, paying the taxes now, and doing the same—whatever that might look like for you, based on your unique situation and stage of life. And if you are still working and your income level is too high to contribute directly to a Roth IRA, investigate whether your company has a Roth option within your retirement savings plan such as your 401(k)or 403(b). More and more companies are adding this option to their qualified plans.

BUY WHAT'S ON SALE

To better illustrate my point, let's start by taking a look at the idea that taxes are currently on sale. Imagine you are reading this book in 1980. If you have a taxable income of $125,000 today, that's an inflation-adjusted equivalent of about $41,000 in 1980 dollars. In other words, $41,000 in 1980 would provide you with the same approximate standard of living as $125,000 today. However, your $41,000 in 1980 would've been subject to a total tax of approximately $10,622, based on the then-current tax tables.

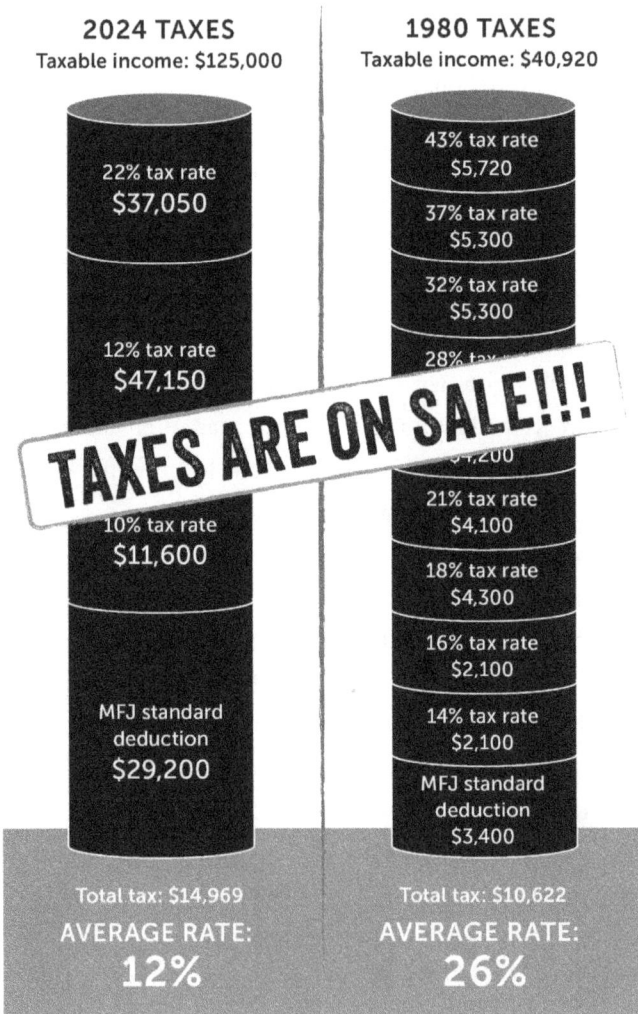

2024 TAXES	1980 TAXES
Taxable income: $125,000	Taxable income: $40,920

2024 TAXES:
- 22% tax rate $37,050
- 12% tax rate $47,150
- 10% tax rate $11,600
- MFJ standard deduction $29,200
- Total tax: $14,969
- AVERAGE RATE: 12%

1980 TAXES:
- 43% tax rate $5,720
- 37% tax rate $5,300
- 32% tax rate $5,300
- 28% tax rate $4,200
- 21% tax rate $4,100
- 18% tax rate $4,300
- 16% tax rate $2,100
- 14% tax rate $2,100
- MFJ standard deduction $3,400
- Total tax: $10,622
- AVERAGE RATE: 26%

TAXES ARE ON SALE!!!

Figure 14.2: Taxes Are on Sale

The highest tax rate you would have experienced for your last dollar earned would've been 43%, while your overall tax burden (effective tax rate) would have been 26%.

Today, by comparison, an inflation-adjusted equivalent income of $125,000 results in a total federal tax of only $14,969. The top tax bracket you'd be exposed to is 22%—versus 1980's 43%—and your overall tax burden is 12% versus 26%. So hopefully you see what I mean when I suggest that taxes are actually on sale.

SPEND YOUR WORST MONEY FIRST

In addition to prevailing US tax rates, you should also consider your own unique, prevailing personal tax rate. Even if tax rates never change, I can say without a doubt that for the average person reading this book (there will always be exceptions), you will likely experience your lowest personal retirement income level and associated tax rate immediately upon your retirement. And over time, your personal income and accompanying tax rate will likely increase.

In other words, immediately upon retirement, many of you won't have any earned income, Social Security, pension, or minimum required distribution income. This is especially true if you retire early. Therefore, you will likely be in the lowest tax bracket that you'll ever experience for the rest of your life. Your taxable income is likely to be totally dependent on what you choose to spend during those early years, whereas later in your retirement, things like pensions and Social Security and required minimum distributions will occur automatically, increasing your personal tax rate. The implications for most people is that the earliest days of your retirement likely present one of the biggest tax-saving opportunities of your lifetime if you plan properly to take advantage of it.

This all leads to the concept of spending your "worst money first." This is a very contrarian approach, because no one likes paying taxes and no one likes spending their nest egg, that is, their tax-deferred retirement savings, which is typically one of their largest assets. This was our pilot's problem. Just as you've been trained to pour as much of your hard-earned money into tax-deferred retirement accounts throughout the course of your working years, only to find out once you retire that these types of assets are now your worst, most tax-disadvantaged assets, you've also been trained, as have most advisors, to spend these tax-deferred assets last. But in thinking long-term, it makes more sense to spend them first.

WORST MONEY FIRST

PRETAX	AFTER TAX	TAX-FREE
WORST	BETTER	BEST
Principle and gains TAXABLE	Gains TAXABLE	Principle and gains TAX FREE

*Restrictions may apply

Figure 14.3: Worst Money First

Typically, once I demonstrate the mathematical reality that this is in someone's financial best interest, the most common objection I get is the idea that doing so will cause you to begin to draw down your nest egg sooner than otherwise. But once again, this is short-term thinking. If you rely on your less-tax-advantaged resources earlier in retirement and defer your more-tax-advantaged resources, like Social Security, until later, you will end up with a much larger, more tax-efficient, guaranteed income base throughout the remainder of your retirement, since delaying these income sources will often result in higher monthly payments down the road. As a result, you will rely less on your nest egg later in retirement, thus actually preserving it for longer. This has been my experience, without exception, for many years.

Not All Income Is Taxed Equally

A simple way to think about spending your worst money first is to work your way from left to right on the chart in Figure 14.3 showing how not all income is taxed equally. This will not only help you visualize the assets you should spend first, but it will also help you visualize the result—which is to preserve and grow your most tax-advantaged assets for later. This will be seen toward the right of the chart. And if you don't ever spend those assets toward the right side of the chart, according to current tax law, the assets in both the middle and right buckets will typically pass to your heirs in a tax-free manner. Saving the best for last makes all the sense in the world!

What about tax rates in the years ahead? I am not a betting person. But if I were, I'd bet tax rates will once again be higher in the future. Our nation is facing an insurmountable level of debt, Social Security is down to just under a 3:1 ratio of contributors to beneficiaries (specifically 2.7 in 2023, estimated to drop to 2.3 covered workers for each beneficiary by

---

5   United States Social Security Administration, "Social Security Fact Sheet," accessed November 8, 2023, https://www.ssa.gov/news/press/factsheets/basicfact-alt.pdf.

2035).[5] Meanwhile, government is bloated and government expenditures are soaring.

In the end, there are only two ways for our government to pay the bills: taxes and borrowing. And government borrowing is simply deferring taxation into the future, when those debts come due. So it all comes down to taxes. That's the only real option. So while I'm not clairvoyant, it's a pretty safe assumption that your taxes will be higher in the future. At the very least, it's highly unlikely that Congress will dramatically lower taxes in the future. In view of this, it's an even greater incentive to spend your highest taxable income sooner rather than later.

A DOUBLE-EDGED SWORD

In many cases, you're highly incentivized to defer drawing on your most tax-efficient sources of income. Social Security and most pensions provide increased benefits to those who defer receiving those benefits. In the case of Social Security, each year you defer your benefit results in somewhere between a 7% and 8% increase. The longer you wait to start it, the greater your initial income will be. That's often the case with pensions, too. Each year you defer, you typically get a slight raise on your initial payment, which will last your entire lifetime.

As your tax-deferred accounts grow, however, so does your associated tax bill. That makes tax-deferred savings a double-edged sword. During retirement, if your tax-deferred investments drop in value, you will undoubtedly be disappointed. And if they grow, your tax liability increases. There is a cost either way.

In contrast, investments in tax-free accounts don't experience this issue. Think of it this way: For every dollar the government agrees not

---

6   Dayana Yochim, "Retirement Account Statistics: 2023," NerdWallet, updated November 6, 2023, https://www.nerdwallet.com/article/investing/retirement-statistics.

to tax you today, they get to tax you on that dollar and any additional growth it experiences down the road—at whatever tax rate *they* chose. Remember, tax-deferred retirement accounts have costs as well as benefits, just like everything else.

Retirement plans are also big money for the financial industry, in that people tend to pour money into these accounts month after month throughout their working lifetimes, not touching it until the latest possible moment, regardless of whether the market is trending up or down. There's currently estimated to be some $36 trillion in tax-deferred retirement accounts, according to the US government.[6] And all that money generates tremendous revenue for the financial industry. So don't be fooled; this is not financial industry or government altruism.

That is not to say that tax-deferred retirement plans are bad. However, there are many other great approaches to saving for retirement, and they come with a variety of different features and benefits. Everyone's situation is unique, and your long-term goals and objectives should dictate how much money you put into these types of plans. If you are the typical retiree who comes to us for help, one of the biggest opportunities is to let us help you defuse the retirement-tax time bomb you've created over the years of following all the mainstream advice of "defer, defer, defer." Essentially, your best money for saving has turned into your worst money for retirement.

R Is for Required

The larger your tax-deferred accounts grow, the larger your required minimum distribution (RMD) will be in the future. More money is better than less money, but in the case of tax-deferred retirement accounts, it just compounds the issue of paying higher taxes over time. By reducing your tax-deferred savings to the lowest level possible by age 70 to 75, you take back the ability to control both your annual income and your level of taxation. This can be done through a variety of spending and conversion strategies. The less you give to Uncle Sam, the more you get to keep. It's that simple.

Last, if you spend your worst money first, hopefully in your lowest tax years, you are more likely to leave the most tax-efficient assets to your beneficiaries. This is a huge win for your estate planning. The difference between leaving your children a traditional IRA or a Roth IRA or other after-tax account can be enormous, especially if they are moderate to high earners themselves.

PLAY THE LONG GAME

Many retirees are blissfully unaware of the high income taxes that await them. Having a lot of income is great, but having to pay tax on all that income is still a problem. As you might imagine, the vast majority of people who come to us have a large percentage of their net worth in tax-deferred retirement accounts. This approach to saving has been ingrained in us for decades. You've been told it's the best and perhaps only way to save for retirement. You are made to feel like you're a fool if you don't maximize your tax-deductible contributions. This thinking, however, is a result of focusing on today's tax bill by deferring a portion of our income to get the deduction now, thereby reducing the tax you will owe this year, with no regard to the long-term tax implications for the 20 or 30 years in which you'll be retired.

But it's not too late to change your thinking and start developing a long-term tax strategy as an integral part of your retirement income plan, rather than continuing to unwittingly kick the can down the road.

Taking Action

Before moving on to the next chapter, use the QR code (page 9) to access the chapter 14 resources, then answer the following questions:

1. What is your current, highest incremental tax bracket— that is, the amount of federal income tax you owe on the very last dollar you receive? (If you're not sure, you can ask your tax preparer.)

2. What is your current average tax ? That is, how much total federal income tax do you pay as a percentage of your total income?

3. How do you feel about those numbers?

4. Do you think those numbers will be higher or lower in the future?

5. Make a list of the strategies in this chapter that you are already incorporating into your tax planning.

6. Make a list of the strategies you learned about that you are not currently incorporating.

7. What, if any, other steps are you taking to mitigate taxes throughout your lifetime that were not included in this chapter?

8. Are you confident your long-term retirement income plan is as tax efficient as it can get?

9. If not, what can you do today to begin to improve your situation?

CHAPTER 15

WHAT COULD POSSIBLY GO WRONG?

Success is the ultimate measure of a strategy.
It doesn't matter how good the plan is or how well executed,
if it doesn't deliver the results, it's a failure.

—JACK WELCH

U p to this point, I've focused almost exclusively on solving the retirement income puzzle, assuming you'll live a long, healthy life and die quietly in your sleep one day. This is the Happily Ever After version of your plan. It's been all about ensuring you have plenty of stable, increasing, tax-efficient lifetime income and lots of extra wiggle room, just in case.

But let's face it. In the real world things don't always go as planned. That's another reason truly comprehensive, holistic planning is so critically important. A great plan must anticipate and allow for contingencies.

If you are like the average retiree, the four most likely ways your finances could be eroded during retirement are as follows—

- Paying too much in taxes
- Inflation eating away at your purchasing power
- Market losses reducing your investment portfolio
- Long-term health care (LTC) expenses consuming your savings

We've covered the first three in detail throughout the previous chapters. But the fourth item here—LTC expenses—begs our attention too. It serves as a reminder that a truly sound plan must include contingencies for all those What-If scenarios.

As I've mentioned a number of times, if your so-called "retirement plan" is limited to investment planning only, then you don't really have a plan and you're leaving a lot to chance. So in the following paragraphs, I'll not only show you how to defend against potentially catastrophic long-term health care costs, I'll also address a number of other, often overlooked threats to your long-term financial success as you transition into retirement.

THE REALITY OF LONG-TERM CARE EXPENSES

Let's start by defining *long-term care* (LTC). Long-term care is the ongoing services and support needed because of a chronic health condition or disability. This is different from an acute health care issue, often addressed in a doctor's office or hospital. In general, if you need help with any two of the following six activities of daily living (ADL): transferring, continence, toileting, bathing, dressing, eating, or if you have a cognitive impairment like Alzheimer's or dementia, you need long-term care.

Contrary to what you might be thinking, it's also important to note that the delivery of LTC services is not limited to a nursing home. Rather, LTC can be provided in a wide variety of settings, including—

- Your personal residence
- An adult day care center
- An assisted living facility
- A nursing home

In fact, according to the United States Department of Health and Human Services (HHS), as of 2017, over 82% of all LTC services are provided in a home-like setting.

I always say there are two kinds of people when it comes to LTC planning—those that have experienced a close friend or family member who has required an extended need for LTC services, and those who haven't. The former, those who *have* experienced this, are quick to want to have a discussion about what they can do to avoid having a similar fate deplete their assets. Those who haven't are certain they'll never need such care, usually citing one of the following two reasons:

1. Neither of my parents required a nursing home, or

2. My kids will take care of me.

Let's take a moment to consider the likelihood of each of these scenarios.

Who Needs It?

It's worth noting that the HHS estimates that over 70% of all people over age 65 will need LTC at some point in their lifetime. So if practically no one

---

7   "Cost of Care Survey," Genworth, 2 June 2022, https://www.genworth.com/aging-and-you/finances /cost-of-care.html.

believes they'll ever need such care yet some 70% actually do, it's safe to say a lot of people are wrong about that. Just look around at the number of care facilities springing up on every corner. Add to this the cost of such care, and you can see why we believe it to be such an important issue to plan for:

- $20,280: Median annual cost for adult day care (five days per week), 2021

- $54,000: Median annual cost for an assisted-living facility, 2021

- $61,776: Median annual cost for a home health aide, 2021 (44 hours/week; 52 weeks/year)

- $108,405: Median annual nursing home cost, private room, 2021

- $141,444: Estimated median annual nursing home cost, private room, 2030 (assuming 3% inflation rate)

- $255,463: Estimated median annual nursing home cost, private room, 2050 (assuming 3% inflation rate)[7]

Relying on Family

The idea that your kids will take care of you sounds great to most people with children, until they really think it through. Although your kids may be more than willing to help you, they may or may not be qualified to do so. At some point, a level of professional expertise is required. And short of the need for such expertise, most people I've worked with simply don't want to be a burden to their loved ones, much less requiring them to help bathe, toilet, and feed them. Even if you can get comfortable with providing such care, relocation, home remodeling for physical accommodations, or professional sacrifices may also be necessary for the caregiver. As you can see, despite the best of intentions, relying on family is much more involved than it appears on the surface.

In the end, my goal in helping you plan for these types of contingencies is not unlike most anything else I do: I am here to educate you about the issue, educate you about the best available options pertaining to that issue, and then you get to decide.

In my opinion, there are few right answers to questions like this, since no one knows what the future holds and everyone's situation is unique. Rather, the most important thing is to be sure you make a well-informed decision, regardless of what that decision is. As I've said before, a well-informed individual tends to make good decisions. The main problem is that most people have not been well informed. That's the advisor's job.

Most Common Ways to Pay For Long-Term Care

Generally speaking, the most popular options for addressing the cost of LTC are:

- Pay out of pocket
- Rely on government programs such as Medicare or Medicaid
- Buy traditional long-term care insurance
- Utilize asset-based or hybrid LTC insurance strategies
- Rely on adult children/family

Let's take a brief look into each of these options, in order to help you better understand them.

Paying Out of Pocket

If you have the wherewithal to pay the potential cost of LTC indefinitely, this may be your best option, as it certainly provides the greatest level of freedom to choose exactly where, how, and by whom your care will be delivered. And although paying out of pocket may sound pretty self-explanatory, there are some important issues to consider:

- Depending on the length of stay and type of care required, the cost can be staggering, and this approach is definitely the most expensive. (I can't begin to count the number of stories I've heard from people whose parents have spent years in a nursing home, depleting much, if not all, of their entire estate.)

- Even if you do have the funds to do so, spending a tremendous sum on LTC services means you'll have less to spend elsewhere or to pass on to your beneficiaries. This is typically not Plan A.

- Probably the most important consideration for paying LTC expenses out of pocket relates to couples. Should one spouse's/partner's need for LTC significantly deplete the couple's savings, the other person may face financial difficulty over the remainder of their lifetime as a result.

Once last note about a less well-known approach to self-funding the cost of potential LTC services is the use of a home equity conversion mortgage (HECM), otherwise known as a reverse mortgage. HECMs are another topic that is beyond the scope of this book but one that's well worth becoming educated about. Suffice it to say, HECMs are probably as poorly understood as annuities, if not more so. For the right person in the right situation, however, a HECM can be an extremely prudent and effective way of addressing a variety of issues, from funding LTC costs, to enhancing your monthly tax-free income, to maximizing the financial legacy you leave to your heirs. This is compounded by the fact that home equity tends to represent one of the largest assets for most retirees, and current interest rates make HECMs an extremely powerful strategy for accessing housing wealth on a tax-free basis, without relinquishing ownership of your home.

As is the case with many missed opportunities, ignorance is often to blame. That's definitively the case with HECMs. And that's why I believe it is important for retirees to at least understand the fundamentals of what they are and how they work.

Relying on Programs Such as Medicare, Medicaid

Contrary to popular belief, Medicare is not a payment solution for LTC, as it provides only limited coverage for such services. Medicare is designed to get you better; that is, rehabilitation. It is not designed for illnesses such as Parkinson's, Alzheimer's, stroke, or chronic arthritis. Therefore, there are significant limitations to Medicare benefits related to the provision of LTC services. For example, Medicare:

- Pays costs only after a three-day hospitalization
- Pays full cost of skilled nursing care for only 20 days
- Pays only partial cost from day 21 to day 100
- Pays nothing after 100 days
- Does not pay for personal or custodial care
- Home health benefits are very limited

Medicaid, on the other hand, will cover the cost of LTC services in some circumstances, but it isn't something you would generally aspire to. After all, by definition, qualifying for Medicaid essentially means you're broke. Moreover, even if you do qualify, you're subject to the following terms—

- Nursing home only; no home care or assisted living facilities are covered
- Limited to a Medicaid-licensed facility
- Limited to a semiprivate room only; usually two residents per room

- Limited to beds specifically designated "Medicaid use" in the aforementioned Medicaid-licensed facility

So even if you do qualify for Medicaid, your facility care options will be severely limited. That brings us to yet another piece of the holistic retirement income planning puzzle—Medicaid planning.

Medicaid planning is the process of *legally* distributing or protecting certain assets in advance, or concurrent with, the need for LTC services, such that you might qualify for Medicaid without having actually spent or depleted all your assets.

This is a more specialized area of planning than is appropriate for the purposes of this book, but there are various strategies you can utilize to accomplish this objective. These strategies vary widely by state, by the amount and type of assets you have, and by your health status and care needs at the time you initiate the planning. We get many panicked calls from family members of people who have failed to do the proper planning and are now facing an imminent long-term care issue. Although by this time their options may be much more limited, they are nonetheless greatly relieved to learn they aren't nonexistent. There are always things that can be done to help protect one's assets, even after a loved one has entered a nursing facility.

There is also a separate Veterans Administration home care/assisted living benefit available to qualifying veterans, spouses, and widows, which has its own application and qualifying process separate from that of Medicaid, although that, too, is beyond the scope of this book. But if you're a veteran, spouse, or widow, it's worth noting you may be eligible.

Traditional Long-Term Care Insurance

The concept of insuring against catastrophic LTC costs isn't unlike any other risk you might choose to insure against; you're paying someone else to assume the risk. When it comes to LTC, there are several different methods of doing so, but like any insurance, it all comes down to the concept of transferring the risk to a third party.

One of the biggest advantages of insuring against the risk of LTC costs is your ability to remain in control of where, how, and by whom your care will be provided. The downside, as with any insurance policy, is the related cost. There is always a cost when transferring risk.

Much like homeowner's or automobile owner's insurance, traditional LTC insurance involves paying premiums for a specified period of time, or for life. If you end up needing to make a large claim, it ends up being a good investment of your dollars. But if you never have to make a claim, you're still out of pocket for the cost of the insurance premiums. For these reasons, and due to the fact that LTC premiums have skyrocketed over the past decade, I am no longer a big fan of traditional LTC insurance.

Back in the late nineties and early 2000s, the cost of these policies was palatable and well worthwhile compared to the potential cost of the risk that was being insured. And even today, if you knew for sure you'd need LTC, the savings would outweigh the cost. However, due to the dramatic increase in the frequency and cost of LTC insurance claims, the number of companies offering this type of coverage has plummeted, while premiums for these traditional policies have soared. As a result, many people who have had these policies for years are now faced with the difficult decision of whether to continue to pay the ever-increasing premiums, reduce their underlying coverage, or drop their policy altogether, essentially forfeiting the premiums they've paid up until now.

Asset-Based LTC Insurance Strategies: A Hybrid Approach

Because of the aforementioned trends, I tend to prefer utilizing a hybrid insurance approach for those who wish to hedge their exposure to LTC expense risk. These strategies combine a life insurance or annuity "chassis" with long-term-care insurance benefits. Hybrid LTC policies come in a tremendous variety of shapes and sizes with many different available options—another subject I can't sufficiently cover here. Instead, I'll simply touch on the highlights to give you a general understanding of the basic concept.

Although this hybrid approach to LTC insurance usually requires the payment of either a significant lump sum premium up front and/or annual premiums over a specified period of time, it typically eliminates the "use it or lose it" dilemma in that your family retains a substantial benefit even if you don't end up requiring LTC services. Most importantly to me, many of these policies lock in your pricing at the time you invoke the policy so you don't need to worry about the cost going up in the future.

For these and other reasons, a few years back my wife and I chose to go this route for our own situation. What's more, I was able to fund our policy with a portion of my traditional IRA funds from an old 401(k). In our case, the policy provides unlimited lifetime benefits for long-term care subject to a monthly maximum, should either of us ever need it. We experience a great deal of peace knowing that if either of us were to ever need LTC services, it won't derail our ability to achieve our long-term retirement and legacy goals, and we won't be a burden to our children.

Although this particular approach made sense for me at the time and I am pleased in having addressed the risk, I'll reiterate that there are no universally right answers to this or any other financial planning issue. In the end, like anything else, the key is to identify the risks to your unique long-term goals and objectives, understand the various options, and make an informed decision.

Friends and Family

I really can't add much to what I've already shared about this option. Most people who reference this as their plan have given little thought to what it would actually look like. In addition to the fact that no one

I've ever met wants to be a burden to their family, few family members actually have the wherewithal to provide a high level of nursing care or the flexibility in their schedule to become a full-time caregiver. So the thought of family is nice, but in my opinion it is limited to a very basic, minimal level of care at best.

ADDRESSING OTHER WHAT-IF SCENARIOS

Other important What-Ifs you should consider when assembling your lifetime retirement income plan can be found on the following Comprehensive Planning Checklist. The Comprehensive Planning Checklist is a great place to start when evaluating your own needs and priorities. We review this checklist annually with every one of our full-service clients. The goal is simply to ensure you clearly understand each of the underlying items such that you can determine which ones matter most to you, and then prioritize when you will address each one.

Comprehensive Planning Checklist

Asset & Investment Planning

- ❏ Balance Sheet
- ❏ Income/Cash Flow
- ❏ Portfolio Analysis/Design

Insurance & Risk Management

- ❏ Life
- ❏ Health/Medicare
- ❏ Disability
- ❏ Home Health, Assisted Living, Long-Term Care
- ❏ Identity Theft Protection
- ❏ Property & Casualty Umbrella

(continued)

Estate & Legal

- ❏ Wills
- ❏ Trusts
- ❏ Powers of Attorney
- ❏ Asset Titling, Entity Structure
- ❏ Medicaid Planning
- ❏ Beneficiary Review
- ❏ Beneficiary Liquidity Plan
- ❏ Legal Expenses
- ❏ Family Estate Organizer

Other Specific Objectives

- ❏ Retirement Planning
- ❏ Survivorship/Legacy Planning
- ❏ Social Security Planning
- ❏ Inheritance Planning
- ❏ Tax Planning
- ❏ Education Funding
- ❏ Debt Reduction
- ❏ Charitable Planning
- ❏ Income Supplementation with HECM

I often tell clients, "Once you hire us and tell us what's important to you, you are essentially giving us permission to 'politely pester' you until the each of the items you care about have been properly addressed." This checklist ensures nothing falls through the cracks that matters to you. Following is a brief overview of some of the most common items.

Estate Planning

I am not an attorney and I don't play one on TV. But I do a lot of estate planning and work closely with our clients' attorneys or refer them to someone we trust, to ensure everything is executed correctly and aligns with their stated objectives. Over the years, we've encountered many people whose estate planning has been completely overlooked or simply fallen through the cracks.

At the very least, I believe everyone should have a will, a general (or financial) power of attorney, a health care power of attorney, a living will, and possibly a trust, depending on their particular situation. If you don't have at least the first three items, or they aren't up to date, that's usually one of the first things we tackle right after we finalize your retirement income plan.

But like most things in life, having them done and having them done correctly are two completely different things. It's critical that they are well designed and coordinated correctly with all your other planning, to achieve everything you desire when and if they're ever needed. For example, we've seen a significant number of people walk through our door with beautifully written trusts but who haven't updated the titling or beneficiary designations of their assets to properly utilize them. In such a case, those wonderful trust documents are completely useless and will accomplish nothing for which they were originally intended. That's because they have no "quarterback"—a comprehensive financial planner—so none of their planning is coordinated, leaving items to fall through the cracks.

Another common problem we encounter is people who had their documents created back when the federal estate tax exemption was much lower than it is today. Many people created what's known as an A/B Trust, which was appropriate and necessary for a much broader group of people than it is today, given the changes that have occurred at the federal level and in most states. Many of these people also had young children at the time, who are now adults. Depending on the details of their current situation, it's extremely likely they either need to update their trust documents or, in many cases, eliminate them altogether. Failure to do so may lead to serious unintended consequences. One way or another, there is a need to take action or their intended desires will not be met.

The bottom line is that estate planning is a critical component of an effective and comprehensive retirement income plan and must be well coordinated with your investment, income, tax, health care, and survivorship planning, just to name a few.

Life Insurance

Do you have a need for life insurance once you retire? Most workers purchase life insurance to protect their families against the possibility of lost income due to the premature death of the worker. Retirement begs the question of whether life insurance is still needed. For many of you, the answer is a simple no. For others, life insurance planning may take on a whole new purpose, including survivorship planning, estate planning, legacy panning, tax planning, pension maximization, debt retirement, or health care funding, just to name a few.

If so, how much do you need? And what kind do you need? Term insurance, which may have been sufficient for income replacement, will likely not fill the bill for any of these long-term goals. Should it be written on one or the other spouse's life or both? And if life insurance is no longer needed to address the traditional risk of loss of income, can any current policies be repurposed to meet other needs, like the LTC examples I provided earlier? Can premiums be discontinued to free up cash flow? These are just a few of the questions that will help you determine if there is a need for life insurance within your current financial plan as you transition into your retirement years.

Medicare Planning

Upon turning age 65, you'll likely become eligible for Medicare. There are, of course, exceptions. Do you qualify based on your employment history? Are you still working and eligible for an employer-sponsored plan? What about your spouse? Does your employer require you to sign up for Medicare immediately upon turning age 65? Does your employer sponsor a health-care plan for retirees? These are but a few of the questions that need to be answered as you turn 65. Waiting longer to find out the answers could be costly, as there are significant financial penalties for not transitioning to Medicare in a timely fashion.

Once you determine it is time to transition to a Medicare plan, what's the best plan for your particular needs? How do your current health, health care providers, and any prescription medications affect that decision? Are you better off with a Medicare supplement or an Advantage plan (and what's the difference?) And what are the most significant determining factors regarding your choice? How will your retirement income affect your Medicare premiums?

A truly holistic retirement income plan must take all these issues into consideration. And a truly comprehensive retirement specialist should have all the answers, which need to be factored into your planning.

Identity Theft

Identity theft is a growing concern for everyone. According to the FBI, identity theft is one of the fastest-growing types of crime in the United States. And once you're retired, you have a target on your back—because you have spent a lifetime accumulating assets. That makes you a more tempting mark for bad actors than younger options who are still working to accumulate.

The resourcefulness of identity thieves is also quite astounding. I've heard some remarkable examples of how such criminals operate. From phishing scams to medical fraud, from gas station debit card skimmers to falsified tax returns, and from unemployment benefits fraud to home equity theft, it never ceases to amaze me how creative those in the business of identity theft can be. New scams seem to be turning up almost daily.

It doesn't matter how great your retirement income plan is if someone steals all your money. For this reason, we believe that everyone—especially those who have just "graduated to the head of the class" when it comes to being a target for identity theft via retirement—should have a robust identity theft protection plan in place.

By robust, I mean one that provides a wide breadth of around-the-clock monitoring services, including scouring the internet, the dark web, credit agencies, and public records for any use of your personal information. My preference is for a service that also provides identity theft mitigation and restoration services for you, not just "guidance." Anyone who's been a victim of identity theft will tell you that the process of identity restoration is incredibly tedious and time consuming. I'd much prefer someone else handle as much of the workload as possible, should that ever be required.

Personal Liability Umbrella Coverage

I've always had personal umbrella liability coverage to extend my personal liability protection over and above that which is provided by my auto and homeowners insurance. I was motivated to do this many years ago after being told a story about someone's child who had been responsible for a traffic accident that involved 10 cars! That's a lot of potential liability! Having two kids of my own, that was all it took for me to rethink my liability coverages.

Just as with identity theft, it's all the more important for those of you who have spent a lifetime accumulating assets and now have much more to lose. If you're like me, an Amazon delivery person visits my house multiple time each week to deliver something to my doorstep. You may also have landscapers, exterminators, window washers, or any variety of other service providers visiting your home—not to mention family, friends, and acquaintances. Unfortunately, in this day and age, we live in a very litigious society. Gone are the days of working things out with a handshake and an apology. It seems everyone is looking for a free lunch. The good news is that this type of coverage is quite inexpensive.

These are just a few of the most common items I see being neglected on a regular basis, which is reflective of a lack of truly holistic retirement planning. And as you can see from the checklist, there are many others to consider. Which items are most important to you and the time line in which you choose to address them is ultimately up to you, but having a comprehensive list helps ensure nothing falls through the cracks, which can lead to significant gaps in your planning and unanticipated risk exposure. The number one priority at this point in your life is protecting what you've accumulated so you can enjoy it or pass it on to the next generation.

FINAL EXPENSES

Many people have either completely planned and prepaid for their financial expenses, or they've given it little to no thought at all. Regardless of where you are on that spectrum, I strongly suggest you give thought to how your final expenses will be paid.

When the last surviving spouse passes, it usually takes weeks, if not months, for the death certificate to be issued and various account beneficiaries to actually have access to their funds. In the meantime, those providing products and services related to final expenses will need to get paid.

There are a variety of ways to deal with this issue, from keeping a stash of physical cash to the creation of a final expense trust. The bottom line is to give it some thought and make sure your beneficiaries have access to sufficient liquidity to handle the situation.

Taking Action

Before moving on to the next chapter, use the QR code (page 9) to access the chapter 15 resources, then:

1. Review the **Comprehensive Planning Checklist** (page 253) to determine which items you have completed, which are not up to date, and which ones you've overlooked completely.

   a. If you are unsure about a topic, make a point to look into it. Ask your advisor to educate you about it. If they are truly a retirement specialist, it should not be a problem for them to do this on the fly.

2. Make a note beside each item describing where things stand.

3. Indicate the level of importance to you for each of the items on the checklist (e.g., 10 is highest importance and 1 is lowest. Or just use high, medium, low.)

4. Now, considering the level of completion (or lack thereof) and level of importance to you, highlight the top three items that currently need your attention.

5. Give those items your attention now—set a deadline for having completed each. Repeat this process once you have completed those top three items, until you have the entire checklist completed.

6. If an item is of little or no importance to you, simply note it and move on.

7. Pat yourself on the back and relax. You're on your way!

CHAPTER 16

FINDING THE RIGHT ADVISOR

Behind every successful person there is
a coach who believed in them and helped them
realize their true potential.

—JOHN WOODEN

Your relationship with your retirement advisor should mirror that of a coach and athlete. This time in your life, retirement, is much like that of the final, decisive moments of a big game. Only you can actually make the play to win the game. But it likely won't happen without a good coach on the sidelines, whose job it is to coordinate all the right pieces in advance—to prepare, to understand the situation, and to make the right calls.

As I explain to all our clients, we have strong opinions based on all our years of experience, but we don't get a vote. It's your money, so you are the only one who gets a vote. As I see it, my job is to ensure you're well-informed relative to the best possible options, given your unique situation, so you're empowered to make the best possible decisions.

As you approach retirement, once you're within about five years of taking the plunge and especially if you're already retired, not having a financial advisor who truly specializes in retirement services becomes exponentially more costly. You only get one chance to get it right. I simply can't overstate the importance of having the right coach. So in this chapter I'm going to provide an overview of how to sort through the thousands of advisors competing for your attention to find the ones that will best help ensure your retirement future.

WHAT TO LOOK FOR

Research says the top three characteristics people look for in a retirement advisor are honesty and trustworthiness, expertise, and experience. That list certainly makes sense. These traits are essential when it comes to working with someone you'll be entrusting your life savings with for the next 20 to 30 years. This will be someone who will guide you through the ever-changing world of things like pensions and Social Security planning, investment planning, tax planning, insurance, health care, and estate planning.

But from my perspective, this is actually more the bare minimum than it is the holy grail of finding the right advisor. Many advisors are trustworthy and experienced, just as there are many who are not. But where the rubber really meets the road is finding an advisor who is all those things as well as being a specialist at what you need, which is truly comprehensive retirement services.

By now you should understand that I have strong convictions about what works well and what doesn't. So strong, in fact, that I've built my entire practice around those beliefs. So as I share what I believe to be the keys to finding the best retirement advisor, it should come as no surprise that I'll largely be describing how we do things within my own practice. Nevertheless, regardless of who you decide to work with, I believe the following four keys will serve you well in your endeavor to establish a long-term relationship with someone who will serve as your financial coach throughout the rest of your lifetime.

The 4 Keys

The right retirement advisor should be:

- **Independent**
  - Not affiliated with a money manager, broker-dealer, bank, credit union, insurance company, mutual fund company, etc.
  - Accredited fiduciaries

- **Focused**
  - Do only one thing and do it very well: Retirement
  - Creation of predictable, increasing, tax-efficient, lifetime income
  - Asset preservation
  - Estate maximization

- **Comprehensive**
  - Investment planning
  - Income planning
  - Tax planning
  - Social security and pension planning
  - Medicare planning
  - Long-term health care planning
  - Survivorship planning
  - Estate planning

- **Excellent teachers**
  - The number one job of an advisor is to educate their clients
  - Well-informed clients make good decisions

Independent

Find an advisor who is truly independent.

What does it mean to be truly independent? A truly independent advisor is not affiliated with a money manager, a broker-dealer, a bank, a credit union, an insurance company, a mutual fund company, or any other financial, insurance, or banking institution. Over the years, I have found that the only way to ensure my ability to operate as a truly objective fiduciary is to have no affiliation with any such entities.

My experience has taught me that any such affiliation comes with an intrinsic conflict of interest. When I began my career in the financial services industry, I worked as an "independent advisor" affiliated with a large broker-dealer and RIA who was also affiliated with a large insurance company and mutual fund company. Every week, this organization sponsored lunch for all of its associate advisors, during which we were all educated about—you guessed it—the products and services of the affiliate companies. As you can imagine, this resulted in a far greater awareness and knowledge of the particular products and services offered by these organizations, which they obviously hoped their advisors would recommend.

A second major limitation that's imposed on advisors who are directly affiliated with a particular broker-dealer is which solutions have been approved by the firm's compliance department. Advisors who are affiliated with a particular broker-dealer are forbidden to offer solutions that aren't approved by their firm's compliance department. This may severely limit the ability for the advisor to act independently, based solely on his or her conviction regarding what's best for their client.

Another example of this type of conflict is evident whenever I review portfolios of a prospective client who is currently working with a large bank, insurance company, broker-dealer, or financial franchise. It's common for the lion's share of their mutual funds, annuities, life insurance, or other financial products to all be with one or a few affiliated companies.

As you can see, not being truly independent can lead to a variety of influences, including incentives, oversight, and organizational structures that make true fiduciary objectivity next to impossible to achieve. Over the years, I've learned the only way to avoid these conflicts of interest is to be truly independent.

Focused

It's been said that becoming an expert at any one thing takes some 10,000-plus hours of practice. That means practice in that one specific area, not just general practice. Being a true expert means having knowledge, experience, wherewithal, and capability in a specific area.

For example, when Tom Brady set out to become the greatest NFL quarterback of all time, he didn't spend an equal amount of time on blocking, tackling, receiving, and rushing. Instead, he focused on those specific skill sets unique to playing the position of quarterback, forgoing most everything else. Of course, he needed to have a certain amount of innate athletic ability to compete at an elite level, but he also had to learn by studying and practicing those specific skill sets over and over until they were literally ingrained into his muscle memory.

It's much the same with any pursuit, including retirement advising. A specialized focus is crucial to being the best. One of the biggest problems you'll encounter is that practically every advisor you meet is going to claim to be whatever it is you're looking for. So for the purposes of this chapter, I'm going to look past the obvious need for someone who's honest and trustworthy, which only you can discern, and focus on the objective, material differences I believe will help you cut through the sea of options to identify those advisors who can serve you best if you are retired or retiring soon.

The first unfortunate truth you need to understand is that most advisors don't specialize. Even if they *say* they do, most will work with anyone who has enough money. And the longer they've been in business, the higher their required minimum investment will likely be. The result is that most advisors become jacks of all trades. But you need to find someone who's truly *mastered retirement*. And since many advisors are either unaware of their lack of expertise in a particular area of focus (they don't know what they don't know) or simply won't acknowledge it, it's up to you to discern the truth.

I believe it's critical to find an advisor who is truly specialized in exactly what you're looking for. They should do one thing and one thing only. This is half the battle of becoming an expert. If they do only one thing, over time there's a much greater likelihood that they will do that one thing *really well*. Whether an advisor is truly specialized should be obvious. If you have to ask, the answer is probably no. Most advisors who are truly specialized waste no time in communicating that vital message through marketing, advertising, and signage. Those who don't are probably trying to appeal to anyone with money, which is exactly what you don't want. Our focus, for example, is extremely narrow, as evidenced by the following client profile, which we share with every prospective new client. After all, it's mutually beneficial that they know what we do best.

Retirement Is Not an Event; It Is a Journey

We work exclusively with people who:

- Are retired or within 5–10 years of retirement
- Have $500,000 or more to invest
- Want predictable, increasing, tax-efficient lifetime income
- Don't want to micromanage their own finances and investments
- Are serious about eliminating the financial uncertainty of retirement (safety versus unnecessary risk)
- Desire a long-term relationship

If you're unsure about an advisor's commitment to retirement services as one unique specialty, you can certainly ask. However, most advisors are going to tell you what they think you want to hear. One pointed question you could ask is, "What does your perfect client look like?" Questions like this should be quickly and easily answerable for an advisor who specializes in retirement services. You might get answers like, "We want to help everyone we can, so we don't limit who we work with;" or, "We have clients from all walks of life;" or, "Our clients just need to have $500,000 in investable assets." Although that sounds nice and altruistic, it really means they'll work with anyone who has money and they'll try to be whatever that person needs, but they *haven't* developed an expertise. That's not what you need. You need an expert.

The previous client profile is something we show every prospective client in our very first meeting. We go through this point by point. They don't have to wonder who we are or guess what we do best. Even if we are an excellent "round hole" and our prospective client is a wonderful "square peg," that doesn't make us a good fit for one another. We want to only work with those people for whom we know we can provide the highest level of value and results. Likewise, you should only want to work with someone who has dedicated their practice to solving the types of problems that you will face throughout your retirement. Anything else and you're taking an unnecessary gamble with your future.

Comprehensive

Another nonnegotiable in your search for the right advisor should be their truly comprehensive approach to retirement services.

> **"The whole is greater than the sum of its parts."**
> —ARISTOTLE

This quote emphasizes the importance of taking a holistic approach to planning, as it suggests that the overall outcome or effectiveness of a plan is not simply the sum of its individual components. Instead, it highlights the idea that a comprehensive approach, taking into account all the inter-related parts and how they work together, can create a greater impact than a piecemeal or isolated plan.

In biology, *holism* refers to the idea that living organisms are more than just the sum of their parts and that their interactions and relationships with their environment and other organisms are critical to their survival and well-being. That's how it is with retirement planning. Just like a healthy living organism, a truly efficient holistic retirement plan requires that each part functions in synchronicity with all the others. Most people erroneously focus far too much on the investment piece of the puzzle, while neglecting most everything else.

There are two problems with this approach. The first is, most do the investing wrong. That's a particularly big problem if it's the only thing you're focused on. But the bigger problem, in my opinion, is that there's far more to retirement planning than investing. And contrary to popular opinion, every part is equally important in determining the outcome. Having a good money manager or attorney or accountant alone won't cut it. You may survive and you may not run out of money (or you may), but in order to make the most of all the resources you've worked your entire life accumulating, each part of the whole must be coordinated with all of the others.

Most people have accumulated a variety of financial, insurance, tax, and legal products and services throughout their lifetimes but have never had everything orchestrated according to a master plan, like the truly wealthy do. Most people's attorneys have never spoken to their investment advisors, and their insurance agents have never spoken to their accountants.

You might be able to get away with this during the accumulation and growth years, so long as you make it out of them alive, but once you reach the preservation and distribution years of retirement, there are no second chances. Coordination of services is no longer optional for those who wish to truly maximize their resources and minimize their exposure to risk. This was the driving force behind our own business model—making everything available under one roof, with us serving as the coaches.

The Real Deal: Your Retirement Blueprint

Making everything available under one roof doesn't mean the advisor needs to do it all themselves. Rather, like a general contractor who's building a house, the only thing that matters is that each task is completed with excellence, regardless of whether it's done in-house or by a third party with whom you have the utmost confidence and a strong working relationship. Either way, all the work is being done well and is coordinated via the master blueprint. Your advisor's primary job is to create that master blueprint and coordinate and oversee all the work.

Now more than ever in your life, you need everything coordinated. For most people, you have no more earned income and no more employee benefits—or at least you're transitioning away from having many of your benefits provided and coordinated through your employer. Time is no longer on your side from an investment perspective, and you're moving from acquiring and growing to protecting and distributing. You get no do-overs, which means the stakes are high.

To give you an idea of what I mean by truly comprehensive, look at the Comprehensive Planning Checklist, page 253. This is a fairly comprehensive list of everything we cover with every full-service client. Some of these items are handled by third parties, but every one is coordinated within the master plan.

The Comprehensive Planning Checklist is a longer-term document that helps you keep track of your progress over time to ensure all the most important issues are addressed and nothing falls through the cracks. It's also a good way to help you prioritize your biggest concerns.

Anyone claiming they have the wherewithal to help you with a truly comprehensive service offering should have a tried-and-true process for managing that process over time. Without such a process, good luck getting everything done, much less in an orderly manner.

Following is a diagram of our process. It is designed to ensure the development of the initial retirement blueprint is completed in a timely and orderly fashion. Although the initial stages of planning are typically executed within the first eight to 10 weeks, truly comprehensive planning is an ongoing process that should occur continuously over time at whatever pace is most comfortable to you, the client.

Our Process

1. Initial Meeting
2. Data Collection
3. Plan Delivery
4. Implementation
5. Initial Review
6. Annual Comprehensive Reviews and Updates
   a. Year-Round Service and Support

Another clue to know if you're dealing with someone who's truly competent at comprehensive planning is what I call "the little things." For example, we provide every full-service client with a binder that includes 15 different sections containing all your planning documents and balance sheet (updated annually) plus all your most important personal documents including bank accounts, retirement accounts, pension and Social Security statements, insurance statements, legal documents, debt statements, tax returns, medical information, and so on.

The binder is helpful not only for keeping things organized during your lifetime, but it also becomes invaluable when the time comes for a surviving spouse (who's not the household CFO), person with power of attorney, or executor to step in and handle your affairs. The point here is that a truly comprehensive advisor will have systems and processes in place to facilitate the types of planning they do. It won't be left up to you, your surviving spouse, or your beneficiaries.

Excellent Teachers

The last of the four most important factors when it comes to finding a great advisor is that they be a great teacher. In my opinion, this is the single most important job of a great advisor. It doesn't matter how good my ideas are if I can't clearly explain them to you so that you truly understand them and can make an informed decision based on your unique personal goals and objectives. A great retirement advisor needs to be able to break everything down into clear, understandable, actionable concepts so that you are empowered to make well-educated decisions. In fact, this is the entire reason I'm writing this book.

I love to teach. My two favorite activities are sitting one-on-one with clients educating them on the concepts that I believe will ensure their retirement success, and teaching classes to empower various groups of people with that same information. But I can only reach so many people with that approach. So it's been my desire for many years to take all the information I love to teach and that I think is so critical for people to understand, and put it into a book that anyone can read and benefit from, whether or not they become a client of ours.

I believe well-informed clients generally make better decisions and have greater peace of mind regarding those decisions than those who are less well informed—who lack that all-important expertise we talked about in an earlier chapter. I also believe it's the advisor's job to do the educating. I often have clients who feel they don't have a strong financial acumen tell me that they've never understood certain financial concepts and probably never will. Some will go so far as to say, "We completely trust you; just tell us what to do." As much as I appreciate someone trusting me, I don't believe anyone should ever make a significant decision without fully comprehending what it is they're doing.

Instead, what we find is that as we go through the process and educate them, most people are pleasantly surprised that they do understand the concepts and feel empowered to make informed decisions. Their ignorance wasn't due to a lack of mental capacity but to a lack of having things explained clearly.

None of this is rocket science. It's just a matter of having someone explain things in a way that you can understand. Everyone is an expert at something. This just happens to be my thing. Unfortunately, it's my experience that the financial industry, among others, tends to unnecessarily complicate matters.

The ability to teach is equally important, if not more so, with individuals who do have a strong financial acumen but who've spent their lives learning what the mainstream financial media has been teaching them. We need to be equally adept at helping them unlearn many of the concepts and principles that they've committed to during their working years, since these very ideas often prove to be the downfall of many retirees.

Whether or not you've found an advisor who's a great teacher should be clear to you by the end of your first meeting. If you come out of the first or second meeting with a prospective advisor and you haven't learned anything or you're not completely sure how they're different from every other advisor, they're probably not the right one for you. And I don't mean just learning things about them as an advisor, but learning things about your particular situation and what you are going to need to know to make good decisions down the road. This should be clear in your very first meeting with them.

AVOID LITMUS TESTS

The other side of the coin of what to look for in an advisor is what *not* to look for. The desire for an advisor to oversimplify the decision-making process creates what I refer to as a tendency toward "litmus tests."

Litmus tests, determining whether a substance is an acid or base, are nice. They're easy. The paper either turns blue or it doesn't. Very little thinking is required. Certainly no discernment.

The only problem with litmus tests when it comes to finding the right advisor is that there is no test paper to return a certain result. It doesn't exist. Nonetheless, there are people who claim it does. They'll tell you that this, that, or the other thing should be all you need to know when it comes to choosing an advisor. This is reminiscent of my example of the 99-cent hamburger in chapter 2, where price mattered more than nutritional value. If you buy into the idea that price is all that matters and therefore all you need to know, they get your business. Likewise, if you believe a certain endorsement, business model, or designation is all that matters when it comes time to choose a retirement advisor, you're likely to be left with a bad taste in your mouth (pun intended).

A great example of this is the CPA designation when it comes to accounting. CPA stands for Certified Public Accountant. It sounds very impressive, and some (CPAs) would suggest you should only work with someone who's a CPA. But it's nothing more than a designation. And most designations are, at their core, for marketing purposes. Behind most designations are organizations, typically composed of professionals from that particular industry, that exist for the sole purpose of creating and maintaining the particular designation.

That doesn't mean designations are meaningless. They can be helpful, for sure. But they are no litmus test. They can't separate the good CPAs from the bad ones. I know many CPAs whose services and advice I would never rely on. And I know others who are extremely competent and trustworthy. Just as I know many excellent tax preparers who don't hold the CPA designation. When it comes to the idea of a litmus test of any kind—using one single variable to judge the overall value of something in its entirety—it simply doesn't exist.

The following are some examples of one-dimensional litmus test–like claims for finding the right financial advisor:

- Endorsements (The advisor was endorsed by an important entity, so they must be good.)
- Licenses (They have such-and-such license, which proves they're trustworthy experts.)
- Certain college degrees (They attended a good college.)
- Specific credentials (The more letters the better, right?)
- A certain number of years of experience (They've been around so long they must know everything; if they were lousy, they would be out of business.)
- A particular business model (They claim their approach ensures your best interests are served.)
- A particular compensation model (They charge fees versus commissions.)
- A particular company or group affiliation (All ACME advisors are great!)

This is obviously not an exhaustive list, but hopefully you get the idea. None of these claims are magic stamps of approval. They prove neither trustworthiness nor expertise. They are all helpful pieces of information when it comes to evaluating your options, but it's up to you to discern the good from the bad and to know what to look for when you seek out a trustworthy and capable retirement advisor.

STOP BEING CODEPENDENT

Another issue we need to address in your search for the right advisor is likely your biggest obstacle—you.

Consider this common scenario:

Someone schedules an initial appointment to either come into our office, or, if they live out of town, have a virtual meeting. (Virtual meetings occur rather frequently in our practice, since we serve clients throughout the United States.) They may have been referred by a friend or family member, or maybe they saw or heard one of our teachings on any number of topics related to retirement, or read one of my books. Either way, they want to learn more about us.

The vast majority of the time, these people already have a financial advisor. About 50% of the time they're coming to us because they're ready for a change. They need something different, and they know it. They know they need to make a change because they're entering into a new phase of life and they understand the need for someone who specializes in their stage of life.

But the other 50% of the time, that's not the case. In these circumstances, they proceed to make sure we know they already have a great advisor who they're really happy with and that they're not looking to make a change. Maybe they just have a question or two about their situation or they want to learn something outside their current advisor's purview.

As I previously mentioned, one of the first questions I usually ask these people is, "If you already have a great advisor and you're not looking to make a change, why are you here?" Almost without exception, the answer is, "My advisor doesn't do [fill in the blank]." Maybe they don't do Social Security planning, or Medicare planning, or tax planning, or estate planning, or charitable planning, or whatever it is the clients think they need that their advisor doesn't provide.

This is when I typically point out the obvious. If their advisor doesn't do those types of things, then they clearly are not a retirement specialist, because you can't be a retirement specialist and not be an expert in those arenas that are most important to retirees. Right? So perhaps it is time for a new advisor . . . ?

The person's next statement undoubtedly leads us directly to one of the two biggest obstacles to finding the right advisor. It usually sounds something like this: "They've been my advisor for years. They've done a really good job and they're really nice. I could never leave them. It would be too hard."

This is called codependence. The expensive kind! Some people just aren't willing to do what they need to do because it's too uncomfortable. They are stuck and will likely stay stuck because doing nothing is the easiest thing to do—certainly easier than feeling they're disappointing someone who has been with them for many years, even if that advisor can't meet their current needs.

I can't help you get over your codependency. I am not a therapist or life coach. (That's my wife, Diane. Perhaps she can help you.) But I *can* provide some reminders that will hopefully help you whenever you feel stuck for all the wrong reasons, whether it's your financial advisor or something completely unrelated. Although these pertain to the issue of financial advice, they can be applied to most any similar professional situation.

- If your advisor did such a great job for you during your working years, then by definition, they can't be a specialist who focuses solely on retirement, and no one can be great at everything. The very fact that they've helped you for all these years, during your accumulation phase, is how you know it's time to move on. And that's okay.

- If your advisor truly wants what's in your best interest, they should be happy for you to work with a specialist who focuses on your specific phase of life. They may be sad to see you leave, but they should be happy to see you getting what you need. If they're not, then maybe your best interest is not their top priority.

- Remember, they've provided you a professional service throughout the course of your relationship. They've gotten paid. They weren't doing the work for free. Hopefully, it's been mutually beneficial, but that doesn't mean it has to be forever.

- The next person who *is* in their wheelhouse will walk through their door. Trust that someone else will be able to benefit from their expertise, even as you move on.

GET OUT OF YOUR OWN WAY

I am reminded of a new client we engaged many years ago from New York. She was an accountant and her husband was an IT executive. They were savvy enough to realize they needed a true retirement specialist and that their current advisor wasn't that. So we embarked on the planning process journey together.

Despite all we accomplished, for the first six months or so of our relationship, she constantly reminded me of all the little things her previous advisor had done that she liked so much, how they had developed such a good friendship, how hard it had been to leave him, how he had asked her to reconsider, and how bad she felt about it. Then one day, about eight months into our relationship, she found out from a friend that he had sold his practice and retired. Suddenly it all became clear to her. Every account he had on his books meant a higher sale price for his practice. To her astonishment, his cajoling was for ulterior motives all along. He was already planning to retire and had never told her. He just needed her to stay around so he would get a higher sale price. Needless to say, she quickly stopped feeling so guilty.

What am I trying to say? The first obstacle to overcome when you're looking for the right advisor is *you*. *You* must first decide what you need. You owe it to yourself to do what's best for you, your family, and your loved ones. So my advice is to decide before you start your search. Decide what you need now, for this time in your life. Write it down. Then make a commitment to yourself that when you find what you need, you'll make the change.

Until you can make that commitment, don't begin your search. Don't waste your time. Or theirs. Just stay where you are. It's like seeing a doctor. There's a time for a pediatrician, a time for a general or family practitioner, and a time for a gerontologist. No one keeps their pediatrician throughout their whole lifetime. Instead, they say this is what I need now, and they move on. Their previous doctor likely loses no sleep over it because if they're really a specialist, the next person who needs exactly what they do best is going to walk through their door tomorrow.

BREAKING UP IS HARD TO DO

As you might imagine, we are often asked by new clients to coach people on how to "break up" with their current advisors. Our answer is always the same. It's as simple as explaining that you're in a different season of life now and your needs have changed. The relationship may have been great and you're very appreciative, but now it's time to move on to what you need during this phase of your life. It's really that simple.

This approach always seems to work well, especially if the other advisor is truly a good person who genuinely cares about you and has your best interests in mind. If, on the other hand, the advisor gets angry or resentful or suggests they can do everything your new advisor can do, then it should just make it that much easier for you to move on.

ADDITIONAL THOUGHTS ON CHOOSING AN ADVISOR

A couple of important but often overlooked additional thoughts for your advisor search. When meeting with a prospective advisor to "kick the tires," ask yourself:

- Did you genuinely enjoy your time with them?
- Did you enjoy visiting their office and their staff?
- Would you look forward to meeting with them again?

These are incredibly important questions to consider. I always tell all prospective clients that it's not enough for us to be good at what we do and for them to fit our profile of a good client. I want to be excited when I see their name on the schedule, and they should feel the same way. After all, we're going to have a long relationship. If that's not the case, maybe we're not the best fit for each other. If that's the reality of the situation, it's okay to walk out the door. Retirement is too long a journey to go it with someone you don't enjoy being with.

One Meeting Should Be All It Takes

I always tell prospective clients that by the time we finish our first two-hour meeting together, they should know if we are a good fit, and vice versa. We either really resonate with one another and want to work together or we don't. Either of those outcomes is fine, but it should be clear when you meet with an advisor for the first time.

When you finish that meeting, you should have a strong sense one way or another. And if you don't have a strong sense, then it's a no and you should keep looking. Whatever you do, don't overcomplicate the process by believing you need to meet with an advisor multiple times in order to decide if they are a good fit. You will know. And you need not meet with a certain number of advisors before making your decision. If the first one you meet resonates, great. Consider yourself fortunate. If not, keep looking until one does. Meeting with too many potential advisors can be equally confusing and needlessly delay your progress. (Unnecessarily drawing the process out can also be a subconscious way of avoiding or procrastinating the change you know you need to make.)

Don't Be Fooled: Bigger Isn't Always Better

Most, but not all, truly independent advisors tend to be smaller than many of their larger counterparts who are affiliated with banks, insurance companies, broker-dealers, and the like. This sometimes begs the question of whether or not larger organizations tend to have access to a greater amount of resources. The short answer to this is no. Today's modern technology enables even the smallest firms to have access to all the same resources as larger firms.

Figure 16.1: You're Not a Number

In fact, because many larger firms tend to have their own in-house resources, they're more likely to limit themselves to only those resources. Whereas smaller, independent firms who don't have as many in-house resources are more likely to avail themselves of a much wider variety of expertise, commensurate with each unique situation, on an as-needed basis.

A great example of this is a large investment firm that has its own in-house research and investment team. Let's call them ACME Capital. Their investment strategies will no doubt always be based on the limited expertise provided by their own team. On the other hand, a smaller firm without their own team can and will choose to investigate, evaluate, and utilize numerous investment strategies from around the globe, including ACME Capital, as needed. Not only are the economics of this approach advantageous, but a firm availing itself of a variety of the best ideas in which there is no conflict of interest means the best ideas always win, regardless of whose ideas they are.

Another thing I enjoy about smaller boutique firms when it comes to any service provider is that their smaller size tends to lend itself to much deeper client relationships. At least that's been my experience from both sides of the equation. One of the main benefits of our purposely smaller business model is the relationships that we develop with those we serve, since it's not a numbers game.

As you can see, it's important to have the right retirement advisor. Odds are it's not the same person who advised you all through your working years. And I get it. If you like your current advisor, it can be hard to let them go. However, some things are just too important to allow your emotions to dictate your decision-making.

When it comes to your retirement, you only get one chance. You shouldn't gamble with your retirement, because there are no do-overs. This is why cutting the proverbial cord and moving on may be vital. Start by meeting with a few prospective advisors and interviewing them while taking the four keys and other ideas you learned in this chapter into consideration.

Taking Action

Before moving on to the next chapter, use the QR code (page 9) to access the chapter 16 resources, then:

1. Take a hard look at your current situation. Is your current financial advisor the right person to guide you throughout your retirement years?

   a. Is it truly their expertise?

2. Look back at your **Retirement Readiness Questionnaire.** Do you like your numbers?

   a. If not, it's time to find a new advisor.

   b. If so, start looking for an actual retirement specialist using the criteria provided in this chapter.

3. Begin with the end in mind: Spend some time thinking about how you would define success with your new advisor two years from now:

   a. What would need to have happened?

   b. What are your top priorities for a successful relationship?

   c. What would give you the greatest peace of mind when it comes to your retirement?

   d. Use the retirement advisor evaluation form cheat sheet—accessible through the QR code—to help you in your search.

CONCLUSION

I hope the information contained in this book has helped you feel better equipped for your retirement—or at least better informed about how to better equip yourself when that day arrives. If it has already arrived, I hope it has provided a plumb line for assessing your readiness. You've been through a crash course in retirement income planning, which is the key to a financially secure retirement. Regardless of whether you have way more money than you'll ever need or you're just hoping you have enough to last a lifetime, you now have the tools to succeed. Remember, the more you have, the more you have to lose—whether it be to taxes, inflation, investment losses, extraordinary health care costs, theft, or legal liability.

Throughout this book, I revealed that most retirees, and their advisors, miss the mark because they treat retirement as an asset-based problem instead of a cash flow problem. That's why I developed and presented a detailed road map for creating stable, increasing, tax-efficient, lifetime income and for maximizing your residual estate value, whether for the eventual benefit of your heirs or just as a means to maintain and maximize your own options throughout your lifetime.

I demonstrated that the key to achieving success within this paradigm is to develop a specific, written, annualized retirement income plan that details exactly how much you'll need and where it will come from, for each and every year, for the rest of your life. There is no substitute for this kind of retirement income planning when it comes to your retirement income security.

I've also explained how, by utilizing the Income Stability Pyramid, you'll be able to identify and quantify your guaranteed, base-level income, your ISR, and your income gap—all of which are keys to building your retirement income plan. This will enable you to understand the difference between your personal "sleep number" and your current situation, which in turn will help you determine precisely how to fill your retirement income gap from year to year. In the end, receiving monthly, stable, increasing, tax-efficient, lifetime income should be as automatic as it was when you were receiving a paycheck, allowing you to focus on enjoying your retirement and not worrying about your finances or cashflow.

I identified a number of myths, hype, and propaganda from the mainstream financial media that have left far too many retirees unwittingly relying on nothing more than luck for their success, including:

- **Social Security & Pensions:** Why many people fail to optimize their benefits
- **Average rates of return:** Why most people focus on the wrong measures of success
- **Benchmarks:** Why they are irrelevant
- **MPT:** Why asset allocation and diversification provide inadequate risk protection
- **Annuities:** Why they are so misunderstood
- **Taxes:** Why you should consider spending your worst money first
- **Investment Risk:** Why it's the No. 1 obstacle to your long-term financial success.

Perhaps most importantly, I've shown you the keys to finding and partnering with the right retirement advisor—one who is truly independent, truly focused, truly comprehensive, and an excellent teacher—who is knowledgeable and capable of educating and helping you navigate the ever-changing maze of retirement.

The ball is now in your court to decide if you're ready to make the changes necessary to secure your desired future. There are plenty of good advisors out there, fully capable of guiding you on your journey. And if you can't find one in your local area that you feel confident about, my team is always just a phone call away. We've been advising retirees throughout the United States for 25 years and we've built our entire practice around the concepts you've just finished reading about.

Regardless of how you choose to proceed, I wish you all the best for a wonderful, fulfilling—and most of all, worry-free—retirement journey. So put it on auto-pilot and go have fun. The best is yet to come!

In your service,
John VanWeelden, MBA, CAP, IAF, NSSA

FINAL THOUGHTS

O ccasionally I am asked the obvious question of when I myself plan to retire. Most are surprised to hear my not-so-obvious answer: Never. I love what I do. We have a great team. And as our lead advisor (also my brother-in-law) likes to say, "We work indoors and there's no heavy lifting." So why would I ever quit? So long as my mind is able to function, I plan to continue.

That's one last piece of advice I'll give you, just as I do anyone who asks (and some who don't): Although I make my living helping people retire and make the most out of their retirement years, I never encourage people to rush out the door to retirement just because they arrived at some magic age or date on the calendar. Unless you hate what you do, don't be in a rush. I strongly suggest anyone planning to retire give some serious thought to what that will look like. Retire *to something*. Not *from something*. Many retirees find themselves somewhat lost, bored, or depressed after they retire if they don't have a plan for this new phase of life. This is particularly true for high achievers, who are often the very people who have accumulated the means to retire in the first place.

And if you are married, no matter how much you may love your spouse, it can be a rude awakening to suddenly realize your normal, personal, daily routines must now coexist.

For some of you, this will be no problem. You're ready and you know it. For others, I strongly recommend you give it some thought before making the leap. In our practice, we're fortunate to have a resident life coach to help clients who wish to work through these things, but that's the exception, not the norm for retirement advisors. As a life coach, my wife, Diane, helps clients who are seeking to adjust to their new reality, find new meaning for their life after their primary vocational work has ended, and even wrestle with their identity and personal value as a retiree. (She can be reached at arise-lifecoaching.com.)

If you have a plan to retire *to* something, you'll be fine. If not, take a step back. Maybe hire a life coach. (I know a great one.) But by all means, have a plan. As the saying goes . . . *"measure twice, cut once."*

ACKNOWLEDGMENTS

I'd like to acknowledge those who helped to make this book possible:

My wife, Diane. Her unwavering optimism, unconditional support, and fearless co-leadership in every area of our lives have been invaluable during this entire process.

My brother-in law, Jim Connell, who's dedication to our clients, daily companionship, professionalism, and support have made this journey exponentially more enjoyable.

Jana Thomas, our client service manager, whose care for our clients, and attention to detail on their behalf, has made it possible for me to set aside time to complete this project.

All of our clients, who have placed their trust and confidence in us over the years, especially in those formative years when we were still learning who we were, through whom I have gained as much as I have given. You're the reason I do what I do and why I enjoy it so much. This book and the wisdom herein is thanks to you, and it is for all those "clients" I may never meet, but who, by reading this book, will gain from the experiences you have provided me.

The entire team at Greenleaf, who guided me every step of the way, from initial drafting to final composition and editing. They have been a pleasure to work with, and their expertise has made this project possible. I have learned so much in this process and I cannot imagine going down this path without them.

ABOUT THE AUTHOR

John VanWeelden is an author, speaker, coach, teacher, and retirement advisor.

John's passion is helping retirees live their best lives ever. By cutting through the myths, hype, and propaganda of the mainstream financial media to reveal the hidden truths about retirement planning and investing, John empowers retirees to make the most of all they've accumulated throughout their working lives through his firm's unique, holistic approach to integrating retirement, income, investment, insurance, tax, health care, survivorship, and estate planning.

John is the owner and principal of VanWeelden Financial Group (VFG), an independent financial services group located in West Chester, Ohio. Established in 1999, VFG includes VanWeelden Wealth Management, LLC, a Registered Investment Advisory firm; and VanWeelden Group, LLC, a licensed insurance agency. Together, VFG specializes in providing truly comprehensive retirement services and fee-only wealth management to individuals and families at or nearing retirement, throughout the United States.

John earned his MBA, as well as undergraduate degrees in both physical and social sciences, from Miami University in Oxford, Ohio. An Accredited Investment Fiduciary, John also holds the designation of

Chartered Advisor in Philanthropy, a post-graduate degree combining advanced studies in estate and charitable planning, and that of National Social Security Advisor.

John and his wife, Diane, a professional life coach, and managing partner of VanWeelden Financial Group, are a dynamic duo in both business and personal endeavors. Together for over 35 years and now empty nesters, they work hard and play hard. When they aren't working in their businesses, you will likely find them working out in the gym, camping, hiking, swimming, gardening, training dogs, or on a beach enjoying the great outdoors.

www.ingramcontent.com/pod-product-compliance
Lightning Source LLC
Chambersburg PA
CBHW030454210326
41597CB00013B/666